CELEBRATING 90 YEARS OF
Stevensons of Uttoxeter

ISBN 978 1905 304 74 5

Contents

FRONT COVER: Originally a Leyland development vehicle, this Olympian prototype, which had a Bristol VR-type lower front panel, was never registered by Leyland Motors and was purchased in an incomplete form by Stevensons. The company removed the centre doorway, then completed the Eastern Coach Works-built shell to PSV standard, and it was registered Q246 FVT (99); it is seen in Rugeley Bus Station wearing its later livery, ready for the short journey to the Springfields Estate. *(EWC)*

TITLE PAGE: Two Cravens-bodied AEC Regent III RTs, KGK 724/5 (14/23), were bought from London Transport Executive in March 1957 when less than eight years old. After setting down a shopping-laden passenger, Stefan Senkow eases no.23 from the bus stop on Lodge Hill at 5.46pm on 29th May 1969 whilst working the 5.30pm Burton to Uttoxeter service via Tutbury. Both vehicles were fitted with doors in 1965 and were withdrawn in 1972 and 1971 respectively, having served Stevensons for nearly twice as long as they had LTE. *(TJ)*

Note: The company name carried an apostrophe, written as Stevenson's, until 1971 when the new company, Stevensons of Uttoxeter Ltd, was formed. For simplicity, the company name is printed without an apostrophe except to indicate possession, when it is shown as Stevensons'.

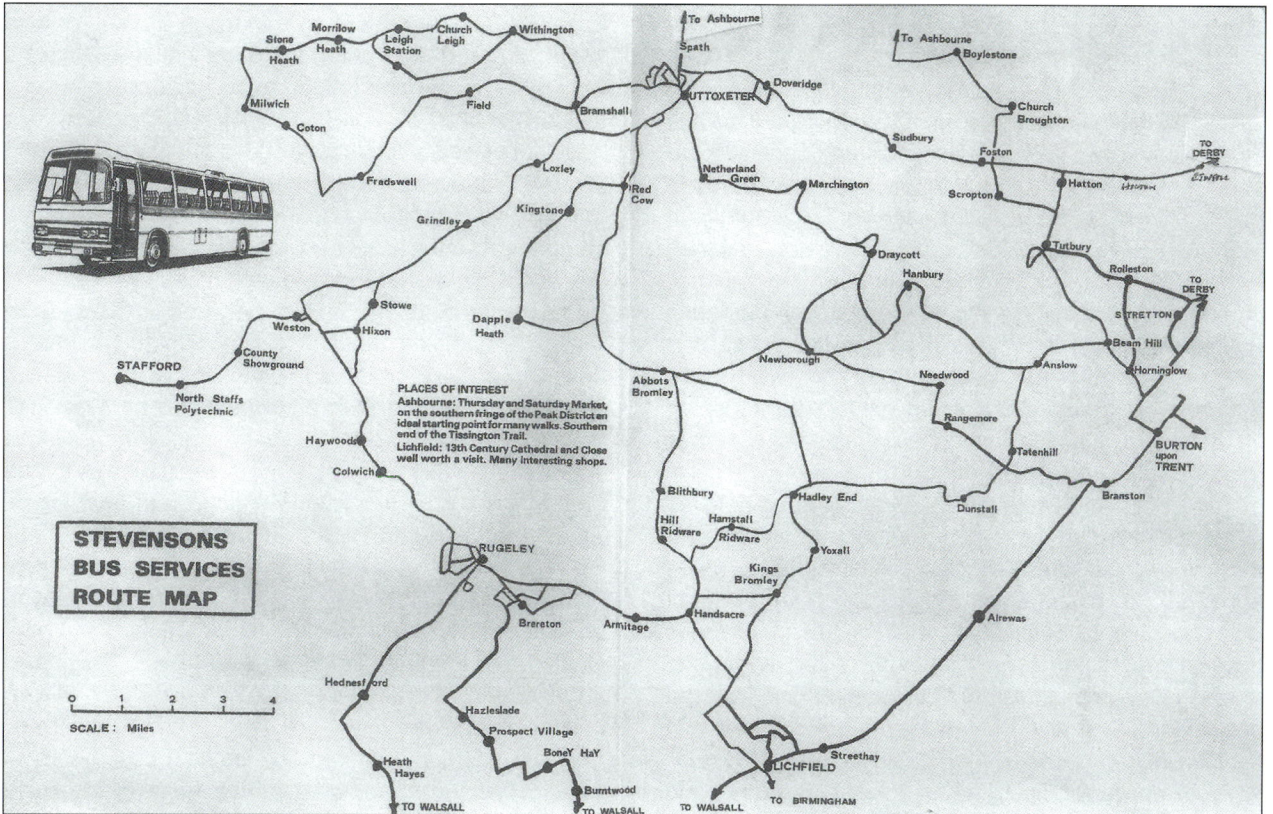

Uttoxeter-Burton operating area, 1980s

JGU 251K is seen in this autumnal view as it climbs from Tatenhill into Rangemore during its journey from Burton on a Saturday service to Abbots Bromley. Behind can be seen the cooling towers of the now-demolished Drakelow Power Station, which had been built on the site of the Gresley family's Drakelow Hall. *(EW)*

Introduction

Stevensons Bus Company was founded in August 1926, the first service operating on Saturday, 11th September between Uttoxeter and Burton-upon-Trent. The company slowly grew in size in and around that heartland, becoming Stevensons of Uttoxeter Ltd in 1971, until by the late 1970s there were over forty vehicles in the fleet. The next two decades saw the company grow quickly, expanding into all the counties bordering Staffordshire, and it became a part of the British Bus group in June 1994. In August 1996 the company passed to the Cowie group, which in November 1997 adopted the name Arriva, and in January 2000 the original garage and head office at Spath, near Uttoxeter, was closed.

Two books and fleet lists on Stevensons, as detailed in the bibliography, have been published over the last thirty years, and many articles on the company have appeared in bus-interest magazines. The aims of this book are to consolidate the content of previous publications, to add considerable new information, and to extend the printed history of the company to the start of operation by British Bus, thence to Arriva. There is a fleet list in the appendices.

From an early age I had an interest in buses and coaches, especially those of privately-owned family concerns. When I lived in Blythe Bridge in the late 1950s and 1960s, many coaches passed through, particularly on summer weekends, and mainly en route to North Wales or Blackpool. These included some black and yellow vehicles with the fleet name of Stevensons; I was not to know at the time that I would work for that company many years later, and I have included in this book some personal reminiscences and anecdotes from that period. This publication has been written as a lasting tribute to a highly regarded and much-missed family company in order to celebrate the 90th anniversary of its founding in August 2016. Interestingly, the date I was offered by the Uttoxeter Town Clerk to view the council's archives was 11th September 2014, exactly 88 years since the start of the Uttoxeter to Burton service!

Acknowledgements

Many people have assisted in the production of this book, including friends and past colleagues, and I extend my sincere thanks to them all wholeheartedly. The importance of the contributions that my good friend and past colleague Tim Jeffcoat has made to this publication cannot be overstated. The majority of the photographs are my own, but from the late 1960s Tim travelled on his bike around Stevensons' area of operation, and took a large number of marvellous colour photographs which, together with his collection of monochrome views, he has now made available to me. Alan Mills, Hon. Librarian of the Omnibus Society, afforded considerable assistance to enable the research of the Society's archive material. In addition to this, I have been able to draw on Tim's extensive archive of company and other literature, and Tim spent an enormous amount of time sorting through his own material and, with me, Omnibus Society archives, and helped to collate everything in a logical manner.

Julian Peddle ultimately became the Managing Director of Stevensons and there is no-one better placed to provide information concerning the later period of the company. As soon as he became aware that I was writing this book, he offered to host some meetings, initially to try to clarify company history between 1926 and the 1970s. At the first meeting Julian commented that a definitive account of the company had to be produced now, in time for the 90th anniversary, since memories may not be as sharp in 10 years' time! I thank Julian especially for his enthusiasm in connection with the project and for his continuing support and assistance. Three grandchildren of the founder, Ruth Day, Basil Stevenson and David Stevenson, have made invaluable contributions, particularly with regard to information on early family and company history, and David very kindly wrote the foreword to the book; it was David who engaged me at Spath in 1978, since his father was on holiday at the time.

David Stanier authored the most recent book on Stevensons and co-authored the first; he allowed the use of some of his own photographs, provided information for some captions, and assisted greatly by providing fleet details to enable the production of the fleet list to June 1994 when the company passed to British Bus. Additionally, the time afforded by John Bennett and Alan Hiley to researching vehicles' histories is greatly appreciated. David Penlington, who co-authored the first Stevensons book, checked the text in this book with particular regard to engineering and technical matters. I thank the many other photographers whose work appears herein, credited where known, and I am very grateful to Derek Lowe for spending considerable time enhancing many early monochrome and some colour photographs. I acknowledge the assistance given by the staff of the 'Magic Attic' in Swadlincote whilst I was researching from old newspapers, and my thanks are also extended to the Editors of the Burton Mail and the Uttoxeter Advertiser for their interest, and for permission to reproduce articles and other content from their newspapers.

My wife Kate, Tim Jeffcoat, Julian Peddle, David Stevenson and Alan Mills kindly proof-read the text (before later additions); all are thanked unreservedly for their time and attention to detail. I express my thanks to Mark Senior and colleagues at Venture Publications for agreeing to publish the book, and particularly to my editor Ian Stubbs for his enthusiasm and assistance in the design of this volume; the proof readers at Venture Publications, David and Mary Shaw, are also thanked for their diligent work, any errors that may remain are mine.

Finally, I thank my dear wife Kate for her support, encouragement and patience, and have great pleasure in dedicating this book to her.

Foreword

I appreciate very much being asked to write the foreword to Eric's book charting the history of Stevensons. I was a part of it for a relatively short period from 1972 until its sale in 1994 but was probably around during the period of most profound change, if not the most endearing period of its existence.

First of all I would like to thank Eric and Tim for the tremendous amount of work they have put in to bring this project to fruition. They of course were both highly valued and well respected members of Stevensons' staff for a good many years. During their research they have uncovered much more than was previously recorded and in some cases brought together people with this common interest; this has given them much pleasure.

The history of Stevensons fits conveniently into three distinct phases. From 1926 to 1972 Stevensons was very much a family business. It must have taken great courage to sell a working farm, buy a bus and build a new house and a bus garage. That is exactly what the founder did, forced by the depressed state of agriculture at this time, and during the following 35 years or so the family was put to work as drivers, conductors or mechanics to keep it going.

The first major change was when George, the youngest son of the founder, bought the family business in 1972 and I joined him. The business prospered on the back of an increasing number of schools contracts and a rapidly growing private hire business. Bus services could not expand due to the licensing system. Towards the end of this phase I was lucky to persuade Julian Peddle to join us, and this very much coincided with the opportunity to develop the bus service network due to Margaret Thatcher's privatisation of the National Bus Company.

The next phase, starting in the early eighties, was the period of seismic change for Stevensons. A merger with the bus undertaking in Burton gave the enlarged company the clout to involve itself in the privatisation process, and this enabled it to acquire a part of the Midland Fox operation in Burton. The rest is history. The company grew rapidly to over 300 vehicles, a modern fleet, not the Stevensons Rockets of old. Julian Peddle became the driving force and it was through his skill and wisdom that the company developed into the marketable commodity that it was when sold.

By this time Stevensons was just like any other large company. It is probably its early history that is the most interesting. The company gained an enviable reputation for reliability, its fares were low, and it boasted for many years loyal, hard working members of staff who endeared themselves to the public.

All these phases are covered in great detail, backed up by some wonderful old photographs, many of which are from Tim's and Eric's collections. I hope that sales will do justice to the hard work it took to produce.

David Stevenson

Passing Chartley Castle near Stowe, whilst travelling between Uttoxeter and Stafford on service 404, is UWW 6X, an ex-West Yorkshire PTE Leyland Olympian with Roe body, bought in May 1987 and numbered 98. Chartley Castle was used for a short while in addition to nearby Tutbury to house Mary, Queen of Scots. *(EW)*

1.A Change of Direction

John Stevenson was born at Hollington House, Hollington, near Uttoxeter, in 1875; he married his wife Mary in 1902 and moved to Fole Farm, near Checkley. By 1926 the country was in the middle of an agricultural slump and it was the year of the General Strike. With poor returns from farming, John Stevenson came to the conclusion that the future was going to be uncertain for his family of four sons and three daughters, so at the age of 51 he considered a change of direction. The only public transport between Uttoxeter (6,000 inhabitants) and Burton-upon-Trent (50,000 inhabitants) fifteen miles distant was the railway, which provided an infrequent and rather inconvenient service necessitating a change of trains at Tutbury station. John decided to start a bus company and provide a through service between the two towns. He sold the farm and purchased seven acres of land at Spath, near Uttoxeter, on which he built a garage large enough for four vehicles, the concrete for the floor being mixed by hand; by 1928 a house, which he called 'Brooklands', was built beside the garage. Hawksworth of Etwall had operated a bus service from 1921 between Tutbury and Uttoxeter on Wednesdays (market day). Trent Motor Traction bought the business in July 1922 and later operated a Derby-Hatton-Uttoxeter service on Wednesdays and Fridays.

Following research of the County Borough of Burton Public Works and Tramways Committee minutes by Tim Jeffcoat, more is now known about the origins of Stevensons' first route and the first vehicle. On 14th July 1926, a Mr WE Wood of Meir, Stoke-on-Trent, had been granted two licences by the County Borough to operate between Burton (New Street) and Uttoxeter via Shobnall Road, New Inn, Draycott and Marchington, but I found no record of this proposed service receiving a licence from Uttoxeter Urban District Council. However,

This advert is from the Uttoxeter Advertiser announcing the first service which would operate from 11th September 1926. *(UA)*

Burton's Minutes of 1st September 1926 record that John Stevenson had purchased the vehicle ordered by Wood (prior to its being registered). On 23rd August 1926, it had been registered new as RF 2202 to John Stevenson who was requesting permission to run the vehicle over the same route; a proprietor's licence and ones for a driver and conductor were then granted to John Stevenson. This first bus was a Reo Pullman 26-seater and carried the legend 'Reo Pullman Saloon' on both sides below the route boards; Reo vehicles, built in America, were quite reliable and were readily available. His application to Uttoxeter UDC to run the service was made on 6th September and an advertisement was placed in the 'Uttoxeter Advertiser' (fondly referred to as 'The Stunner') that the starting date for the service

The first vehicle was RF 2202, a 26-seater Reo Pullman new on 23rd August 1926, and it is seen in Uttoxeter Market Place; of note is the fleet name 'Reo Pullman Saloon' on the side of the bus. An advert for a dance at Burton in 1926 referred to the 'late night Reo buses to Uttoxeter'. It was in Uttoxeter Market Place where the famous lexicologist Dr Samuel Johnson stood bare-headed in bad weather, doing penance to atone for refusing to assist there at the family's book stall when he was younger and his father was ill. *(TJC)*

would be Saturday 11th September 1926, although the route as described in that advertisement was to be via Tutbury, not Draycott!

However, internal combustion engines were completely new to the family, and a driver was required for the bus. Earlier, when John had lived in Hollington, he knew another farmer, Charlie Whieldon, who had a model T Ford; he taught Bernard, John's eldest son, how to drive the vehicle and also assisted the company by driving when possible. Bernard drove the first bus, with his sister Marjorie, aged 15, as conductress. Initially, fares were 1s 4d (7p) single and 2s (10p) return, and the first timetable provided for six return journeys daily, which amounted to over 1,000 miles each week. Then on 6th October the Burton Town Clerk reported that Stevensons were not adhering to the licensed route, instead traversing Shobnall Street then Belvedere Road to gain access to Tutbury Road, the service continuing thereafter via Tutbury, Hatton and Sudbury (this latter part being the route licensed by Uttoxeter UDC and potentially more lucrative). John Stevenson was informed that he could not be allowed to use the route via Belvedere Road, but fortunately, following correspondence and a meeting, it was agreed that the service between Tutbury and Burton could proceed instead via Horninglow Road to terminate in Horninglow Street, a proprietor's licence and a driver's licence being duly granted. With the opening of Wetmore Road Motor Park on 1st October 1927, that became the terminus instead. There were restrictions on journeys within Burton, the 'Burton-on-Trent Standard Conditions', which placed picking up and other restrictions on operators running into the town, in order to protect council-operated services.

It is very rare to have first-hand accounts of these early days. However, in 1984 Mr LGJ Layberry (by then living out of the area) wrote to the company reflecting on the period, and the following extracts provide interesting reading.

"I remember the advent so well. I was twelve years old in 1926 and my home was in High Street, Tutbury, but I spent most of my time at my uncle's smallholding on the Tutbury Road close to where the Beacon now stands. We could not only see the buses from inside the house, but when outside had a good view of them for a couple of hundred yards as they approached down the hill on their way to Burton. The first bus, the Reo Pullman Saloon RF 2202 seemed to us the last word in luxury, for it was far superior to the vehicles of Burton Corporation, the Trent, and the Midland Red, which ran buses into Burton from the Mining villages. At that time all the buses parked in Horninglow Street outside Trinity Church on both sides of the road, and on Saturdays double-banked on the near-side when facing the river. The new yellow bus ran so smoothly and silently that my brother and I named it 'The Cat'.

A competitor started an identical service with an ugly, lumbering, grey-green bus (possibly a Guy) which

we nick-named 'The Elephant'. We were indignant that such an opportunist should seek to cash in on the enterprise of John Stevenson who had blazed the trail, and we were very pleased when the interloper was forced out of business in a week or two. This was achieved by another Reo Saloon RA 1765 which ran just a minute or two ahead of the Elephant. This Reo was a slightly smaller model than RF 2202 and because of this we called it 'The Kitten'. We could not imagine any passengers choosing to ride on the Elephant when they could take the Cat or the Kitten.

The drivers in those days were very considerate. I remember one summer evening, quite late, when I was at home in Tutbury, and on its last trip to Burton the service bus stopped at the Dog and Partridge opposite our house to pick up a large crowd. Eighteen or twenty people remained who could not be squeezed on and the driver pleasantly said "Stay where you are, I'll be back in about twenty minutes!" This speed seemed like lightning to us, for many of the other buses ran on solid rubber wheels and only crawled along. By the way, in Tutbury the bus was known simply as 'The Yeller'; I have never heard the name 'Stevenson' mentioned in conversation although of course it was quite conspicuous on the bus itself, on the rear panels.

We boys all had bikes by this time and a ride on a bus was a rare and unnecessary luxury. However, I remember one occasion when I boarded RF 2202 at Tutbury High Street and rode to Beam Hill corner. The fare was twopence (half-price); the conductor was a young lady, in itself a startling departure from custom in those days, one of Mr. Stevensons' daughters, presumably Marjorie. She was an attractive girl, but alas I was only thirteen! At week-ends, when the bus was often crowded, she frequently stood on the top step, hanging on with the door open. We used to hope that as the bus gathered speed down the hill the slip-stream would lift her skirt; sometimes it did, to our great joy! In 1932 I left the district, but on my infrequent visits I always noticed that 'The Yellers' had become bigger, brighter, and more numerous".

THE YELLOW BUS
will run to
TEAN DANCE
ON FRIDAY, MARCH 9,
Leaving Uttoxeter 7.15 p.m.
Return Fare 1s. 6d.

Advertisement- The Yellow Bus, 7th March 1928. (UA)

It was previously believed that the Reo RA 1765 mentioned in the above letter was acquired from Woolliscroft, Darley Dale in 1929. However, recent research shows that not to have been so, and it would appear that it was acquired from Williamson, the Reo and Bristol agents in Heanor, shortly after being registered by them in March 1927. This coincides with an application by John Stevenson to Uttoxeter UDC in February 1927

An example of an early Uttoxeter Saloon Service ticket.

C 9707
Uttoxeter Saloon Service
J. STEVENSON, UTTOXETER.

INWARD SINGLE OUTWARD
INWARD RETURN OUTWARD

Bell Punch Company, London. B5568

Stevensons timetable, after the Ashbourne to Sudbury service started in 9/28, but before a Uttoxeter to Somersal Herbert service had been started at some time between then and 6/31.

Tel.: 131 Uttoxeter.

Uttoxeter
Yellow Bus Service.

TIME · TABLES.

Uttoxeter—Salt Box—Burton.
Uttoxeter—Hanbury—Burton.
Sudbury—Ashbourne.

PRICE ONE PENNY.

Marjorie and Bill Stevenson are seen with a rather dapper Les Brighouse beside the first vehicle, RF 2202. *(TJC)*

UTTOXETER & BURTON TIME TABLE.

		X a.m.	X a.m.	X a.m.	a.m.	X a.m.	p.m.	p.m.	p.m.	p.m.	p.m.	p.m.	p.m.	S p.m.
Uttoxeter	Dep.	6 50	7 50	9 30	11 0	12 15	1 0	2 0	2 45	4 0	5 40	7 0	8 30	9 30
Doveridge		7 0	8 0	9 40	11 10	12 25	1 10	2 10	2 55	4 10	5 50	7 10	8 40	9 40
Sudbury		7 10	8 10	9 50	11 20	12 35	1 20	2 20	3 5	4 20	6 0	7 20	8 50	9 50
Foston		7 15	8 15	9 55	11 25	12 40	1 25	2 25	3 10	4 25	6 5	7 25	8 55	9 55
Salt Box		7 20	8 20	10 0	11 30	12 45	1 30	2 30	3 15	4 30	6 10	7 30	9 0	10 0
Tutbury		7 30	8 30	10 10	11 40	12 55	1 40	2 40	3 25	4 40	6 20	7 40	9 10	10 10
Burton	Arr.	7 50	8 50	10 30	12 0	1 15	2 0	3 0	3 45	5 0	6 40	8 0	9 30	10 30

		X a.m.	X a.m.	X a.m.	p.m.	X p.m.	p.m.	p.m.	p.m.	p.m.	p.m.	p.m.	p.m.	S p.m.
Burton	Dep.	8 0	9 30	10 35	12 0	1 30	2 30	3 15	4 15	5 30	7 10	8 15	9 35	10 30
Tutbury		8 20	9 50	10 55	12 20	1 50	2 50	3 35	4 35	5 50	7 30	8 35	9 55	10 50
Salt Box		8 30	10 0	11 5	12 30	2 0	3 0	3 45	4 45	6 0	7 40	8 45	10 5	11 0
Foston		8 35	10 5	11 10	12 35	2 5	3 5	3 50	4 50	6 5	7 45	8 50	10 10	11 5
Sudbury		8 40	10 10	11 15	12 40	2 10	3 10	3 55	4 55	6 10	7 50	8 55	10 15	11 10
Doveridge		8 50	10 20	11 25	12 50	2 20	3 20	4 5	5 5	6 20	8 0	9 5	10 25	11 20
Uttoxeter	Arr.	9 0	10 30	11 35	1 0	2 30	3 30	4 15	5 15	6 30	8 10	9 15	10 35	11 30

X—Does not run on Sundays. S—Runs Saturdays and Sundays only.
Buses start from Wetmore Road Park, Burton, and from Market Square, Uttoxeter.

UTTOXETER, HANBURY AND BURTON.
Mondays, Thursdays and Saturdays.

	a.m.	a.m.	p.m.	p.m.	X p.m.	S.O. p.m.	
Uttoxeter Dep.	9 0	†11 0	2 0	4 45		†8 30	S.O. Denotes Saturdays only.
Doveridge	9 10	†11 10	2 10	4 55		†8 40	
Sudbury	9 20	†11 20	2 20	5 5		†9 0	X Denotes Thursdays and Saturdays only.
Draycott	9 30	11 30	2 30	5 15	7 0	9 10	
Hanbury	9 45	11 45	2 45	5 30	7 15	9 20	† Denotes change at Sudbury.
Anslow	10 0	12 0	3 0	5 45	7 30	9 35	
Burton Arr.	10 15	12 15	3 15	6 0	7 45	9 50	

	a.m.	p.m.	p.m.	p.m.	X p.m.	S.O. p.m.	
Burton Dep.	10 20	12 15	3 30	6 15	8 0	10 0	The Proprietor does not hold himself responsible for loss or injury which may arise from delay.
Anslow	10 35	12 30	3 45	6 30	8 15	10 15	
Hanbury	10 50	12 45	4 0	6 45	8 30	10 30	
Draycott	11 0	12 55	4 15	7 0	8 45	10 40	
Sudbury	†11 5	1 5	4 20		8 55	10 45	
Doveridge	†11 15	1 15	4 30		9 5	10 55	
Uttoxeter Arr.	†11 20	1 25	4 40		9 15	11 0	

ASHBOURNE AND SUDBURY, via Cubley.
In connection with Burton.

Monday to Friday.						Saturdays and Sundays Only. N.S. Denotes not Sundays.							
		a.m.	a.m.	p.m.	p.m.		N.S. a.m.	N.S. a.m.	p.m.	p.m.	p.m.	S.O. p.m.	S p.m.
Sudbury	Dep.	8 10	10 15	4 35	6 10	Dep.	8 10	10 15	12 45	3 10	6 30	8 35	8 0
Cubley		8 25	10 30	4 45	6 20		8 25	10 30	1 0	3 20	6 40	8 45	8 15
Clifton		8 45	10 50	5 5	6 40		8 45	10 50	1 20	3 40	6 50	9 5	8 40
Ashbourne	Arr.	8 50	11 0	5 10	6 45	Arr.	8 50	11 0	1 30	3 45	7 0	9 10	8 45

		X a.m.	X a.m.	X p.m.	X p.m.		N.S. X a.m.	N.S. X a.m.	X p.m.	X p.m.	X p.m.	S.O. X p.m.	S X p.m.
Ashbourne	Dep.	9 15	11 45	5 10	6 45	Dep.	9 15	11 45	2 15	3 45	7 15	9 15	9 15
Clifton		9 20	11 50	5 20	6 50		9 20	11 50	2 20	3 50	7 20	9 20	9 20
Cubley		9 40	12 10	5 40	7 10		9 40	12 10	2 40	4 10	7 40	9 40	9 40
Sudbury	Arr.	9 50	12 25	5 55	7 20	Arr.	9 50	12 25	2 55	4 20	7 50	9 50	9 50

WEDNESDAYS.—Market Bus leaves Uttoxeter at 3.30 and 4.15.

for a licence for an additional vehicle, and ties in with Mr Layberry's observations. The arrival of this second vehicle allowed the frequency to be doubled. John's second son, also named John, was granted a driver's licence by the Uttoxeter Urban District Council (UUDC) in March 1927 and was sent to Williamsons, where he undertook a six month course to become a mechanic and learned how to strip a Reo chassis and build it up again. The youngest daughter, Gertrude, also became a conductress; third son Bill started as a driver. The eldest daughter Hannah was married by the time the company

The second vehicle was RA 1765, a Reo 20-seater new in March 1927 (later 24 seats), bought from Williamsons, Heanor who were Reo agents, shortly after being registered by them and it worked until December 1937. The driver, John Stevenson Jnr, is seen perched on the wing, with an unknown lady opposite. *(TJC)*

Harry Blood is seen with TO 4626, one of two used 18-seater Reos, bought in August 1927 when only five months old. Being sprightly vehicles, referred to by the drivers as 'flying hen pens', they were often used when 'tabbing' the competitor's vehicle, although on this occasion TO 4626 is seen on the Ashbourne to Sudbury service. This and sister vehicle TO 4624 were recorded at Spath by a visitor in 1934, and this vehicle was seen again in 1937, but may have been withdrawn. *(TJC)*

This magnificent vehicle was RF 5178, a three-axle Guy CX with a Guy 41-seat body, new in November 1928, and the body bears the legend 'Uttoxeter Saloon'; the seating was reduced to 36 in 1930. Tragically, this vehicle and the original Reo were destroyed in the garage fire in February 1930. Bill Stevenson is sitting in the cab, and it is believed to be Harry Blood standing beside the bus. Les possibly started as a driver but was Garage Foreman by 1936. *(TJC)*

started and played no part in the business, although her husband, Ben Wright, became involved for a few years in the 1960s after her father's death; their son, Kenneth, worked in the garage from 1946 onwards.

On 4th July 1927 John Stevenson received licences from UUDC to increase further the number of buses operated; two more of the reliable Reos were acquired second-hand in August 1927 which allowed for some still necessary duplication. By September five of the eight staff were Stevenson's family members. However, after driving for Stevensons for a while, Charlie Whieldon left to operate his own Green Bus Company from 9th May 1927, initially from where he lived at Hollywood Farm in Hollington, then from premises in Uttoxeter and later on in Rugeley also, the route being Uttoxeter to Hednesford. Referred to originally as the Reo Pullman Saloon Bus Service, John Stevenson's company was being advertised as The Yellow Bus in March 1928, since the livery was yellow and cream with black relief and as The Yellow Bus Service by February 1930.

When Roy Marshall was General Manager for East Staffs District Council's bus operation, he researched various old council minutes and he found that Roberts

of Newborough, who had been operating a Thursday-only service from Hanbury to Burton via Anslow and Shobnall Road, ceased to operate from 14th January 1928 in view of constant breakdowns. The service was replaced by Stevensons from Thursday 19th January 1928, with one from Uttoxeter to Burton (New Street) via Doveridge, Sudbury, Draycott, Hanbury, Anslow and Shobnall Road. By January 1929 at least, the service operated on Monday, Thursday and Saturday. Roberts' vehicle RF 1798, make unknown but new in April 1926 to Bush, Abbots Bromley, was acquired at the time, but one of Stevensons' own 20-seaters was used instead on the new service. Roy Marshall's notes also revealed that a new Bristol 32-seater was acquired for use on the main route via Tutbury from February 1928; there is no record in published fleet lists of such a vehicle in the fleet at the time, but the following articles most likely provide the answers.

In a 'Modern Transport' article of 2nd June 1928 entitled 'Motor Omnibus Services in the provinces – Burton and District', the author of the article described John Stevenson's operation, which comprised ten round trips to Burton. In addition to the Reos operated, he

RA 4996, a Bristol B with Roe 32-seat body, is believed to have been bought from Williamson Heanor, early in 1928. It is seen in front of the replacement garage which was built in 1930, although the date of the photo has to be after July 1936, in view of the people seen. To the left is driver Joe Wildsmith, conductor Les Harper is on the step, and to the right is garage hand Bill Foden, a cousin of John Stevenson. *(TJC)*

This advert from the Uttoxeter Advertiser of 19th March 1930 announced the Potteries Electric Traction Company's short-lived competing service from Hanley via Uttoxeter to Burton. *(UA)*

Bamford's Ltd of Uttoxeter produced agricultural machinery, as seen in this advert of 15th May 1929. *(UA)*

gave a full description of two 'Bristol Superbuses' of the Light Passenger type (Bs), which had Roe 32-seat bodies. Additionally, an article in the January 1948 issue of 'Bus & Coach' states that "*Within a matter of days a second Reo was order (sic) and the frequency of the Uttoxeter-Burton service was doubled. There were, however, times when the capacity of this two-bus service was strained beyond all reasonable standards of seating and accommodation, and this caused Mr Stevenson to go in for 32-seaters. The first of these was a Bristol acquired in 1928, with a body by Charles Roe*".

These were surprising revelations, since that type was only introduced in the previous year, and the first recorded example in Stevensons' fleet was RA 4996, previously reported as being acquired a year later in February 1929 from Brooks Brothers of Gresley, which preceded a new Lawton-bodied example. These articles and recent research give much weight to the belief now held that this vehicle was in fact registered by Williamsons, and that it was sold early in 1928 to Stevensons (there being no record of its operating for Brooks). Furthermore, it would now appear that the body was removed from its chassis in later years and fitted to a newer and longer one of 1930 acquired from a dealer in 1937, whereupon the body was lengthened and rebuilt to dual-purpose specification. This is afforded significant credence since the 1948 article referred to continues "*It is not unusual for a chassis to outlive a body, but this Roe body outlived the 1928 Bristol chassis and was transferred to a newer Bristol chassis, which is still running, and the body - over 19 years old - still looks good for a year or so*". It was in fact withdrawn in 1952. Additionally, Williamsons took four of the Bristol Bs with Roe 32-seat bodies for their own fleet. It is known that when Williamsons became a subsidiary of Midland General, (and possibly before) they loaned Bristol Bs to other operators, either from their fleet or in the capacity as Bristol agent, and it is speculated that the other bus mentioned in the 1928 article could indeed have been on loan from Williamsons, particularly since John Stevenson was already a customer. Presumably, he was sufficiently pleased with the performance of the vehicles, hence the later purchases. In November 1928 a magnificent new Guy CX three-axle saloon was purchased; the Guy body seated 41 (reduced to 36 in 1930) and 'Uttoxeter Saloon' was written boldly on the sides. That fleetname was carried by several buses around that time, and also replaced the original one on RF 2202.

From September 1928 there was a service from Sudbury to Ashbourne, which in due course was amended to include some through running from Uttoxeter; however, between 10th September 1928 and 22nd January 1929 there was quite intense competition from Slater of Mayfield who operated a route between Ashbourne, Sudbury and Burton.

RF 7091, was a Bristol B with a Lawton body seating 32, which was delivered new in April 1930; at some time between 1937 and 1941 it was given fleet number 3. The words 'Yellow Bus' can be seen in the aperture beside the destination blind; the driver is believed to be Harry Blood. (RH)

This imposing Minerva, VO 390, was purchased by Stevensons in April, 1930, and carries the 'Uttoxeter Saloon' fleetname. It had been new to the Arnold Motor Bus Company in February 1929 and passed to Nottingham Corporation Passenger Transport one year later, but was not operated by them. It is thought that the driver could be Joe Wildsmith. (TJC)

Stevensons then employed a 'tabbing' tactic using a very fast Reo to protect their revenue; Slaters then withdrew and the status quo was restored. Fourteen other operators held licences for services into Uttoxeter in 1929, many of which ran only on market days. The Potteries Electric Traction Co (PET) was admonished by UUDC for starting a Hanley–Uttoxeter–Burton service on 4th November 1929 without licences, and for using vehicles they had acquired with the business of W. Proctor of Longton on 16th May 1929 (run as a subsidiary until 1932), and which still carried their original liveries. PET was advised that their service had to be suspended until licences had been granted for three buses to run on the route, and that unless they discontinued using the Proctor's buses in Proctor's livery on the service, further action would be taken. In retaliation John Stevenson applied for a bus licence to run from Uttoxeter to Longton, which the council granted on 2nd December, being authorised to operate between Uttoxeter and Longton until the end of the year, although it is doubtful that this was acted on since there was no subsequent renewal. PET withdrew for the time being. However, in March 1930 PET started their service again, as per the advertisement shown; two journeys also operated from Hanley to Derby at 10.00am and 4.45pm. It is not known when PET's Burton service finished, but a Hanley to Derby (only) licence was granted on 5th August 1931 and a PET timetable of March 1932 shows that there was only a service to Derby with connections to Burton, presumably with Trent.

This is the aftermath of the garage fire in February 1930; it is possible to make out the remains of the three-axle Guy amongst the wreckage. (GSC)

YELLOW BUS SERVICE

There are a Few Seats Vacant for LLANDUDNO on THURSDAY, AUGUST 14. Return Fare 8s.
There are also a Few Vacant Seats for BLACKPOOL on AUGUST 16, to return August 23. Return Fare 16s.
A Bus will run to SHREWSBURY FLOWER SHOW on THURSDAY, AUGUST 21. Return Fare 5s. 6d.

An advert of 6th August 1930 for excursions by the Yellow Bus Service. These would have been operated by RF 7352. (UA)

RF 7091 had a long life, and in 1949 it was taken out of service and fitted with a Gardner 4LW engine. In 1951 it received a second-hand ECOC body with rear entrance, which came from North Western Road Car; a past employee recalled that the replacement radiator and various other parts at the front came from an ERF lorry. It re-entered the fleet as no.7 and the view near St Mary's Church in Uttoxeter shows that it has sustained some damage below the windows. Withdrawal came in April 1954. *(RHC)*

The first new purpose-built coach, a Sunbeam Motor Company (SMC) Pathan, RF 7352, was bought in June 1930; it had a 32-seat Burlingham body which had two hinged doors, and a roof luggage rack was also fitted. The Stevensons' house 'Brooklands' is in the background. *(RHC)*

THE YELLOW COACH.

Special Trip to BLACKPOOL ILLU-MINATIONS, MONDAY, OCT. 13. Depart Uttoxeter 8.30. Return Fare 8s. Seats may be booked at Morin's Kiosk, Market-place, or at Stevenson's, Spath.

By 8th October 1930 the company was using the 'Yellow Coach' name in its adverts for excursions. *(UA)*

The Proof of Value
is in the Quality of Wear.

Geo. Orme & Sons, Ltd., have a reputation for quality—which is your guarantee of good value. No matter what price you pay, you cannot get better value than we can give you.

See Windows of Our Three Shops
for
Special Displays of Autumn Outerwear and Underwear.
("Wolsey" Display Next Week.)

Geo. Orme & Sons,
Outfitters for Men, Women and Children,
Market Place and High Street,
UTTOXETER.

In 1928 the Uttoxeter Advertiser carried this advertisement for George Orme of Uttoxeter which shows a typical style of the period for ladies' clothes. *(UA)*

An advert from 16th May 1928 for the Public Benefit Boot Company. From the early 1930s, Stevensons' services departed from the Market Place by their shop, which in time was acquired by George Orme. *(UA)*

for footwear for all the family - - call first at one of the Benefit shops. All the styles at economy prices.

Public Benefit
BOOT CO. LTD.

The youngest son, George, born on 16th July 1915, wished to carry on with secondary education, but he had his hopes dashed and was persuaded to join the company instead, which he did when aged fourteen in 1929. He was not pleased at having to finish education, but could always boast high quality handwriting as well as the ability to compose a good letter, both of which would stand him in good stead in later life. George was keen to become a footballer, and when at school had spent many hours practising after his schoolwork was finished; he had played on Burton Albion's ground, and proved to be good enough for a trial with Stoke City FC. At age seventeen he spent a week there, in company with another hopeful, but unfortunately young George was not successful; his companion went on to make quite a name for himself, one Stanley Matthews! In order to be able to play for Uttoxeter on Saturdays, George worked as a conductor on the early shift then, after playing, returned to work in the evening. Cartilage trouble and the advent of war eventually put paid to George's football activities.

All seemed to be going well for the company until the early hours of Thursday 13th February 1930. A policeman passing the garage shortly before 1.00am noticed a light, and thought that someone was working late on a vehicle. On closer inspection he found that a fire had started in the centre of the garage and he roused the family. Driver Horatio ('Rache') Nelson drove one bus to safety then motored to the Fire Station at Uttoxeter. As no-one was around he started the fire engine and sustained a severe blow to his chest from the starting handle. However, living up to his illustrious name, he drove the appliance to Spath before collapsing, after which he was taken to hospital where he recovered. In spite of the best efforts of all concerned the first Reo, the Guy and a Morris car were destroyed but the other buses and another car were saved, although the garage was burned down and all the parts and equipment were lost. The cost of the damage was at least £3,500. Hugh Wilshaw of Cheadle immediately loaned a vehicle and, with the remaining buses, services were maintained and eventually the garage was re-built, incorporating longer bays and inspection pits. It was Rache Nelson who suggested to John Stevenson that the workmen's returns be extended to unemployed men when they had to travel to and from Burton on Fridays to collect their dole money. That was agreed to, and they travelled on a special bus at the workman return fare on condition that they returned immediately they had drawn their money. Rache became Marjorie Stevenson's husband in August 1934, and Marjorie relinquished her conducting duties at that time.

A new Lawton-bodied Bristol B, RF 7091, was bought in March 1930, as was a one-year-old Minerva, VO 390; the Bristol was re-bodied with an ex-North Western ECOC body in 1951 which gave it three more years' service. At least by 1930, most likely from much earlier, the company was carrying out private hire work, so in June that year a new Sunbeam Pathan with a stylish Burlingham dual-door coach body was purchased; registered RF 7352, it carried an 'S' in a circle within a triangle on each side. Above the 'S' was a very small rising sun, the first use of that motif that has been noted; this feature was perhaps inspired by the emblem of the Sunbeam Motor Co, to which it bore a striking resemblance. It evolved into Stevensons' well known larger rising sun emblem, with 'STEVENSON'S' in a semi-circle round the points of the sun's rays, but there were many versions of this over the years, with a script Stevensons painted through the sun's rays later being adopted.

Fleet livery was mainly yellow and black with cream or white relief, but there were occasional variations. Some early coaches bore the name 'Yellow Coaches' and 'Stevensons Bus Services' appeared on the buses on many occasions, often with 'SBS' at the front; at some stage in the 1940s maroon briefly appeared in the livery. Locals also referred fondly to the company as 'Stevensons' Rockets' or simply, and most often 'Stevos'. From the 1960s until the 1980s the fleetname was generally omitted on service buses, as everyone knew to whom the 'Yellow Rockets' belonged.

Rather surprisingly, John Stevenson never drove any vehicle and rarely travelled on his own buses and coaches. In later years Mary owned a Wolseley car, but since she did not drive either, a bus driver or mechanic was used to chauffeur them around as necessary. John concentrated particularly on body repairs and maintenance, and was extremely proficient at working on the wooden-framed bodies. The workshops were well fitted out with appropriate modern machinery, and almost all work on the vehicles was done on the premises. From early days, any damage was rectified as soon as possible, since the vehicles were regarded as Stevensons' shop-window; that philosophy continued for the life of the company. Equally important in John Stevenson's view was good timekeeping, particularly on the country routes with lower frequencies.

In August 1930, in view of increasing traffic problems, Uttoxeter Urban District Council allocated bus stops around the Market Place for the various operators. On 1st September John complained about his designated stand by the Public Benefit Boot Company (the premises later becoming Orme's shop), saying that it was inconvenient, but to no avail. He refused to make use of the stand, but on 3rd November the Council requested the Superintendent of Police to take proceedings if John Stevenson did not conform. When licences were granted to Stevensons under the 1930 Road Traffic Act on 17th June 1931, the company received licences to run services, which were identified as follows:
D881 Uttoxeter-Doveridge-Sudbury-Tutbury-Burton
D882 Uttoxeter-Doveridge-Sudbury-Draycott-Hanbury-Anslow-Henhurst Hill-Burton
D883 Uttoxeter-Somershall (actually Somersal Herbert)
TER 713/1 Ashbourne-Sudbury

A condition was attached to the licences that John Stevenson's vehicles must use the stand allotted to him

YELLOW BUS SERVICE.

Uttoxeter—Ashbourne Service,
via Sudbury, Cubley and Clifton.
On and after Tuesday, August 8th, 1933.

TIME TABLE.

To operate on Tuesdays, Thursdays, Saturdays, and Sundays only.

Tuesdays and Thursdays only.

		a.m.	a.m.	p.m.	p.m.	p.m.			
Uttoxeter	(dep.)	8 30	—	—	4 15	—	—	—	—
Doveridge		8 40	—	—	4 25	—	—	—	—
Sudbury		8 50	10 20	12 45 TO	4 35	6 10	—	—	—
Cubley		9 0	10 40	12 55 TO	4 45	6 20	—	—	—
Clifton		9 20	11 0	1 15 TO	5 5	6 40	—	—	—
Ashbourne	(arr.)	9 30	11 10	1 25 TO	5 10	6 45	—	—	—

		a.m.	a.m.	p.m.	p.m.	p.m.			
Ashbourne	(dep.)	9 30	11 45	1 30 TO	5 10	6 45	—	—	—
Clifton		9 40	11 55	1 40 TO	5 20	6 50	—	—	—
Cubley		10 0	12 15	2 0 TO	5 40	7 10	—	—	—
Sudbury	(arr.)	10 10	12 25	2 10 TO	5 55	7 20	—	—	—
Doveridge		—	12 35	2 20 TO	—	7 30	—	—	—
Uttoxeter		—	12 45	2 30 TO	—	7 40	—	—	—

TO—Thursdays only.

Saturdays and Sundays only.

		a.m.	a.m.	p.m.	p.m.	p.m.				p.m.
Uttoxeter	(dep.)	8 30 SO				5 50 NS	6 10 SO			8 30 SO
Doveridge		8 40 SO				6 0 NS	6 20 SO			8 40 SO
Sudbury		8 50 SO	10 15 SO	12 45	3 20	6 10 NS	6 40 SO	8 5		8 55 SO
Cubley		9 0 SO	10 30 SO	1 0	3 40	6 20 NS	6 40 SO	8 10		9 5 SO
Clifton		9 20 SO	10 50 SO	1 20	3 40	6 50 NS	8 30			9 25 SO
Ashbourne	(arr.)	9 30 SO	11 0 SO	1 30	3 45	6 45 NS	7 0 SO	8 40		9 30 SO

		a.m.	a.m.	p.m.	p.m.	p.m.				p.m.
Ashbourne	(dep.)	9 30 SO	11 50 SO	2 15	3 45	6 45 NS	7 15 SO	9 20		9 30 SO
Clifton		9 40 SO	11 50 SO	2 20	3 50	6 50 NS	7 20 SO	9 20		9 40 SO
Cubley		10 0 SO	12 0	2 40	4 10	7 10 NS	7 40 SO	9 40		10 0 SO
Sudbury	(arr.)	10 10 SO	12 20 SO	2 55		7 20 NS	7 50 SO	9 50		10 10 SO
Doveridge						4 30	8 0 SO	10 0		10 20 SO
Uttoxeter						4 40	8 10 SO	10 10		10 30 SO

SO—Saturdays only. NS—Not Saturday.

FARE TABLE.

		Doveridge		Sudbury		Boylestone Lane End.		Cubley		Darley Moor		Clifton		Ashbourne	
		S.	R.	S.	R.	S.	R.	S.	R.	S.	R.	S.	R.	S.	R.
Uttoxeter		3d	4d	5d	9d	7d	1s	8d	1s 2d	10d	1s 6d	1s	1s 8d
Doveridge		—	—	3d	4d	5d	8d	6d	11d	8d	1s 2d	10d	1s 6d	1s	1s 8d
Sudbury		—	—	—	—	2d	—	4d	7d	6d	11d	8d	1s 2d	10d	1s 4d
Boylestone Lane End		—	—	—	—	—	—	2d	—	4d	9d	6d	1s	8d	1s 2d
Little Cubley		—	—	—	—	—	—	—	—	3d	5d	5d	9d	6d	11d
Cubley		—	—	—	—	—	—	—	—	3d	5d	5d	9d	6d	11d
Darley Moor		—	—	—	—	—	—	—	—	—	—	4d	7d	5d	9d
Clifton		—	—	—	—	—	—	—	—	—	—	—	—	2d	7d

UTTOXETER
YELLOW BUS SERVICE.

Market Service, Wednesday only, to Uttoxeter.

Between Norbury Lane End and Uttoxeter via :—
Cubley, Somersal, Doveridge.

		a.m.	a.m.	p.m.	p.m.	p.m.
Norbury Lane End	(dep.)	10 0		12 10		3 10
Cubley		10 5		12 15		3 15
Boylestone Lane End		10 10		12 20		3 20	4 45
Somersal		10 30			2 0	
Doveridge		10 40	11 10	12 35	2 0	3 35	5 0
Uttoxeter	(arr.)	10 50	11 20	12 45	2 10	3 45	5 10

		a.m.	a.m.	p.m.	p.m.	p.m.
Uttoxeter	(dep.)	11 0	11 30	1 10	2 30	4 0
Doveridge	(arr.)	11 10	11 30	1 10	2 40	4 10
Somersal					2 50	
Boylestone Lane End		11 55		3 0	4 25	
Cubley		12 0		3 5	4 30	
Norbury Lane End	(arr.)	12 5		3 10	4 35	

FARES.

		UTTOXETER Single	Return
Norbury Lane End		9d	1s 4d
Cubley		8d	1s 2d
Boylestone Lane End		7d	1s
Somersal		6d	11d
Doveridge		3d	4d

STEVENSON'S GARAGE,
SPATH, UTTOXETER.

TELEPHONE: 131 UTTOXETER.

KELLY'S X.L. PRINTING WORKS, UTTOXETER.

3703   UTTOXETER YELLOW BUS SERVICE

UTTOXETER AND BURTON TIME TABLE.

		x	x	x	*x		x								s
		a.m.	a.m.	a.m.	a.m.	a.m.	a.m.	p.m.	p.m.	p.m.	p.m.	p.m.	p.m.	p.m.	p.m.
Uttoxeter	dep.	6 0	650	750	930	11 0	1215	1 0	2 0	245	4 0	540	7 0	830	930
Doveridge		6 5	7 0	8 0	940	1110	1225	110	210	255	410	550	710	840	940
Sudbury		615	710	810	950	1120	1235	120	220	3 5	420	6 0	720	850	950
Foston		625	715	815	955	1125	1240	125	225	310	425	6 5	725	855	955
Salt Box		630	720	820	10 0	1130	1245	130	230	315	430	610	730	9 0	10 0
Tutbury		635	730	830	1010	1140	1255	140	240	325	440	620	740	910	1010
Burton	arr.	7 0	750	850	1030	12 0	1 15	2 0	3.0	345	5 0	640	8 0	930	1030

		x	x	x	x		x								s
		a.m.	a.m.	a.m.	a.m.	p.m.	p.m.	p.m.	p.m.	p.m.	p.m.	p.m.	p.m.	p.m.	p.m.
Burton	dep.	7 0	8 0	930	1035	12 0	130	230	315	415	530	710	815	935	1030
Tutbury		715	820	950	1055	1220	150	250	335	435	550	730	835	955	1050
Salt Box		725	830	10 0	11 5	1230	2 0	3 0	345	445	6 0	740	845	10 5	11 0
Foston		730	835	10 5	1110	1235	2 5	3 5	350	450	6 5	745	850	1010	11 5
Sudbury		735	840	1010	1115	1240	210	310	355	455	610	750	855	1015	1110
Doveridge		745	850	1020	1125	1250	220	320	4 5	5 5	620	8 0	9 5	1025	1120
Uttoxeter	arr.	755	9 0	1030	1135	1 0	230	330	415	515	630	810	915	1035	1150

x—Does not run on Sundays.   s—Runs Saturdays and Sundays only.
Buses start from Wetmore Road Park, Burton, and from Market Square, Uttoxeter.

3704   UTTOXETER, HANBURY AND BURTON.
MONDAYS, THURSDAYS AND SATURDAYS.

				x	so
		a.m.	a.m.	p.m.	p.m.	p.m.	p.m.
Uttoxeter	dep.	9 0	*11 0	2 0	445	...	*830
Doveridge		910	*1110	210	455	...	*840
Sudbury		920	1120	220	5 5	...	*9 0
Draycott		930	1130	230	515	7 0	910
Hanbury		945	1145	245	530	715	920
Anslow		10 0	12 0	3 0	545	730	935
Burton	arr.	1015	1215	315	6 0	745	950

				x	so
		a.m.	p.m.	p.m.	p.m.	p.m.	p.m.
Burton	dep.	1020	1215	330	615	8 0	10 0
Anslow		1035	1230	345	630	815	1015
Hanbury		1050	1245	4 0	645	830	1030
Draycott		11 0	1255	415	7 0	845	1040
Sudbury		*11 5	1 5	420	...	855	1045
Doveridge		1115	115	430	...	9 5	1055
Uttoxeter	arr.	*1120	125	440	...	915	11 0

so—Denotes Saturdays only.
x—Denotes Thursdays and Saturdays only.
*—Denotes change at Sudbury.

The Proprietor does not hold himself responsible for loss or injury which may arise from delay.

The Publishers will use every care, by personal supervision, to ensure the general correctness of the Tables, but they do not hold themselves responsible for the accuracy of the times given, or for any alterations or errors that may arise herefrom or be found herein.

---

by the Uttoxeter UDC, and thereafter all the company's vehicles departed from or near to the stand until Uttoxeter Bus Station was built in 1970. Excursions and Tours from Uttoxeter were licensed as D884; the first licensed tour was to Blackpool, to operate between April and October.

GH Webb of Somersal Herbert had operated a service from there to Uttoxeter via Doveridge on market days from at least May 1924, and on 4th July 1927 Uttoxeter UDC had renewed his licence (for using vehicle R 7277). Either Webb had ceased to operate that service or John Stevenson had acquired it from Webb by June 1931, but the vehicle was not acquired. On 1st December 1930, Trent Motor Traction Ltd advised Uttoxeter UDC that they had acquired Bayliss & Sons' bus company and received permission to operate to the same timetable for the Ashbourne to Uttoxeter service via Rocester. In the other direction, PET had services to Abbots Bromley, Coton-in-the-Clay, and Kings Bromley, as well as between Uttoxeter and the Potteries. From September 1926 Harry Wood of Newborough Road, Hanbury, had operated a Burton to Newborough service via Tatenhill, Rangemoor, Anslow and Hoar Cross (Monday to Saturday, and summer Sundays), as well as a Wednesday only service from Burton via Shobnall, New Inn, Newborough and Thorney Lanes to Uttoxeter. By January 1932 Stevensons had been granted a licence for eighteen more excursions and tours, which

The second of Stevensons' Sunbeam Pathans, CRF 349 (10), was bought in March 1934; it had a rear-entrance 32-seat Burlingham coach body with a roof-mounted luggage rack and was fitted with wiring on the roof as a radio aerial. At some time it was fitted with a Leyland petrol engine, but surprisingly, in view of the extra vehicles required at the time, this good-looking vehicle and the earlier Sunbeam were withdrawn in February 1941. No.10 was sold to Worthington Motor Tours, Stafford, later passing to Sutton Motor Services (Stoke) Ltd in March 1946, from where it was withdrawn in March 1949. The earlier Sunbeam was not so fortunate, being scrapped on withdrawal in 1941. Standing in front of the coach are (l to r) Bill Fraser, Tom Birch, and Bob Atkin who joined in February 1936. *(TJC)*

Seen by St Mary's Church, Uttoxeter, in the 1950s is CRE 13 (11), a Maudslay SF40 new in July 1935, which had a stylish Burlingham dual-purpose body featuring an entrance right at the front by the engine; that configuration allowed for the fitment of 40 seats but by 1946 this had been reduced to 38. After a life of twenty-two years it was withdrawn in September 1957 following an accident in August and scrapped. *(OS)*

Conductor Arthur Charlesworth stands on the step of **VT 1195**, a Bristol 'B' with Lawton body of 1928, purchased from Tilstone, Tunstall in May, 1935. It is seen outside the garage at Spath, and the near-side front tyre seems to be ready for replacement. *(TJC)*

One of the vehicles bought in 1938 was **VT 4759**, a Leyland Lion LT2 with Lawton 34-seat body, which was ordered by J. Pritchard, Stoke-on-Trent, but delivered to Tilstone's, Tunstall in 1930; the seating had been reduced to 32 by 1948. Bearing fleet number 9, it is seen in 1949 in Balance Street, Uttoxeter, presumably on a Wednesday market day, and it served for 15 years before withdrawal on 21st December 1953. Reputedly, the town name has had 79 spellings since it was mentioned in the Domesday Book as 'Wotocheshede', although the favoured pronunciation by local people is 'Uhcheter'. The Market Charter dates from 1308. *(CW)*

VT 9766 (6), a Lawton-bodied TSM B39A, was new to Hawthorne, Stoke-on-Trent in 1933; it was acquired in 1938 and is seen in 1944 opposite the Spath garage. In the following year a Leyland radiator was fitted. The body was extensively rebuilt in 1946 to a modern style, including flared lower panels, and the removal of the roof luggage rack, and it was renumbered 2 *(GHB/RM)*

The only vehicle bought in 1937 was EVT 422 (12), a Bedford WTB with a Duple 25-seat coach body which cost £850, and it is seen resplendent at Spath when still quite new. Of note are the wires on the roof for the radio aerial. This stylish coach lasted until 29th March 1960. *(TJC)*

operated between April and October, and in April that year a licence for an express service from Uttoxeter (Market Place) to Blackpool was added, which was only operated on Saturdays in July, August and September, with a maximum of two vehicles on each timing. By that time forecourt petrol sales were taking place, which provided extra income; diesel was still being sold in the 1980s. Another local operator was Fox and Gallimore of High Street, Uttoxeter, which operated two town services in the 1920s, but it does not appear that licences were applied for in 1930/1. It became GA Fox in 1930, then in December 1934 GA Fox snr. & GA Fox jnr, from which time a service was operated between Uttoxeter and Leigh, until the company ceased around 1939.

The service from Uttoxeter via Hanbury to Burton (New Street Bus Park) left the main road at Sudbury and ran via Draycott-in-the-Clay, Hanbury, Anslow, Acorn Inn and Henhurst Hill. Sometimes this service and the Ashbourne service connected with the 'main road' buses at Sudbury, necessitating a change of vehicle there for passengers travelling to and from Burton, or Uttoxeter. Also, an application was made in April 1933 to extend the Wednesday market day service between Uttoxeter and Somersal to Cubley Common (Darley Moor), and that had taken place at least by August. Additional taking-up points for tours and excursions were granted in March 1934, at Draycott-in-the-Clay, Stramshall, Beamhurst, Checkley and Fole, the last four points also being included in the Blackpool express licence; the 1935 timetable for this service shows a journey time of 5½ hours! The Cash Book for June 1934 gives an insight into the extent of private hires and excursions from the general area around Uttoxeter and Burton, there being just over thirty in the month. At the time there was a fleet of eight vehicles and examples of destinations and coach hire prices are: Chatsworth (£7 5s), Rhyl (£8 11s 6d), Lickey Hills (£5 12s), Matlock (£5), Port Sunlight (£6 12s), Llangollen (£8 10s), Southport (£10 6s 6d), Coventry (£4) and Liverpool (£10), together with many local destinations. A licence for a Saturday evening service between Burton and Scropton via Tutbury was granted on 11th June 1934.

From 11th February 1935 Uttoxeter UDC decreed that on Wednesday market days, during the period of the market, until 6pm, buses would have to use Balance Street as the terminal point for services. This affected Whieldon's services to Rugeley and Stafford, but their service to Marchington and beyond would have departed as usual from the entrance to their garage opposite Stevensons' stand by the Market Place. In 1935 John Jnr took over as General Manager, relieving his father of the administrative and managerial tasks. Sam Barlow joined the company in the following year as a conductor and he had become the longest-serving employee at the time of his retirement in 1978, albeit with a short break in service.

Until 1937 vehicle intake generally alternated between new and used purchases each year. There was a steady increase in business including private hire and excursion work, reflected in the purchase of a Morris Dictator, and another Sunbeam Pathan, both being new vehicles with Burlingham coach bodies. The Sunbeam coach, CRF 349, was bought in 1934; it had been built in 1933 for that year's Coach and Bus Show, and served as a demonstration vehicle for a while. A new Maudslay SF40, CRE 13, was bought in July 1935; it had a Burlingham 40-seat dual-purpose body, the entrance of which was right at the front by the engine. The chassis cost £675 and Burlingham received £543 for the body. By contrast, a seven-year-old Lawton-bodied Bristol B service bus was bought from Tilstone's, Tunstall, in May 1935 for just £50. On 14th November 1936 a new and very limited service was started from Burton via Beam Hill to Anslow (Bell Inn), which ran on Thursdays, Saturdays and Sundays. A Tilling Stevens B10A (VT 4482), Bristol B (VT 1195), and a normal-control Leyland Lioness (TE 4414) were second-hand purchases, preceding a new Duple-bodied Bedford WTB coach, which came in June 1937, and in that year the chassis of Milton Bus Co's Bristol B, VT 4202, was bought, apparently being used in the rebuilding of RA 4996.

An application was made in November 1937 to run a service to carry workers from Burton to the Air Ministry Works (RAF) at Fauld, near Tutbury. Temporary licences

1940

Telephone: Uttoxeter 131

Uttoxeter Yellow Bus Service

Proprietor : JOHN STEVENSON,

The Garage, Spath, Uttoxeter.

War Emergency Time Tables.

1—Uttoxeter, Hatton, Tutbury, Burton
2—Uttoxeter, Hanbury, Burton
3—Uttoxeter, Sudbury, Ashbourne
4—Uttoxeter, Somersal, Cubley
5—Burton, Tutbury, Scropton
6—Burton, Outwoods, Anslow, Beam Hill

KELLY, PRINTER, UTTOXETER.

Service No. 1—UTTOXETER AND BURTON TIME TABLE.

This Service starts from Wetmore Road Park, Burton, and from Market Square, Uttoxeter.

Stops (first table): Uttoxeter Dp., Doveridge, Sudbury, Foston, Salt Box, Tutbury, Burton arr.

Stops (second table): Burton Dp., Tutbury, Salt Box, Foston, Sudbury, Doveridge, Uttoxeter arr.

X—Does not run on Sundays. W—Runs Wednesdays and Saturdays only. S—Runs Saturdays only. T.S.—Runs Thurs. and Sats. only. Extra Bus for Uttoxeter, Saturdays only—Depart Doveridge 5-30 p. Extra Bus from Burton daily at 6-30 p.m. to Tutbury (Sundays excepted).

were granted for six weeks until the full licence came into effect on 10th January 1938; three vehicles were required initially, and four more used vehicles were bought from operators in the Potteries in 1938 due to this increased workload. During the Second World War many vehicles were required to transport workers to and from new military camps at Marchington, Sudbury and Foston, some workers travelling from as far afield as Stoke-on-Trent and Derby, although details of the wartime services are not available. Much of that military-generated work increased and continued for the next two or three decades as more camps were built in the area.

It was obvious that it was now desirable to base some vehicles at the Burton end of the operations, so in September 1938 temporary accommodation for five vehicles was provided in hired premises off Horninglow Street, Burton-upon-Trent, near the Drill Hall; this was short-lived, since on the first day of the war it was requisitioned for war use and used as a billet for the 6th North Staffordshire Territorial Regiment. After a brief spell in another location in Horninglow, in June 1940 the garage was re-located at Horninglow canal wharf, where vehicles had to be reversed along the canal side by the garage building. I am told that this was particularly unpleasant when it was foggy! Whilst based there, the company owned two lorries which were used to transport corn, mainly for Silcox the farm merchant, one of the wharf buildings being used

for corn storage, and there was a lorry contract with Tutbury RDC at least between 1949 and 1950. The lorry operation had ceased by about 1963 and one of the drivers, Ron Alderson, worked thereafter at the Spath garage. Rache Nelson left Stevensons on at least one occasion, but re-joined the bus company after military service, although he too spent some years driving the lorries. Gertrude Stevenson married in 1939 and gave up her conducting job; at about the same time Bill Stevenson also left the business to go into farming, although at busy periods he helped out as a driver when he could. In December 1938 a workers' service was granted to run from Uttoxeter to the RAF works at Fauld but strangely that licence was surrendered on 14th August 1939, although the service re-appeared later. By September 1939 the company was operating school contracts from Marchington, Abbots Bromley and Morrilow Heath to Uttoxeter and fourteen vehicles were in the fleet at that time.

By 1939, service numbers were being shown on the timetables as follows:
1. Uttoxeter-Tutbury-Burton
2. Uttoxeter-Hanbury-Burton
3. Uttoxeter-Sudbury-Ashbourne
4. Uttoxeter-Somersal-Cubley
5. Burton-Tutbury-Scropton
6. Burton-Beam Hill-Anslow

2. A Limited Company

With the advent of war and fuel supply difficulties, excursions and tours were suspended and reductions in service levels were made, an example of the alterations being on the previous page. With good foresight a quantity of seasoned ash had been bought just before the war; this certainly helped the company to keep wooden-framed vehicles on the road during the hostilities. Likewise, there was a stock of hides to enable the repair of seats. The biggest problem was the terrible shortage of staff with so many men, including family members, being in the armed forces. George Stevenson had been enlisted into the Royal Engineers, and in 1940 Joan Ryder had become his wife; eventually the family managed to convince the authorities that George was required to keep the business running and he was released from the Army. In due course he and Joan moved into Spath House which was opposite the garage; one room in the house was used as a mess room by the employees. In November 1941 a new company, John Stevenson (Uttoxeter) Limited, was formed; this took over the business, although the vehicles remained licensed to John Stevenson. 'Brooklands' was the registered office and it remained so to the end. Four elderly vehicles were acquired between November 1943 and September 1944, these being two Leyland LT2s, a Bristol B and a Morris Dictator.

Mention has already been made of Fauld, which lies between Tutbury and Draycott-in-the-Clay. Gypsum had been mined there for hundreds of years and a large area of old underground workings had been requisitioned for war use by the RAF as an underground munitions storage depot. On Monday 27th November 1944 at 11.11am, 3,670 tons of ordnance, mainly high-explosive filled bombs ready for use in France and Germany, exploded; it was one of the largest non-nuclear explosions in history and the largest ever to occur on UK soil. Seventy-eight lives were lost, including RAF staff, civilian workers, Italian prisoners-of-war, rescue workers and people from two farms which, together with all the livestock, were obliterated. Thirty-seven of the fatalities were workers of Peter Ford & Sons Plaster and Lime Works, and others in the surrounding countryside, most of whom drowned when the explosion destroyed the dam of a large reservoir. The Cock Inn at nearby Hanbury had to be re-built and a large number of buildings, some many miles away from the explosion, had to be repaired. The resultant 'Hanbury crater' is still a restricted area.

The connection with buses is that Stevensons provided transport to the site for RAF personnel and civilian workers. George Stevenson said that on the day of the explosion two vehicles had been left there ready for later return journeys. Both were severely damaged and some time later 'an official' visited the company and established the value of the two vehicles. An amount was paid on the understanding that no details were released. Perusal of the fleet list shows that a Leyland Lioness, TE 4414, left the fleet at an unknown date in 1944, and that has to be one of the vehicles concerned. Basil Stevenson (George Stevenson's nephew) recalled that the other vehicle was a 'Tall Tillings', which could only have been VT 6211 (previously recorded as withdrawn in July 1944), or EH 9136. Basil thinks that it was the latter vehicle, which coincidentally is seen in the photo overleaf with TE 4414. EH 9136 is recorded as being withdrawn, at an unknown date, and sold to Templeton, Birmingham, and then used as a lorry until December 1950. If that was the second vehicle involved

GO 4307 was a Leyland LT2 which had been new to RF Knight (White Line Coaches), London, in April 1931, and it was in Stevensons' fleet by March 1944, becoming no.15. The make of the interesting body is not known, but it could be by Petty or Wycombe. At some stage Stevensons fitted the Cov-Rad radiator seen in this view at Spath, and the vehicle was withdrawn in 1950. (TJC)

The company also introduced workmen's weekly tickets, an example being shown here. An updated version was used on the Burton to Birmingham express service from the 1980s; although issuing them was time-consuming on Mondays, the use of them certainly assisted timekeeping for the rest of the week. (EWC)

The only Leyland Lioness owned was TE 4414, a PLC1 with a Strachan & Brown 26-seat body. New in 1928 to Colne Corporation Transport, it came to Stevensons in 1936 becoming no.8. Previously understood to have been converted from normal control to forward control prior to entry to service, this view taken in 1944 shows it still as built, and Basil Stevenson has no recollection of its being converted. The other vehicle in view is EH 9136, a Tilling Stevens (TSM) B10A with a Lawton 32-seat body new in 1927 (Lawton's first 'overtype' body), which was acquired from Tilstone, Tunstall, in 1932. The buses are parked on the grass verge, opposite the garage, that practice later being the subject of complaints; the name of the dog is unrecorded. *(GHB/RM)*

VT 4482, a TSM B10A which had a 34-seat bus body, make unknown, was new to Hawthorn's Bus Company (Central), Stoke-on-Trent in 1930. It passed to PMT, from where it was bought in 1936, becoming no.14. At some stage thereafter it had been withdrawn and converted into a henhouse, but following the loss of two vehicles in the Fauld explosion, was resurrected, fitted with wooden slatted seats, and returned to the road. It had received a Leyland radiator by 1949 and was withdrawn in June the following year, being sold on 29th August 1950 for £26; not bad for an old henhouse! The vehicles to the left are VT 9766, RF 8719 and RB 6093. *(RM/OS)*

In February 1945 a utility double-decker was allocated to Stevensons; the first such vehicle to be owned. It cost £2,300 and was a Park Royal-bodied Guy Arab II, registered LRE 199 (17), which had a Gardner 5LW engine, and is seen at the Horninglow Canal Wharf garage, Burton. Withdrawal of no.17 came in August 1964. *(EWC)*

in the explosion, then possibly only the body of the bus was badly damaged, but it could have been suitable for conversion for use as a lorry. At the time VT 4482, a Tilling Stevens which had been acquired in 1936, had been withdrawn and was in use as a hen house but it was resurrected and put back on the road, minus its hens! Quoting Basil Stevenson "We cut up, patched up or rebuilt so many buses during the war years; you just used what you could get and put the pieces together".

The situation was improved considerably when the Ministry of Supply allocated a new vehicle to the company. It was the first double-decker in the fleet, a Guy Arab II 5LW with Park Royal high-bridge body built to relaxed-utility specification, which arrived in February 1945; this bus remained in the fleet for nearly twenty years. The passing of the 1944 Education Act led to an increase in the number of school contracts, and by 1948 Stevensons was operating seven in the Uttoxeter area.

STEVENSON'S BUS SERVICE No. 2

Uttoxeter - Burton-on-Trent.

Route — Uttoxeter, Doveridge, Sudbury, Draycott, Hanbury, Anslow, Beam Hill and Burton.

TIME TABLE—DAILY

	X am	X am	X am	pm	pm	TS pm	pm	TS pm	pm	pm	SS pm	SS pm
Dep UTTOXETER	7 45		11 0		1 15				4 45	7 0		9 15
„ DOVERIDGE	7 50		11 5		1 20				4 50	7 5		9 20
„ SUDBURY	8 0		11 15		1 30				5 0	7 15		9 30
„ DRAYCOTT	8 10		11 25		1 40				5 10	7 25		9 40
„ HANBURY	8 20		11 35		1 50				5 20	7 35		9 50
„ ANSLOW, BELL	8 30	9 0	11 45	12 0	2 0	2 15	3 30	5 15	5 30	7 45	9 15	10 0
„ BEAM HILL	8 35	9 5	11 55	12 5	2 5	2 20	3 35	5 20	5 35	7 50	9 20	10 5
Arr. BURTON	8 45	9 15	12 0	12 15	2 15	2 30	3 45	5 30	5 45	8 0	9 30	10 15

	X am	X am	am	X pm	TS pm	pm	pm	TS pm	pm	pm	SS pm	SS pm
Dep. BURTON	8 45	10 0	11 45	12 15	2 0	3 15	4 0	5 0	5 45	8 0	9 0	10 15
„ BEAM HILL	8 55	10 10	11 55	12 25	2 10	3 25	4 10	5 10	5 55	8 10	9 10	10 25
„ ANSLOW, BELL	9 0	10 15	12 0	12 30	2 15	3 30	4 15	5 15	6 0	8 15	9 15	10 30
„ HANBURY		10 25		12 40			4 25		6 15	8 25		10 45
„ DRAYCOTT		10 35		12 50			4 35		6 25	8 35		10 55
„ SUDBURY		10 45		1 0			4 45c		6 35	8 45		11 5
„ DOVERIDGE		10 55		1 10			5 0c		6 45	8 55		11 10
Arr. UTTOXETER		11 0		1 15			5 15c		6 50	9 0		11 15

X—Means not Sunday. TS—Means Thursday and Saturday only.
SS—Means Saturday and Sunday only. C—Means change at Sudbury.
2. 15 p.m. Arrive Burton to proceed to Burton Infirmary on Thursdays and Sundays at 3.55 p.m. Depart Burton Infirmary to Bus Park.
Buses Terminate at Wetmore Road Motor Park, Burton-on-Trent, Sudbury and Market Place, Uttoxeter.

Proprietor - JOHN STEVENSON, THE GARAGE, SPATH, UTTOXETER. (Tel. Uttoxeter 131)

Timetable dated late 1948.

TELEPHONE: UTTOXETER 131

JOHN STEVENSON

PROPRIETOR OF THE YELLOW COACH SERVICES

REGULAR SERVICES TO
BURTON-ON-TRENT
AND ASHBOURNE

MODERN COACHES
FOR HIRE

BRANCH OFFICE:
CANAL WHARF GARAGE
HORNINGLOW ROAD NORTH
BURTON-ON-TRENT

THE GARAGE, SPATH, UTTOXETER, STAFFS

Nov 5th 1946

The Clerk to the Commissioners
West Midland Traffic Area,
York House,
Gt. Charles Street,
Birmingham 3.

RECEIVED
6 NOV 1946

Ref D9922

Dear Sir,

Stage Service Uttoxeter - Burton-on-Trent

I beg to submit an application to vary the Time Table on the above service for which a copy of the proposed variation together with a copy of the existing time table are enclosed herewith, thanking you,

Yours faithfully

[signature] Stevenson

Returned for slight alter.

George Stevenson had many talents, and from the mid-1930s applied most of the signwriting, including the 'rising sun' emblems, on Stevenson's vehicles, particularly during the war except during his time in the armed forces. He was also an excellent welder and occasionally undertook some welding work for Joe Bamford, who had left the family's agricultural machinery business and started J C Bamford (later JCB) in a small garage in Uttoxeter in 1945. He moved the company to Rocester where he was able to develop the business, and it has now become a world-wide multi-million pound concern famous for its excavators and other innovative machinery. The foreman painter at Bamfords was Harold Foster, and he may have done some signwriting for Stevensons before the war. In any case, from the late 1940s until his death in 1973, Harold carried out more or less all the signwriting for the company; this included advertisements on the buses as well as preparing destination blinds.

From 19th October 1946, service 2 was altered to run via Anslow village and Beam Hill instead of via The Acorn Inn, the timings between Anslow and Burton on service 6 being incorporated. Between 1946 and 1950 Leylands and some Guys featured in the fleet; three were used examples but there was a new Burlingham-bodied Leyland Titan PD1 and two new Leyland Tiger PS1s with Barnard coach bodies. Two of the three new Guy Arab IIIs had coach bodies, one by Santus and one Burlingham; the third received a Massey high-bridge body which was to be the last new double-decker for over thirty years. The operation of double-deckers brought its own problems, in that the garage had been built for single-deckers. Part of the garage was rebuilt during 1945 and 1946 to accommodate four double-deckers, approval having been given in July 1945; a KNE low-voltage inspection lamp system was incorporated in the pits, and workshop machinery was updated, which enabled larger jobs, including rebuilds, to be tackled. In 1946 there were problems with vehicles having to be parked on the grass verge of the road at Spath, and a plan was put forward to convert a field across the road from the garage into a vehicle park. There were council objections, but it was completed around mid-1947. Nationwide, the winter of 1947

This 1947 view by Scropton Lane, Hatton shows **NRE 36** (4), a **Leyland Titan PD1** with Burlingham body which cost £3,926 when new in April of that year; it went on to achieve 19 years' service. Note the stylish gas lamp in the picture. *(B&C)*

Two identical Leyland Tiger PS1/1s, **PRE 607/8**, (8 and 20) with Barnard 33-seat bodies were bought in June 1948 for £3,990 each, and the latter vehicle is seen on market day in Balance Street, Uttoxeter with conductor Ken Charlesworth sporting his **TIM** ticket machine. *(EWC)*

This Santus-bodied **Guy Arab III** (5LW), **MRE 391**, was new to Stevensons in October 1946 as no.18 and cost £3,017. It arrived painted only in black and white, and John Stevenson would not go near it until it had been correctly painted! Unfortunately, Santus bodies were not brilliant, and it can be seen that the sliding roof has been removed in an attempt to improve the rigidity of the coach. This may have helped it to achieve nineteen years' service. *(EWC)*

New in May 1949 was RRF 773, a Meadows-engined Guy Arab III which carried a stylish 56-seat Massey body, the total cost being £4,247. At some time it received a replacement Gardner 5LW engine, and platform doors were fitted in May 1965; it served in the fleet until April 1969. Roy Marshall recorded the vehicle at Wetmore Bus Park, Burton on 12th April 1952; perhaps the lady, young girl and teddy bear were waiting for the 'Blue Bus Service' (Tailby & George) vehicle to arrive at its accustomed location in the bus park. The bus in front is GE 7222, which was withdrawn in July 1954. *(RM/OS)*

was exceptionally severe, and Stevensons' services were affected, although the drivers kept going as best they could in atrocious conditions. One day George Stevenson was driving the last bus from Ashbourne; he and his conductor waited for time, but carried no-one, and eventually had to leave the bus in a drift and make their way back on foot. It then took ages for the road to be cleared so that the bus could be rescued.

A Morris Dictator, RF 8719, which had been new to the company in 1931, was extensively rebuilt in 1949 to a modern style inside and out, and received a Leyland radiator. Thereafter, it was often the vehicle of choice by private hire organisers and was still used on long-distance work in 1952, visiting Blackpool twice, London

and Cardiff! A Tilling-Stevens, VT 9766, was similarly rebuilt. In the late 1940s a number of vehicles received Gardner 4LW or 5LW engines and Leyland or Cov-Rad radiators as replacements for original equipment; Gardner engines became increasingly popular over the next ten years or so. An acquired Leyland Tiger coach and one of the Barnard-bodied PS1s received new Burlingham bodies (1950/3), the latter being a full-fronted example. Perusal of the Coach Bookings Diary for Saturday, 11th June 1949, reveals that there were fourteen private hire or excursion bookings for the day from a fleet of twenty-four vehicles; therefore, over half the fleet was engaged on coaching work. A booking to Skegness was for two coaches and cost £46 10s in total. Some other destinations and prices were as follows: Rhyl (£21 15s), the equivalent price in 1935 being £8 11s 6d, London (£33 15s), Manchester (£20 5s), Belle Vue (£18 4s 6d), Warwick (£13 4s). All these jobs were covered by new or re-bodied coaches, local work being covered by more elderly vehicles, even a Bristol B of 1927! A large proportion of this work was from the Burton area, but one job for a 25-seater was sub-contracted from Warrington's Coaches of Ilam.

Stevensons' services sat neatly in the area bounded by Trent Motor Traction, BMMO (Midland Red) and Potteries Motor Traction (PMT). The latter company also operated into Uttoxeter from Longton and Hanley, the Hanley service being extended to Derby, and they ran a number of country routes to the town, mainly on market days. In the late 1940s new housing estates were being built on the west side of Uttoxeter; both Stevensons and PMT expected to benefit from this potential increased patronage, as did Whieldon's and, after some disputes, much paperwork and many meetings, new arrangements were brought in. From October 5th 1946, despite PMT opposition, Stevensons started a new

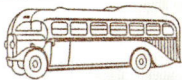

STEVENSON'S TOURS

In July 1931 Stevensons purchased this new Morris Dictator, RF 8719 (4), which carried a Burlingham body seating 32. Previously quoted as having a front entrance, an early photo shows it with one at the rear. Here we see it after being extensively rebuilt in 1948, as described earlier for VT 9766; also, the doorway has been moved to the front, and bus-type seats are fitted. It was renumbered 21, and served the company until December 1952. *(PY/OS)*

service from Bramshall via Bramshall Road and Holly Road to Uttoxeter which was allocated the vacant service number 6; from June 1948 it was extended to Doveridge, thereby providing a service into Doveridge village for the first time, as the Burton services passed by on the main road. PMT started their Town Circular, which at that stage served Park Avenue and New Road, around November 1948, but Whieldon's lost out completely with these new services.

From early 1948, following a request from Tutbury RDC for buses to serve the Park Lane and Redhill Lane area of Tutbury, where the council was building new houses, the Burton to Scropton service 5 was enhanced considerably becoming a daily operation, and was diverted via these roads. On 2nd December 1949 a new Wednesday-only service was granted between Church Broughton, Hatton, and Scropton to Uttoxeter, which provided for one return journey. However, passenger numbers did not justify its continuance, and it had ceased by 22nd September 1950. By contrast, in 1948 patronage on service 1 was such that a request was made to the Traffic Commissioners for substantial licensed duplication on every day of the week, and this was granted on 22nd October 1948 as follows: Mondays, Tuesdays, Fridays – 12 journeys; Thursdays – 16 journeys; Wednesdays – 15 journeys; Saturdays – 26 journeys; Sundays – 16 journeys. Some duplicates ran between the termini, Uttoxeter and Burton, whilst others operated between either Tutbury or Hatton and Burton, or between Tutbury or Sudbury and Uttoxeter. Many of these duplicates were operated by double-deckers!

In 1950 Joan Stevenson's sister, Madeline (Miss Ryder or "Madge') joined the company to run the office at Spath, and worked there for nearly thirty years; she passed away in 2010, age 96. An insurance document reveals that in July 1950 the value of the fleet was £26,481. On 1st February 1950 a daily service was started between Burton and Ashbourne via Ironwalls Lane and Park Lane in Tutbury, thence via Scropton, Cubley and Clifton, which generally afforded connections at Sudbury to and from Uttoxeter, thereby replacing the earlier Uttoxeter to Ashbourne and Burton to Scropton services; it retained the latter's service number 5. The terminal point in Ashbourne was Station Road until the

STEVENSON'S BUS SERVICE No. 6

Doveridge - Uttoxeter - Bramshall

Starts from Market Place, Uttoxeter, Bell Inn, Doveridge and Dagdale Lane, Bramshall.

TIME TABLE from 1st SEPT., 1951

	X a.m.	X a.m.	X a.m.	a.m.	a.m.	p.m.	X p.m.	X p.m.	X p.m.	X p.m.	p.m.	p.m.	p.m.	p.m.	p.m.
Dep Doveridge ...		7 40	8 45	10 5		12 35	2 5	2 35	3 35	4 5		6 5		8 5	9 20
Arr Uttoxeter ...		7 50	8 55	10 15		12 45	2 15	2 45	3 45	4 15		6 15		9 15	9 30
	MF	X	X	X	SO	X	SUN	X							
Dep Uttoxeter ...	7 15	7 50	9 0	10 30	11 15	12 45	2 15	3 0		4 15	5 30	6 15	7 20	8 45	10 0
,, Wharf ...	7 18	7 53	9 3	10 33	11 18	12 48	2 18	3 3		4 18	5 33	6 18	7 33	8 48	10 3
,, Dollis Hill ...	7 20	7 55	9 5	10 35	11 20	12 50	2 20	3 5		4 20	5 35	6 20	7 35	8 50	10 5
,, The Heath ...	7 22	7 57	9 7	10 37	11 22	12 52	2 22	3 7		4 22	5 37	6 22	7 37	8 52	10 7
,, Stone Road ...	7 24	7 59	9 9	10 39	11 24	12 54	2 24	3 9		4 24	5 39	6 24	7 39	8 54	10 9
,, Kiddlestitch ...	7 26	8 1	9 11	10 41	11 26	12 56	2 26	3 11		4 26	5 41	6 26	7 41	8 56	10 11
Arr Bramshall ...	7 30	8 5	9 15	10 45	11 30	1 0	2 30	3 15		4 30	5 45	6 30	7 45	9 0	10 15
	MF a.m.	X a.m.	X a.m.	X a.m.	SO a.m.	X p.m.	SUN p.m.	X p.m.	p.m.	p.m.	p.m.	p.m.	p.m.	p.m.	p.m.
Dep Bramshall ...	7 30	8 25	9 15	10 45	11 30	1 15	2 30	3 15		4 45	5 45	6 30	7 45	9 0	10 15
,, Kiddlestitch ...	7 34	8 28	9 19	10 49	11 34	1 19	2 34	3 19		4 49	5 49	6 34	7 49	9 4	10 19
,, Stone Road ...	7 36	8 31	9 21	10 51	11 36	1 21	2 36	3 21		4 51	5 51	6 36	7 51	9 6	10 21
,, The Heath ...	7 38	8 33	9 23	10 53	11 38	1 23	2 38	3 23		4 53	5 53	6 38	7 53	9 8	10 23
,, Dollis Hill ...	7 40	8 35	9 25	10 55	11 40	1 25	2 40	3 25		4 55	5 55	6 40	7 55	9 10	10 25
,, Wharf ...	7 42	8 37	9 27	10 57	11 42	1 27	2 42	3 27		4 57	5 57	6 42	7 57	9 12	10 27
Arr Uttoxeter ...	7 45	8 40	9 30	11 0	11 45	1 30	2 45	3 30		5 0	6 0	6 45	8 0	9 15	10 30
	X	X				X	X	X	X						
Dep Uttoxeter ...	7 30	8 40	10 0		12 30	2 0	2 30	3 30	4 0		6 0		8 0	9 15	10 30
Arr Doveridge ...	7 40	8 45	10 5		12 35	2 5	2 35	3 35	4 5		6 5		8 5	9 20	10 35

MF—Monday to Friday. X—Does not run on Sunday. SUN—Sunday only. SO—Saturday only.

Connections for Derby, Longton, Rugeley, Cannock, Stafford and Lichfield.

Proprietor - JOHN STEVENSON, THE GARAGE, SPATH, UTTOXETER. (Tel. Uttoxeter 131)

KELLY'S X.L. PRINTING WORKS, UTTOXETER.

TIME TABLE

DAILY

		X a.m.	X a.m.	X a.m.	X a.m.	a.m.	X a.m.	WTS p.m.	p.m.	p.m.	p.m.	p.m.	p.m.	p.m.	p.m.	p.m.	p.m
Uttoxeter	dep.	6. 0	7. 0	8. 0	9.30	10.35	11.45	12.15	1. 0	2. 0	2.45	4. 0	5.30	6.30	7.35	8.35	9.30
Doveridge	,,	6. 5	7. 5	8. 5	9.35	10.40	11.50	12.25	1. 5	2. 5	2.50	4. 5	5.35	6.35	7.40	8.40	9.35
Sudbury	,,	6.15	7.15	8.15	9.45	10.50	12. 0	12.35	1.15	2.15	3. 0	4.15	5.45	6.45	7.50	8.50	9.45
Foston	,,	6.25	7.20	8.20	9.50	10.55	12. 5	12.40	1.20	2.20	3. 5	4.20	5.50	6.50	7.55	8.55	9.50
Salt Box	,,	6.30	7.25	8.25	9.55	11. 0	12.10	12.45	1.25	2.25	3.10	4.25	5.55	6.55	8. 0	9. 0	9.55
Tutbury	,,	6.35	7.30	8.30	10. 0	11. 5	12.15	12.50	1.30	2.30	3.15	4.30	6. 0	7. 0	8. 5	9. 5	10. 0
Burton	arr.	7. 0	7.50	9. 0	10.20	11.25	12.35	1.10	1.50	2.50	3.35	4.50	6.20	7.15	8.25	9.25	10.15
		X a.m.	X a.m.	X a.m.	X a.m.	WTS a.m.	p.m.	X p.m.	p.m.	p.m.	p.m.	p.m.	p.m.	p.m.	p.m.	p.m.	p.m.
Burton	dep.	7. 0	8. 0	9. 0	10.30	11.15	12.15	1.15	2.30	3.15	4.15	5.30	6.30	7.15	8.30	9.30	10.20
Tutbury	,,	7.15	8.20	9.20	10.50	11.35	12.35	1.35	2.50	3.35	4.35	5.50	6.50	7.35	8.50	9.50	10.35
Salt Box	,,	7.25	8.30	9.25	10.55	11.45	12.45	1.45	2.55	3.45	4.40	5.55	7. 0	7.45	8.55	9.55	10.40
Foston	,,	7.30	8.35	9.30	11. 0	11.50	12.50	1.50	3. 0	3.50	4.45	6. 0	7. 5	7.50	9. 0	10. 0	10.45
Sudbury	,,	7.35	8.40	9.35	11. 5	11.55	12.55	1.55	3. 5	3.55	4.50	6. 5	7.10	7.55	9. 5	10. 5	10.50
Doveridge	,,	7.45	8.50	9.45	11.15	12. 5	1. 5	2. 5	3.15	4. 5	5. 0	6.15	7.20	8. 5	9 15	10.15	11. 0
Uttoxeter	arr.	7.50	9. 0	9.55	11.25	12.15	1.15	2.15	3.25	4.15	5.10	6.25	7.30	8.15	9.25	10.25	11.10

X—Not Sundays. WTS—Wednesdays, Thursdays and Saturdays only.

DUPLICATE SERVICE

MONDAYS, TUESDAYS AND FRIDAYS

		p.m.	p.m.	p.m.	p.m.	p.m.	p.m.
Uttoxeter to Burton	dep.	5.30	6.15	—	—	—	—
Uttoxeter to Tutbury	,,	4. 0	—	—	—	—	—
Burton to Hatton	,,	4.15	5.30	9.30	—	—	—
		a.m.	a.m.				
Sudbury to Uttoxeter	,,	7.35	8.40	—	—	—	—
Tutbury to Burton ..	,,	7.30	—	—	—	—	—
			p.m.				
Hatton to Burton	,,	8.25	3.10	9.55	—	—	—

THURSDAYS

		p.m.	p.m.	p.m.	p.m.	p.m.	p.m.
Uttoxeter to Burton ..	,,	5.30	6.30	—	—	—	—
Uttoxeter to Tutbury..	,,	4. 0	—	—	—	—	—
Burton to Hatton	,,	4.15	5.30	7.15	9.30	10.20	—
		a.m.	a.m.				
Tutbury to Burton ..	,,	7.30	—	—	—	—	—
Hatton to Burton	,,	8.25	9.55	1.25	3.10	9.55	—
Sudbury to Uttoxeter	,,	7.35	8.40	—	—	—	—

WEDNESDAYS

		p.m.	p.m.	p.m.	p.m.	p.m.	p.m.
Uttoxeter to Burton	,,	5.30	2.45	4. 0	6.30	—	—
		a.m.	a.m.				
Burton to Uttoxeter	,,	9. 0	10.30	—	—	—	—
		p.m.	p.m.	p.m.	p.m.	p.m.	
Burton to Hatton	,,	4.15	5.30	9.30	10.20		
		a.m.	a.m.				
Tutbury to Burton ..	,,	7.30	—	—	—	—	—
Hatton to Burton	,,	8.25	9.55	—	—	—	—
Sudbury to Uttoxeter	,,	7.35	8.40	—	—	—	—

SATURDAYS

		a.m.	p.m.	p.m.	p.m.	p.m.	p.m.
Uttoxeter to Burton	,,	9.30	1. 0	2. 0	4. 0	5.30	6.30
		p.m.					
Burton to Uttoxeter	,,	1.15	2.30	10.20	—	—	—
Burton to Sudbury....	,,	12.15	—	—	—	—	—
Burton to Hatton	,,	3.15	4.15	5.30	6.30	7.15	8.30
		9.30					
Hatton to Burton	,,	3.10	9.55	—	—	—	—
		a.m.					
Tutbury to Burton ..	,,	7.30	1.30	—	—	—	—
			a.m.				
Sudbury to Uttoxeter	,,	7.35	8.40	3.55	7.10	—	—
		p.m.					
Uttoxeter to Sudbury	,,	7.35	—	—	—	—	—

SUNDAYS

		p.m.	p.m.	p.m.	p.m.	p.m.	p.m
Uttoxeter to Burton	,,	1. 0	5.30	6.30	7.30	—	—
Burton to Uttoxeter	,,	4.15	5.30	6.30	8.30	10.20	—
Burton to Hatton	,,	2.30	7.15	9.30	—	—	—
Hatton to Burton	,,	3.10	4.25	9. 0	9.55	—	—

8

FARE TABLE

ORDINARY FARES

	Uttoxeter		Doveridge		Halfway		Sudbury		Foston		Hatton		Tutbury		Lodge		Beamhill	
	S	R	S	R	S	R	S	R	S	R	S	R	S	R	S	R	S	R
Burton	1/4	2/-	1/-	1/10	1/-	1/8	10d.	1/6	8d.	1/2	6d.	11d.	5d.	9d.	3d.	5d.	3d.	5d.
Horninglow	1/2	2/-	1/-	1/8	10d.	1/6	9d.	1/4	6d.	11d.	5d.	9d.	4d.	7d.	2d.	4d.		
Beamhill	1/-	1/10	10d.	1/6	9d.	1/4	8d.	1/2	5d.	9d.	4d.	7d.	3d.	5d.	1d.			
Lodge	1/-	1/8	9d.	1/4	8d.	1/2	6d.	11d.	4d.	7d.	3d.	5d.	2d.	4d.				
Tutbury	10d.	1/6	8d.	1/2	6d.	11d.	5d.	9d.	3d.	5d.	2d.	4d.						
Hatton	9d.	1/4	6d.	11d.	5d.	9d.	4d.	7d.	2d.	4d.								
Foston	8d.	1/2	5d.	9d.	4d.	7d.	2d.	4d.										
Sudbury	5d.	9d.	3d.	5d.	2d.	4d.												
Halfway	4d.	7d.	2d.	4d.														
Doveridge	3d.	4d.																

WORKMENS RETURN

	Burton	Tutbury	Hatton	Foston	Sudbury	Halfway	Doveridge
Uttoxeter	1/9	'1/-	1/-	11d.	6d.	5d.	4d.
Doveridge	1/9	11d.	8d.	—	—	—	—
Halfway	1/6	8d.	7d.	—	—	—	—
Sudbury	1/-	7d.	6d.	—	—	—	—
Foston	11d.	—	—	—	—	—	—
Hatton	6d.	—	—	—	6d.	—	—
Tutbury	6d.	—	—	—	7d.	8d.	11d.
Horninglow	—	5d.	6d.	11d.	1/-	1/4	1/6

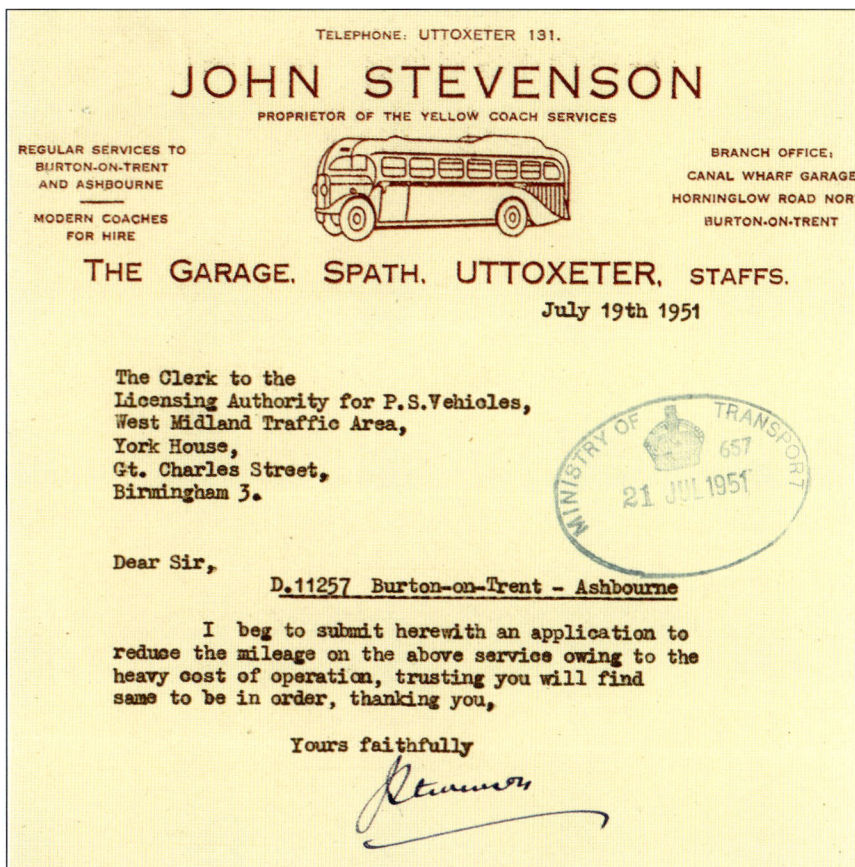

TELEPHONE: UTTOXETER 131.

JOHN STEVENSON

PROPRIETOR OF THE YELLOW COACH SERVICES

REGULAR SERVICES TO
BURTON-ON-TRENT
AND ASHBOURNE

MODERN COACHES
FOR HIRE

BRANCH OFFICE:
CANAL WHARF GARAGE
HORNINGLOW ROAD NORT
BURTON-ON-TRENT

THE GARAGE. SPATH. UTTOXETER, STAFFS.

July 19th 1951

The Clerk to the
Licensing Authority for P.S.Vehicles,
West Midland Traffic Area,
York House,
Gt. Charles Street,
Birmingham 3.

Dear Sir,

    D.11257 Burton-on-Trent - Ashbourne

    I beg to submit herewith an application to
reduce the mileage on the above service owing to the
heavy cost of operation, trusting you will find
same to be in order, thanking you,

    Yours faithfully

(MINISTRY OF TRANSPORT stamp, 657, 21 JUL 1951)

Brian Kershaw, a coach driver from Burton depot, told me of an occasion when he had taken the market day service to Ashbourne. He was just about to depart for his long break when he saw the Land Rover of George Stevenson (Mr George) pull up by his saloon. He explained that he needed the bus and, leaving his vehicle for Brian to use during his break, promised to be back in good time. True to his word he was back just in time, but when Brian looked inside there was straw and dirt on the floor. George kept some cattle on his land and he explained that he had needed to use the bus to take two calves to market. When Brian complained about the mess George replied that the passengers in the main would be farmers' wives who would, no doubt, be used to a bit of mess! It was not unknown for hens and small livestock to have been carried on market days.

new Bus Station opened on 1st October 1955. However, the service provision was extremely over-optimistic, and a reduction in frequency was soon applied for. There would have been some traffic associated with the RAF airfield and camp at Darley Moor, and between Burton and Scropton, but with the closure of the camp, and increasing ownership of cars (fuel rationing for cars ceased in May 1950), patronage declined considerably. In 1953 the service was cut back drastically but still ran below cost, and in 1965, reflecting further poor returns, the service became a Thursday and Saturday only operation (Ashbourne market days).

The first underfloor-engined coach was a Leyland Royal Tiger with Burlingham 'Seagull' coach body, bought new in 1951; the next new coach, a Plaxton-bodied Bedford SB, was bought in June 1953 and in 1956 a Duple-bodied example arrived. Remarkably, the fare table for the Uttoxeter-Tutbury-Burton service 1, dated 4th February 1952, shows that the single fare between the termini was 1/4d, exactly the same as it had been when the service started in 1926! However, this stability in fares was soon to change. The table of costs reproduced on this page reveals the situation in 1953/4, which it was hoped would be remedied in part by the new fare tables.

YRF 871, a Bedford SB with a Plaxton Venturer 37-seat body, was new in June 1953 (26), and gave over sixteen years' service. It is seen in Uttoxeter ready for a journey via Tutbury to Burton, possibly on a Sunday. Stevensons' Town Office was on the first floor to the left of the coach. (EWC)

25

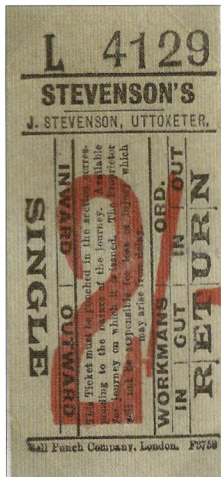

Tickets courtesy of DJ Stanier.

From March 1953, services were operated from Hanley, Alton and Derby to Marchington Camp, and from Meir and Alton to Foston Camp; these were weekday services for civilian workers at the camps. Between August 1953 and about May 1963 Stevensons operated express services to Manchester and Birmingham from Sudbury Camp for servicemen returning home for, and coming back off, weekend leave. Also, from April 1955 works services for civilian workers were jointly operated by Stevensons and Whieldon's between Uttoxeter and Sudbury Camp via Abbots Bromley, and between Mayfield and Sudbury Camp via Ashbourne. After one year Stevensons exchanged their share in the Abbots Bromley route for exclusive operation of the Ashbourne one; the latter service continued until 1967. During the 1950s many used single-deckers, some of which were coaches, on Dennis, Daimler, Leyland, and Guy chassis, were bought. A Leyland TD6 and two all-Leyland TD7 double-deckers were purchased from Birmingham City Transport in 1954, then the first of many double-deckers to be bought from London Transport Executive (LTE) came in 1957. These were seven-year-old 'RT' type AEC Regent IIIs with five-bay Cravens bodies, KGK 724/5, which were being disposed of early because the body make was non-standard for LTE. A four-bay Park Royal-bodied Leyland 7RT, also surplus to LTE's requirements, arrived in 1959 and more were to follow in due course; they worked for many more years with Stevensons than they had done with LTE. There were problems caused by the Suez Crisis from late 1956; this resulted in some service journeys being temporarily withdrawn, in

---

STEVENSON'S BUS SERVICES.   4th February 1952

FARE TABLE. No. 1 ROUTE. Uttoxeter to Burton via Tutbury

ORDINARY FARES.

	NKT PLACE UTTOXETER	DOVERIDGE	HALF WAY	SUDBURY	ASTON LANE	FOSTON	SALT BOX	HATTON	TUTBURY	FIDD. LANE	LODGE	BEAM HILL	HORNINGLOW
	Sin	Sin	Sin	Sin	Sin	Sin	Sin	Sin	Sin	Sin	Sin	Sin	Sin
BURTON	1/4	1/3	1/1	11d	11d	9d	7d	7d	6d	5d	4d	4d	3d
HORNINGLOW	1/3	1/1	1/-	10d	10d	8d	6d	6d	5d	4d	3d	3d	
BEAM HILL	1/3	1/1	1/-	9d	9d	7d	5d	5d	4d	2½	1½		
LODGE.	1/-	10d	9d	8d	7d	5d	4d	4d	3d	1½			
FIDD. LANE	11d	10d	8d	8d	7d	6d	4d	3d	2d				
TUTBURY	11d	9d	7d	6d	6d	4d	2½	1½					
HATTON	10d	8d	6d	5d	5d	3d	1½						
SALT BOX	9d	7d	6d	5d	5d	3d							
FOSTON	8d	6d	5d	4d	3d								
ASTON LANE	7d	5d	4d	2½									
SUDBURY	6d	4d	2½										
HALF WAY	5d	3d											
DOVERIDGE	3d												

CHILDREN'S FARES.
Children under 5 years of age, free providing they do not occupy a seat required by an adult Children who have attained the age of 5 years but have not yet attained the age of 14 years half the adult fare.

WORKMEN'S RETURN FARES to be issued up to 9am only.

	UTTOXETER	DOVERIDGE	HALF WAY	SUDBURY	FOSTON	SALT BOX	HATTON	TUTBURY	LODGE	BEAM HILL
	Rtn	Rtn	Rtn	Rtn	Rtn	Rtn	Rtn	Rtn	Rtn	Rtn
BURTON	1/9	1/8	1/6	1/3	1/-	11d	10d	10d	7d	6d
BEAM HILL	1/8	1/6	1/5	1/1	10d	8d	8d	7d		
LODGE.	1/6	1/5	1/3	1/-	10d	8d	8d	6d		
TUTBURY	1/3	1/1	10d	9d	7d					
HATTON	1/3	10d	9d	8d						
SALT BOX	1/1	10d	9d	8d						
FOSTON	1/-	9d	8d							
SUDBURY	8d	6d								
HALF WAY	7d.									

For HATTON read Church Lane Scropton Lane and Tutbury Stn.

COSTS 1953-54 (PENCE)

Traffic expenses: per mile
Office and managerial 1.00
Platform staff wages 6.75
Cleaning 0.125
Garage expenses 1.30
Oiling and greasing 0.15
Miscellaneous 0.15
                                                9.475

General expenses:
Rent and rates 0.10
Postage, telephone, printing 0.15
Light, heat and power 0.05
Insurance 0.50
Audit 0.06
Miscellaneous 0.35
                                                1.21

Repairs and maintenance:
Rolling stock 2.50
Buildings and fixtures 0.15
Tyres 0.525
                                                3.175

Fuel (including tax) 5.65
Licences 0.75
Depreciation 1.325

Total 21.585

Current fleet: Six double-deckers, 21 single-deckers.

Stevensons' tickets from 1955. AW Monk collection, courtesy Roger Monk

Also from London Transport came KGU 216, a 7RT (Leyland) with Park Royal body of 1949, bought when ten years old in November 1959 (29). Doors were fitted in October 1965 and it is seen passing through the pretty village of Sudbury on 3rd April 1969 at 10.49am, whilst working the 10.30am from Uttoxeter via Tutbury to Burton. After the Sudbury by-pass was completed three years later, the village was occasionally used for period films, at which time modern signage would be removed, and sawdust or such like would hide the modern road and pavement surfaces. The bus became something of a period piece since it lasted in service (mainly on contracts) until May 1976, at which time it was nearly twenty-seven years old. Leyland PD2 and PD3 chassis types would feature in the fleet for many years, the last one operating in 1993! (TJ)

view of fuel restrictions. Hostilities had ended by December that year, and the canal was fully reopened to shipping on 24th April 1957, fuel rationing ceasing in the following month, but the temporary service reductions were not reinstated since those journeys had been un-remunerative anyway. Interestingly, advertising of petrol on the recently-introduced ITV channel was banned for a year. Bell Punch tickets were used initially but they were replaced in the mid-1950s by 'TIM' machines (Ticket Issuing Machine Company), obviating the need for pre-printed tickets, and in due course by Setright machines, which in turn would eventually be superseded by electronic Wayfarer equipment in the late 1980s.

Summer express services ran to North Wales from Burton and the Ashbourne area, as well as to Blackpool from Uttoxeter and some points en route. Tours and excursions were operated over a wide area, and on Saturday 11th June 1955 the Coach Bookings Diary reveals that, from a fleet of twenty-seven vehicles, there were twenty-two bookings, one being for an advertised tour to Nottingham. Coaches travelled to London, Manchester and Blackpool, and the Bedford WTB, EVT 422, then eighteen years old, ventured from Ellastone to Aberystwyth! Six coaches were on hire to Lymers of Tean, and one job from Abbotsholme School was sub-contracted to Whieldon's.

Following a breakdown in national PSV industry wage negotiations, a national bus strike was called with effect from Saturday 20th July 1957. Stevensons' employees received a bonus on top of the national wage and, in common with most independent operators, the company attempted to maintain their services, but pickets were on duty along the main roads, and also in Uttoxeter, where police were on duty to keep the peace. Even so, drivers and conductors were jostled and abused, and attempts were made to immobilise the vehicles with nail boards under the tyres and by putting sand in the fuel tanks. The situation was worse by Monday when about 200 pickets turned up at Stevensons' garages. Some pickets boarded a Burton-bound bus as passengers; a police car followed the bus, but once into Derbyshire, the pickets alighted and stopped the vehicle from proceeding, and the police from Uttoxeter were unable to intervene. It was now virtually impossible to run a reasonable service and Stevensons ceased to operate after 3.00pm on Tuesday, when the last bus on the road returned to Burton garage. It was agreed that certain school buses from outlying areas would be allowed to operate under the supervision of pickets. However, national wage negotiations were progressing favourably and by Friday, with the police now outnumbering pickets, normal services resumed to Burton, Ashbourne, Hanbury, Bramshall and Doveridge, but Stevensons' buses were the only ones to be seen. A wage settlement was agreed and the strike was called off, services returning to normal nationally on Monday, 29th July. Three buses had been parked at Bill Stevenson's farm premises at the Highwood, just outside Uttoxeter, but it is understood that they were not used during the strike.

Around this time Stevensons also advertised their self-drive Dormobile caravans and car hire, highlighting the 'reasonable terms, modern cars, and AA membership'. Over a two-year period from early 1957 discussions took place between Stevensons, PMT and Uttoxeter UDC over the modification of PMT's Town Circular and Stevensons' Bramshall service, in view of the new housing being built in the Byrds Lane and Pennycroft Road areas. Agreement was reached in December 1959 after which the Bramshall service was changed to operate through part of the estate along Byrds Lane, by-passing part of Bramshall Road.

On 28th November 1960 the 'main road' Uttoxeter to Burton service 1 was modified to follow a clockwise loop in Tutbury round Holts Lane and Park Lane, which served additional new housing. At the same time the route of service 5, Burton to Ashbourne, was similarly modified. From around that time Ford coaches became popular choices, both new and used examples being bought. Used double-deckers purchased in the decade included AEC Regent IIIs and Vs as well as Leyland PD1s and PD2s, many being fitted with platform doors by the company. Underfloor-engined single-deckers acquired in the 1960s included the prototype AEC Reliance with a Park Royal body, 50 AMC. Others comprised an AEC Regal IV, a Daimler Freeline, a Leyland Tiger Cub and various Leyland Royal Tigers, with coach or bus bodies. This allowed for the progressive introduction of some driver-only operation, which helped towards containing costs. By 1961 the fleet strength was twenty-eight; there were sixteen school contracts and eleven military contracts,

The first Ford coach was 4799 RF, a Thames 570E with Duple body seating 41, which was new in June 1960 (12); this was the first vehicle owned which had the new style curved windows at the front and back. Bill Chell was setting down some passengers from a private hire at Church Broughton Chapel on 17th October 1974, about six months from the vehicle's withdrawal date of April 1975. (TJ)

HTF 822 was an all-Leyland PD2/1 new in 1947 to Accrington Corporation. It was acquired in January 1961 (9), platform doors being added in March 1964, and was photographed working the 1.30pm Uttoxeter to Burton via Hanbury service in Horninglow Road, Burton at 2.24pm on 5th April 1969. (TJ)

New to De Luxe Buses, Mancetter, near Atherstone in 1951, KUE 950 was a Burlingham-bodied AEC Regal IV, bought by Stevensons in November 1961. This was the first vehicle in the company fitted out for one-person operation, as indicated by the notice in the front window, and is seen in Wetmore Bus Park, Burton, ready for a run to Anslow on 14th October 1962. (TJ)

New to ACV Ltd, Southall in 1953, 50 AMC was the original AEC Reliance demonstrator, the body seating 44 passengers being built by Roe on Park Royal frames. It had passed to Armstrong's Motor Services Ltd, Newcastle upon Tyne by August 1954 and was bought from them in November 1962 becoming no.15. The bus was fitted for one man operation (as it was then termed) and is seen in Wetmore Bus Park, Burton on 23rd July 1963, ready for a journey on the Hanbury route. Withdrawal came in June 1967 when fourteen years old. (EWC)

which obviously were inter-worked with regular services where possible. The Army camps at Marchington, Sudbury and Foston were run down progressively through the 1960s, and simultaneously work was transferred to a new location further east, Hilton Central Vehicle Depot. By 1970, this was the only Army location still served by Stevensons' contracts, one route from Alton, and one from Uttoxeter. These services were operated until early 1990; two part-time drivers who worked full time at Hilton CVD drove the buses. In railway circles Spath is notable for being the site of the first automatic (train operated) railway level crossing in the United Kingdom, opened on 5th February 1961; the crossing was situated just behind the bus garage.

When the plans for the Burton by-pass were announced, the Burton garage at Horninglow Wharf was found to be on the course of the new road and so would have to be vacated. Some old maltings buildings in Rolleston Road, Horninglow, were acquired in June 1963 and were modified to accommodate six buses inside, others having to remain outside in a yard; up to sixteen vehicles would be based there in due course. The Canal Wharf depot was compulsorily-purchased in 1964, and was vacated at some time between October that year and February the following year. A surprise purchase in 1963, considering the recently-acquired underfloor-engined vehicles, was that of two Leyland PS1s with Willowbrook dual-purpose bodies, which were used mainly on contracts. One unusual vehicle was MXX 371, an ex-LTE Guy Special single-decker of 1954, bought in 1965.

John Stevenson, the founder of the company, died on 10th November 1966 aged 91, his wife Mary having predeceased him in February 1962. In his younger days John did some entertaining for charity; he loved music and was a keen supporter of Uttoxeter Choral Society. George and Joan Stevenson

---

WEST MIDLAND TRAFFIC AREA

Cumberland House, 200 Broad Street, BIRMINGHAM 15

Telephone: Birmingham MIDLAND 5011

T.62

Please address any reply to
THE CLERK
and quote:
Your reference:

PUBLIC SERVICE VEHICLES AND TROLLEY VEHICLES (CARRYING CAPACITY) REGULATIONS 1954, (S.I. 1954/No.1612) AS AMENDED BY S.I. 1958/No.472 AND S.I. 1966/No.674

PUBLIC SERVICE VEHICLES (EQUIPMENT AND USE) REGULATIONS 1958 (S.I. 1958/No.926) AS AMENDED BY S.I. 1966/No.676

The Traffic Commissioners for the West Midland Traffic Area hereby certify that in their opinion a conductor is not necessary on the undermentioned stage carriage services operated by ___John Stevenson___ provided that the following conditions are observed:- (Uttoxeter) Ltd.

(1) Only vehicles which have been approved by the Traffic Commissioners as being suitable for one-man operation and detailed in Certificate dated _____13th September 1968_____ shall be used.

(2) Fares shall be collected only when the vehicle is stationary.

(3) NOT MORE THAN EIGHT STANDING PASSENGERS SHALL BE CARRIED.

* D.9915 Bramshall (New Inn) and Doveridge (Bell Cottage).
* D.9922 Uttoxeter (Market Place) and Burton-upon-Trent (Wetmore Park).
* D.11257 Burton-upon-Trent (Wetmore Park) and Ashbourne (Bus Station).

* Only on that section of the route which lies within this Traffic Area.

This certificate shall remain valid until revoked by the Traffic Commissioners.

Dated this 5th day of March 1969

for and on behalf of the Traffic Commissioner
West Midland Traffic Area

John Stevenson (Uttoxeter) Ltd.
The Garage
Spath
UTTOXETER
Staffs.

This very atmospheric view shows Horninglow Canal Wharf circa 1963. The two Stevensons buses are Burlingham-bodied Leyland PD1 NRE 36 (4) on the left, and an ex-Burton Corporation Guy Arab with Brush body of 1946 to the right. Behind the Guy single-decker can be seen Olive Stevenson's office, referred to as 'the shed on wheels', standing alongside Horninglow Road North. The warehouse by the Guy was used to store grain, which would be distributed by Stevensons' lorries, and the building to the left was used as a bus garage. Within a year all this would be swept aside when construction of the Burton by-pass commenced. (MAC)

GAY 170 and 171, Leyland Tiger PS1/1s with Willowbrook dual-purpose bodies seating 35, were new in 1950 to Allen's Motor Services, Mountsorrel, from where they were acquired; they entered service as 21 and 28 in June and May 1963 respectively and worked for nine years with Stevensons. The latter vehicle is seen on Horninglow Road, Burton at 5.32pm on 25th June 1968 whilst on the 5.30pm Burton to Uttoxeter via Tutbury duplicate, and is followed by KGK 724 returning to Rolleston Road garage off the 5.00pm Scropton to Burton service. GAY 171 is under restoration in Leicestershire at the time of writing, and will be out-shopped in Allen's livery. (TJ)

MXX 371, a Guy 'GS' Special with 26-seat Eastern Coach Works body, was new to London Transport in 1954. It entered service with Stevensons in March 1965 (27), and was just the vehicle for this apparently empty journey; it is seen in front of the Church of St Paul, Scropton at 4.07pm on 8th February 1969, when working the 3.30pm Burton to Ashbourne service. The road conditions would most likely become worse nearer to its destination. The company had approached London Transport to see if any of their RF class AEC Regal IVs were to be sold, which proved not to be the case. However, it was found that some of the Guys were to be sold, hence this purchase. (RJ)

had lived in Holly Road, Uttoxeter for some time, but after John's death they moved into 'Brooklands'. Most of the family wanted to sell the company, all except George Stevenson and his brother John. However, agreement could not be reached, since according to a clause in the will, anyone who left the company would receive nothing. Therefore, the company continued in its then current form for another six years, the vehicles being licensed to the 'Executors of John Stevenson (deceased)' until June 1968, after which they were licensed to John Stevenson (Uttoxeter) Ltd. One of the executors was Ben Wright, Hannah Stevenson's husband. The fuel tax remission scheme, which had been introduced in 1964, would have helped the financial situation for a while, but operating costs continued to increase, and the October 1967 fare table for the Uttoxeter-Tutbury-Burton service shows that the single fare between the termini had risen to 2s 6d. For many years thereafter, applications for fare increases became at least annual events. The first minibuses for the fleet arrived in 1968 and 1969, a Ford Transit with Martin Walter body and a BMC 250JU with BMC body, both seating twelve people. 1968 saw the purchase from Trathen, Yelverton, of CTT 423C, an AEC Reliance with a lovely Duple Northern coach body which was only three years old; it gave twelve years' exemplary service before passing to local operator BC Travel, and was a wonderful vehicle to drive. More AEC Reliances, Regent Vs, Leyland PD2s and the first PD3s as well as Leyland Leopards appeared in the 1970s, some coming from Sheffield Corporation; 1500 WJ, with a Weymann 'Fanfare' body, which became no 15, had the prototype Leyland Leopard L1 chassis.

The Stevenson family at John and Mary's Golden Wedding Anniversary Dinner on 2nd April 1952. Top row (l to r): John, George, Gertrude (Mrs Farmer), Bernard, Bill. Bottom row (l to r): Hannah (Mrs Wright), John, Mary, Marjorie (Mrs Nelson). *(RDC)*

CTT 423C was an AEC Reliance with a classic Duple Northern Continental body seating 51 passengers, which was new in March 1965 to Trathen, Yelverton, from where it was purchased in June 1968 when just over three years old, becoming Stevensons' no.4. At some time it was fitted with an AH 691 11.3 litre engine, and I was fortunate to experience driving this wonderful machine on two occasions, the latter being a journey on 10th May 1980 from Alleyne's High School, Uttoxeter to Leek, where this photo was taken. Two months later it was withdrawn and in November that year was sold to Bill Stanton (BC Travel). *(EW)*

The second **AEC Regent V** bought was 966 CWL, new in March 1958 to City of Oxford Motor Services. Bought by Stevensons in January 1970, its Weymann 65-seat body was up-seated to 73, and electrically-operated platform doors were fitted prior to entry into service on 9th February as no.8. It is seen during its first run on Dove Bank, Uttoxeter at 12.50pm when returning from Doveridge on the 12.40pm journey to Uttoxeter, with driver Brian Fern and conductor Ken Charlesworth. This bus was highly regarded by the drivers and it worked until August 1977 when it was nineteen years old. *(TJ)*

STEVENSON'S BUS SERVICE No. 1.
Uttoxeter - Burton-on-Trent

TIME TABLE

Depart	X a.m.	X a.m.	MF a.m.	X a.m.	X a.m.	a.m.	X a.m.	S a.m.	p.m.	p.m.	p.m.	p.m.	p.m.	p.m.	p.m.	p.m.	p.m.
Uttoxeter	6.00	7.00		8.00	9.30	10.30	11.45	12.15	1.00	2.00	2.45	4.00	5.30	6.30	7.30	8.30	9.30
Doveridge	6.05	7.05		8.05	9.35	10.35	11.50	12.20	1.05	2.05	2.50	4.05	5.35	6.35	7.35	8.35	9.35
Sudbury	6.15	7.15		8.15	9.45	10.45	12.00	12.30	1.15	2.15	3.00	4.15	5.45	6.45	7.45	8.45	9.45
Foston	6.20	7.20		8.20	9.50	10.50	12.05	12.35	1.20	2.20	3.05	4.20	5.50	6.50	7.50	8.50	9.50
Hatton (Salt Box)	6.25	7.25	7.57	8.25	9.55	10.55	12.10	12.40	1.25	2.25	3.10	4.25	5.55	6.55	7.55	8.55	9.55
Hatton Scropton Lane	6.27	7.27	7.59	8.27	9.57	10.57	12.12	12.42	1.27	2.27	3.12	4.27	5.57	6.57	7.57	8.57	9.57
Tutbury Post Office	6.30	7.30	8.02	8.30	10.00	11.00	12.15	12.45	1.30	2.30	3.15	4.30	6.00	7.00	8.00	9.00	10.00
Tutbury Holts Lane	6.32	7.32	—	8.32	10.02	11.02	12.17	12.47	1.32	2.32	3.17	4.32	6.02	7.02	8.02	9.02	10.02
Tutbury Park Lane	6.35	7.35	—	8.35	10.05	11.05	12.20	12.50	1.35	2.35	3.20	4.35	6.05	7.05	8.05	9.05	10.05
Tutbury Post Office	6.37	7.37	—	8.37	10.07	11.07	12.22	12.52	1.37	2.37	3.22	4.37	6.07	7.07	8.07	9.07	10.07
Burton Lodge	6.40	7.40	8.05	8.40	10.10	11.10	12.25	12.55	1.40	2.40	3.25	4.40	6.10	7.10	8.10	9.10	10.10
Beam Hill	6.42	7.42	8.07	8.42	10.12	11.12	12.27	12.57	1.42	2.42	3.27	4.42	6.12	7.12	8.12	9.12	10.12
Arr — Burton on Trent	6.50	7.50	8.15	8.50	10.20	11.20	12.35	1.05	1.50	2.50	3.35	4.50	6.20	7.20	8.20	9.20	10.20

Depart	X a.m.	X a.m.	X a.m.	X a.m.	S a.m.	p.m.	p.m.	p.m.	p.m.	p.m.	MF p.m.	p.m.	p.m.	p.m.	p.m.	p.m.	p.m.
Burton on Trent	7.00	8.00	9.00	10.30	11.15	12.15	1.15	2.30	3.15	4.15	5.00	5.30	6.30	7.30	8.30	9.30	10.20
Beam Hill	7.08	8.08	9.08	10.38	11.23	12.23	1.23	2.38	3.23	4.23	5.08	5.38	6.38	7.38	8.38	9.38	10.28
Burton Lodge	7.10	8.10	9.10	10.40	11.25	12.25	1.25	2.40	3.25	4.25	5.10	5.40	6.40	7.40	8.40	9.40	10.30
Tutbury Post Office	7.13	8.13	9.13	10.43	11.28	12.28	1.28	2.43	3.28	4.28	5.13	5.43	6.43	7.43	8.43	9.43	10.33
Tutbury Holts Lane	7.15	8.15	9.15	10.45	11.30	12.30	1.30	2.45	3.30	4.30	—	5.45	6.45	7.45	8.45	9.45	10.35
Tutbury Park Lane	7.18	8.18	9.18	10.48	11.33	12.33	1.33	2.48	3.33	4.33	—	5.48	6.48	7.48	8.48	9.48	10.38
Tutbury Post Office	7.20	8.20	9.20	10.50	11.35	12.35	1.35	2.50	3.35	4.35	—	5.50	6.50	7.50	8.50	9.50	10.40
Hatton Scropton Lane	7.23	8.23	9.23	10.53	11.38	12.38	1.38	2.53	3.38	4.38	5.16	5.53	6.53	7.53	8.53	9.53	10.43
Hatton Salt Box	7.25	8.25	9.25	10.55	11.40	12.40	1.40	2.55	3.40	4.40	5.18	5.55	6.55	7.55	8.55	9.55	10.45
Foston	7.30	8.30	9.30	11.00	11.45	12.45	1.45	3.00	3.45	4.45	5.23	6.00	7.00	8.00	9.00	10.00	10.50
Sudbury	7.35	8.35	9.35	11.05	11.50	12.50	1.50	3.05	3.50	4.50	5.28	6.05	7.05	8.05	9.05	10.05	10.55
Doveridge	7.45	8.45	9.45	11.15	12.00	1.00	2.00	3.15	4.00	5.00	5.38	6.15	7.15	8.15	9.15	10.15	11.05
Arr — Uttoxeter	7.50	8.50	9.50	11.20	12.05	1.05	2.05	3.20	4.05	5.05	5.43	6.20	7.20	8.20	9.20	10.20	11.10

MF – Mondays to Fridays
S – Saturdays Only
X – Not Sundays

	a.m.	
Dep. Tutbury Post Office	8.45)	
Tutbury Holts Lane	8.47)	Operates on
Tutbury Park Lane	8.50)	School days
Arr. Tutbury Burton St. School	8.55)	only

Service 1 timetable, circa 1970.

Seven Leyland Leopard L1s were bought from Sheffield Corporation in 1971/1972. 1500 WJ was the prototype of the chassis type and was new in July 1959 with this classic Weymann Fanfare coach body; it took fleet number 15 and entered service in June 1971. John Sharpe was the driver when the vehicle was photographed on 9th March 1979, setting off along Rolleston Road, Horninglow, to take up a Hatton School contract; three months later it was withdrawn and this historically-important vehicle was lost to the scrap man. *(TJ)*

STEVENSON'S BUS SERVICE No. 2.
Uttoxeter to Burton via Hanbury

Starts from Uttoxeter and Wetmore Road Motor Park, Burton-on-Trent

WEEKDAYS ONLY   NOT SUNDAYS
COMMENCING 4TH JANUARY 1971
TIME TABLE

MONDAY TO SATURDAY (NO SUNDAY SERVICE)

Depart	A.M.	A.M.	A.M.	SO A.M.	SO P.M.	MF * P.M.	P.M.	TS P.M.	P.M.
Uttoxeter	7-40			11-00	1-30	1-00			5-00
Doveridge	7-45			11-05	1-35	1-05			5-05
Sudbury	7-55			11-15	1-45	1-20			5-15
Draycott	8-05			11-25	1-55	1-25			5-25
Hanbury	8-15			11-35	2-05	1-35			5-35
Anslow	8-25	9-00	11-45	11-45	2-15	1-45	3-50	5-15	5-45
Beam Hill	8-30	9-05	11-50	11-50	2-20	1-50	3-55	5-20	5-50
Arriv. - Burton	8-40	9-15	12-00	12-00	2-30	2-00	4-05	5-30	6-00

	A.M.	A.M.	A.M.	SO P.M.	SO P.M.	P.M.	MF P.M.	TS P.M.	P.M.
Burton	8-40	10-00	11-30	12-15	4-00	3-35	4-30	5-00	6-00
Beam Hill	8-50	10-10	11-40	12-25	4-05	3-40	4-35	5-05	6-10
Anslow	8-55	10-15	11-45	12-30	4-15	3-50	4-45	5-15	6-15
Hanbury		10-25		12-40	4-25		4-55		6-25
Draycott		10-35		12-50	4-35		5-05		6-35
Sudbury		10-45		1-00	4-45		5-15		6-45
Doveridge		10-55		1-10	4-55		5-25		6-55
Arriv. - Uttoxeter		11-00		1-15	5-00		5-30		7-00

NOTES. SO means Saturday only. TS means Thursday, Saturday   MF means Monday to Friday

* Travel out from Uttoxeter at 1 p.m. on Service No. 1 (via Tutbury) and change at Sudbury, Station Road.

3. Formation of a New Company

Approaches had been made in 1967 to Trent Motor Traction and later to PMT, with attempts to sell the business to them, but they were not interested. By 1971 agreement had still not been reached on the future of the company, the two executors had both died and the bank of the last-surviving one had become the new executor. The bank wanted the long-standing problem resolved quickly and wished to dispose of the company bit by bit; instead it was persuaded to put the company up for auction, which it did on 23rd November that year in Hanley. George Stevenson was the successful bidder and purchased the business, the house and the vehicles for £26,000, which was a very low price. A new company, Stevensons of Uttoxeter Limited, was formed that year with George and his wife Joan as directors. Their son David graduated in Economics, which he taught for several years, then had his own business in Leicester; he joined the family business in 1972, responsible particularly for the Burton side of the company, and he also became a director. Prior to his arrival Stevensons was just about paying its way, but he introduced extra work such as feeder work for Shearings, obtained other local contracts, and helped the business to grow and prosper.

George and Joan Stevenson *(TJC)*

Under instructions from John Stevenson (Uttoxeter) Limited and the Executors of John Stevenson, deceased.

Of particular interest to haulage undertakings, bus operators and similar organisations.

The Valuable Freehold Properties

at

Uttoxeter and Burton-on-Trent

together with the

Vehicles, Equipment and other Assets

used in connection with the old established Bus, Coach and Car Hire business

Lot 1— Freehold property at Uttoxeter including a petrol sales forecourt, repair garages, a cottage, the fine detached five-bedroom residence, agricultural land and the vehicle park. Also included are approx. 30 coaches or buses and 15 other vehicles.

Lot 2— The freehold bus garage, vehicle park and enquiry office situate at Rolleston Road, Burton-on-Trent.

Viewing by arrangement with Louis Taylor & Sons.
Vacant Possession on Completion (subject to four minor tenancies on Lot 2).

Joint Auctioneers— Chesshire, Gibson & Co., 63 Temple Row, Birmingham 021-643-9351.

Vendors Solicitor— Messrs. Tinsdill & Co., 4 Brook Street, Stoke-on-Trent 0782 48561.

Vendor's Accountants— Messrs. A. Cropp Hawkins & Co., F.C.A., 5 Brook Street, Stoke-on-Trent 0782-44113.

LOUIS TAYLOR & SONS

will offer the above for sale by Public Auction at their

PROPERTY ROOMS PERCY ST., HANLEY

on the 23rd NOVEMBER, 1971
at 7 o-clock in the evening

For further details apply to— LOUIS TAYLOR & SONS, Percy Street, Hanley. Tel. Stoke-on-Trent 22373

This advert for the forthcoming sale of the company by auction appeared in local newspapers in November 1971. *(EWC)*

Also, with the continually-growing population, additional and larger vehicles were required, including for school contracts, and the company was successful in that area. David said that his father had been very loyal to the family, becoming the lynch pin of the company despite being the youngest, and that without his efforts Stevensons would not have survived. Being able to purchase the company, albeit at age 55, was just reward for those efforts. George was a hard-working practical man with great stamina, and a man of ideas. His bark was worse than his bite, and he rarely sacked anyone, but drivers often took advantage. Although he would have been up and about before 6.00am, he could often be found finishing the late turn for a driver, which meant an 11.30pm finish. Recalling his own younger days when living at Spath, David said that he often travelled with drivers on local contracts, such as that between Denstone College and Uttoxeter Station; whilst he was a student he had passed his Class 1 PSV test, and the first vehicle he drove for Stevensons was no.29, KGU 216, an ex-London Transport RT. It is worthy of note that Denstone College must have been one of the most regular hirers of Stevensons' coaches for over sixty years.

In October 1973 OPEC (the Organisation of Petroleum Exporting Countries) declared an oil embargo which lasted until March 1974, at the end of which the price of oil had risen from $3 to nearly $12 per barrel. However, by then the UK was a net exporter of oil so fuel rationing was not necessary on that occasion, but the added cost to operators would result in more regular applications for fare increases over the coming years, as seen in the accompanying letter of July 1979. Some service mileage was pruned and in January 1976 special Sunday fares were introduced. There were also significant increases in fares on the express services.

Following the Government's introduction of the New Bus Grant scheme, companies would only pay half the

This **AEC Regent V** with 69-seat Roe body, **6349 WJ**, was also bought from Sheffield Corporation, having been new to them in April 1960. It arrived in June 1972 but did not enter service until November that year; numbered 27 and now fitted with platform doors, it is seen in Burton, very near to the original terminus in Horninglow Street, bound for Tutbury and Uttoxeter. *(EWC)*

The first new vehicle to be bought whilst taking advantage of the New Bus Grant was **LRE 783K (21)**, a Ford R192 which had a Duple Viceroy 45-seat coach body built to grant specification, and which entered service in July 1972. On 7th July 1973 Cyril Hollins is seen waiting at the top of Red Hill, Doveridge whilst on the way to a private hire. It proved to be a most useful and well-liked vehicle, was re-numbered 16 in January 1981, and after receiving an 'A' suffix in May 1982 was withdrawn in December that year. *(TJ)*

A surprise purchase in March 1974 was **WBF 842M (25)**, a Seddon Pennine 6 which had a Duple body to the new maximum length of 12 metres, with seats for 57 passengers and which was bought in view of the short supply of Ford coaches at the time. However, it was not successful and was sold in April 1977 to Graham's Coaches, Kettering after only three years' service. *(RM/OS)*

35

TEH 761R, a Ford R1114 with Plaxton Supreme 53-seat body, was purchased in April 1977 (25) ready for the summer season. On 28th April 1980 it was photographed being driven by Dave Royall, turning off Dovecliff Road into Church Road at Clay Mills whilst on a Stretton baths contract. In January 1981 it was renumbered 8, and on withdrawal in December 1983, it passed via Yeates (dealer) to Bennett, Gloucester, and thence to Llansilin Motor Service. George Stevenson's view was that Plaxton produced the best coach bodies available at that time. *(TJ)*

cost of a new bus or coach, providing that it was built to a specification which made it suitable for use on stage service work, and providing that at least half of its mileage was on such work. Stevensons was quick to take advantage of this, and two Ford coaches, then a Bedford YRT coach were bought. Two Massey-bodied Daimler CCG5 double-deckers came from Burton Corporation and were normally used on contracts; these were followed by a solitary AEC Renown with forward-entrance Park Royal body from City of Oxford Motor Services which was used on service and contract work. A 12-metre Seddon Pennine 6 with a Duple 57-seat coach body was bought in 1974, since Ford chassis were in short supply at the time, but it was replaced after only three years. Some Plaxton-bodied Ford R226 coaches, which were only two years old and very good

purchases, came from the Shearings group; more new Ford coaches appeared later, as did two Hawson-bodied Bedford J1Z2H minibuses, and various Ford Transits.

Whieldon's Green Bus Service had passed to Midland Red on 5th November 1973; following changes made by the latter company in April 1975, from 21st April Stevensons' Hanbury service 2 was altered to travel via Marchington instead of Sudbury between Uttoxeter and Draycott. August that year saw the arrival of the first rear-engined double-decker, an MCCW-bodied Leyland PDR1 Mk2 Atlantean, which had been new to City of Portsmouth Passenger Transport Department in 1963; two identical vehicles followed in 1976. Trent Motor Traction had announced that their Sunday service through Rolleston was to be withdrawn from 11th January 1976. Staffordshire County Council

The first rear-engined double-decker for the fleet was 204 BTP, a Leyland Atlantean PDR1/1 (Mark II) with 76-seat MCCW body which was new to City of Portsmouth Passenger Transport Department in 1963. It was purchased through Burton Corporation (they had some for their fleet) and arrived in August 1975 (14); in April 1976 217/9 BTP were bought direct from Portsmouth (7 and 27). Bill Chell was in charge, with Coral Davies as conductress, when 219 BTP was captured on Horninglow Road, Burton, whilst working the 1.00pm Uttoxeter 'Main Road' to Burton on 4th April 1977. This was the first of the three to be withdrawn, in January 1981. The Burton Daimler to the rear wears the livery introduced by General Manager Roy Marshall. *(TJ)*

then approached George Stevenson to see whether service number 1 could be re-routed to serve the village from the same date. Arrangements were made to do that and a revised timetable was widely advertised at Stevensons' own cost. However, Trent reversed their decision following union opposition, and Stevensons had to withdraw their plans.

Just after World War Two, an office had been opened beside Orme's shop at the Market Place in Uttoxeter, situated above the old Labour Exchange. From 1947 it was run by Tony Snart who issued timetables as required and took bookings for express services and tours; he was also responsible for the wages and accounts and was a part-time driver. After the new Bus Station was opened on 6th September 1970 (on the site of the long-disused Bunting's Brewery) that office was inconveniently located, and was closed when a new Stevensons Travel Office, managed by Tony, was opened in the High Street in 1976. In Burton, Olive Stevenson (wife of Bernard) had run the office (referred to as 'a shed on wheels') at Canal Wharf depot; following the move to Rolleston Road a small brick office was built there, and this eventually also became a Travel Office. That and the Uttoxeter Travel Office were ABTA bonded, and in due course an office was opened in Station Street in the centre of Burton. Ironically, it opened just before the Council declared Station Street a pedestrian area, and the bus services were moved to New Street.

Uttoxeter Travel Office, shortly before closure on 29th November 1996. (EW)

From the start of service operations from Burton depot, there was one unusual 'passenger' which commuted every day, Monday to Saturday, between the depot and the Uttoxeter Town Office, this being 'The Tin' (originally an ex-WW2 ammunition box, later a Setright ticket machine box) which carried the takings from Burton depot, that practice still taking place in the 1980s. The company became involved in the purchasing and refurbishment of ex-Post Office Telephones golden yellow-painted Morris Minor vans, which were then sold.

Additional revenue came from the carriage of parcels on the buses. I recall sitting at Uttoxeter Bus Station late one afternoon in the 1980s, waiting for departure time to Burton, when there was a loud noise, as bound copies of the Uttoxeter Advertiser were dropped onto the step at the front. These parcels would be dropped off at newsagents along the route. Interesting items are known to have been carried in the past, including a piano, which met a disastrous and noisy end whilst being off-loaded!

The only AEC Swift to be operated was NJW 709E which had a Strachan 54-seat dual-door body (partial 3x2 seating) when new to Wolverhampton Corporation in 1967. It was bought from Sykes (dealer) Barnsley in December 1975, whereupon the centre door was removed, the seating was increased to 58, and it entered service in May 1976 as no.29. On 11th May 1978 it was being driven by Robin Young when photographed at Tutbury Station whilst working the 8.50am Hatton to Burton journey. Withdrawn as 29A in February 1981, by September it had passed via a dealer to Brutonian, Bruton (TJ)

An AEC Swift with Strachan 54-seat dual-door body, new to Wolverhampton Corporation in 1967, latterly with West Midlands PTE, was bought from Sykes (Dealer) in 1975, and Stevensons re-built it to 58 seats with a single doorway prior to entry into service. Between 1976 and 1978 eight Leyland PD2As with forward-entrance bodies by NCME and East Lancs were purchased from Burnley and Pendle Joint Transport Committee, all but one being operated. In the late 1970s, the company held licences for services to all the major seaports and airports, including Heathrow and Gatwick, as well as for express services to Blackpool and North Wales, although with declining patronage the latter service was passed to Barton Transport in May 1979 and absorbed into their timetable; also, excursion and tours licences were held covering over 200 destinations. Following implementation of the 1980 Transport Act, express services were started to many other destinations around the country.

Another Leyland Atlantean, but with Alexander body, came from Greater Glasgow PTE in 1977 but only lasted for two years. A Leyland Leopard with Plaxton Highway

bus body, 6 MPT (18), was acquired from The Eden Bus Services Ltd, West Auckland, in 1977 and worked for nearly five years; it is now preserved. Although it had a narrow cab, it was the favourite vehicle at the time of Keith Russell of Burton Depot. It was always referred to by him in his usual way as 'coach' 18 and a Plaxton window sticker, most likely off the next-mentioned new coach, mysteriously appeared in the front window of no 18. On 15th December 1977 a Thursday-only service number.3 was started between Burton and Abbots Bromley via Marchington and Draycott, an additional Saturday operation starting two years later. Around this time a new fleet logo appeared showing 'StevensonS', below which in yellow on a black line was written 'Uttoxeter & Burton'.

During 1977 the garage at Spath was increased in size again, allowing two 36ft single-deckers to be worked on, and incorporating a third inspection pit. A set of Hywema vehicle lifts was bought, and twelve-ton jacking beams in two of the pits allowed underfloor-fitted engines to be removed and refitted.

November 1977 saw the purchase of XRE 305S, a Leyland Leopard PSU3E/4R with Plaxton coach body, but at first Dave Barratt, Workshop Foreman at Spath, was not satisfied with the vehicle's performance. This was taken up with Leyland Motors, and their Field Service Engineer, Maurice Brown, fitted a new differential. This resolved the problems, and henceforth it was widely recognised as being the best new coach

ever bought by the company; however, it did not enter service until March 1978. A Duple-bodied Bedford SB5 coach preceded two Weymann bus-bodied Leyland Leopard PSU3/3RTs which came from East Midlands Motor Services Ltd.

I started my PSV training in August 1978 in Burton and Swadlincote, with coach driver Norman Tucker as my instructor. My vehicle was ex-Burnley and Pendle Leyland PD2 PCW 945, in which I passed my test in The Potteries on 13th September that year, and I started at Spath to work part-time on private hires and contracts. At that time drivers were given a duplicated trip sheet, on which the driver was requested to ask the organiser on completion of the hire to 'SING', an interesting mis-spelling which often raised a chuckle! In January 1979 I was asked to try some service work and on the evening of 12th January, with Stefan Senkow as my guide, I learnt the 'main road' service, driving Leopard FVO 434D. The following day, using Bedford YRT, JRF 785N, I worked on both of the Uttoxeter to Burton services, and thereafter I was engaged in a pleasant mixture of duties. Stevensons was a good family company for which to work, eventually supplying uniforms to permanent part-timers, and at length I became a full-time employee.

In 1978 Midland Red carried out a Market Analysis Project (MAP) on their Swadlincote garage services operating in the Forest of Needwood area, west of Burton. They concluded that most of them were to be withdrawn, leaving Staffordshire County Council to decide upon replacement arrangements. The Council

An example of a woven badge for the coach drivers' uniform.

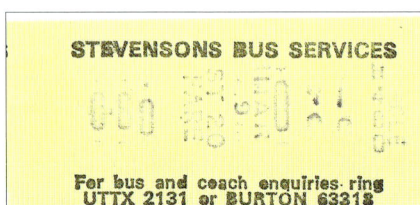

One of my Setright tickets

STEVENSONS BUS SERVICES

For bus and coach enquiries ring UTTX 2131 or BURTON 63318

realised that the services did not perform as well as they should because the Burton Standard Conditions prevented their access to the town centre (creating a long walk to the shops for their passengers) and decided to try to overturn this restriction. So when the licence applications were sent in for the replacement services, all the operators involved specified a town centre route down Station Street. East Staffordshire District Council vigorously opposed the plans, claiming that the roads were unsuitable for large saloons. The Chairman of the Traffic Commissioners disagreed, after riding round the town in a Midland Red Leyland National, and granted the applications. ESDC then obtained permission to apply to the High Court for an order of certiorari (a legal device to quash the decision), but withdrew after taking further legal advice. The Burton Standard Conditions were modified, and on 17th February 1979 the services of Stevensons and Midland Red (and others) in Burton were diverted to serve Station Street and the town centre, although conditions regarding picking up and setting down passengers within the old borough area remained. Stevensons started a new Thursday-only route between Kings Bromley and Burton, the Abbots Bromley and Hanbury services were revised extensively and re-routed via Newborough, and a new Tuesday-only express service commenced between Uttoxeter and Birmingham via Abbots Bromley, Lichfield, and the Carrefour Hypermarket at Minworth. At the same time the County Council re-numbered the services in Stevensons' area of operation into the 400 series, the main Burton service becoming 401.

Blizzards badly affected the area on 16th February 1979; this caused problems on two school journeys and a diversion had to be used on the Hanbury route, but the services were maintained. Stevensons had a reputation for turning up in all weathers, often in atrocious conditions when other operators had ceased to run. Many roads used by the service buses were not gritted early enough and so Stevensons took it upon themselves to apply grit where necessary, this eventually being supplied officially by the Council. I once drove the gritting lorry early in the day with a mechanic on board who gritted the sloping bus station at Uttoxeter, and the necessary roads in the Uttoxeter estates. John Stevenson had once recalled a time when a driver said that it was too bad to take a bus out, and he replied that if passengers had been taken to Burton, the company would have to fetch them back again. David Stevenson gave an example of the public's faith in the company when one day he took a 'phone call at the Burton office at 6.00pm. The caller said "the 4.30pm bus has not turned up", and was still waiting, firmly believing that 'Stevos' always turns up!

One day I was asked to drive the return market day service to Church Leigh and Milwich, using a Leopard saloon. I knew the road to Morrilow Heath and was told that there was a left turn near the water tower there to Milwich. There was one passenger remaining at the front of the bus, clutching her shopping bag, as I turned at the signpost towards Milwich. After crossing another road and rounding a number of bends into the valley, we were suddenly confronted by a ford flowing across the road, which widened somewhat at that point. My passenger, a regular on the service, had never uttered a word when I mistakenly took what turned out to be the wrong road; a lady came rushing from the farm across the ford shouting "The bus doesn't come down here", to which I replied "It does today dear". Reversing up the winding country lane was not a preferred option, so I used the full available width of the road and had nearly crossed the ford when that scraping noise was heard! On arrival at Milwich my phone call to Spath was answered by 'Mr. George' who asked if it was safe to carry on, and I am sure that I heard him chuckling when he told me to swap buses on my return at Uttoxeter so that my re-designing of the lower panel could be rectified.

Five Massey-bodied Atlanteans, new to Maidstone Corporation in 1967/68, arrived in 1979. However, the most significant acquisitions in that year were the Daimler Fleetlines (DMS), with either Park Royal or MCW dual-door bodies, which had been new to London Transport Executive (LTE) from 1971 onwards. LTE had started to dispose of them after only eight or so years' service as they had difficulties with them in service and with their maintenance. Nine, one of which was for spares, were bought in 1979; the first three were bought direct from LTE and cost £4,250 each; the next six came via Wombwell Diesels, after which virtually all others were bought via Ensign (dealer), Grays. First into service in September 1979 was JGU 284K (17) which retained its centre doors for some time.

For some customers, Ensign had started to remove the centre doors on DMSs, re-panel them and fit a window which was noticeably smaller than the original windows, then fitted three seats where the doorway had been. When Stevensons were preparing the next bus for service they carried out a similar conversion but, using a window from the DMS bought for spares, Stevensons' bodybuilders perfected the 'invisible' conversion to single doorway and five additional seats were fitted. This vehicle received a white band between decks as did the following two, but the next to be modified, JGF 196K (45), received a new striped livery. It won awards at bus rallies, the most prestigious being the Telma Trophy for best in class at Showbus on 7th September 1980 when it was held at Thorpe Park, London, where it could be compared with an Ensign conversion in Derby Corporation's livery by which it stood. Shortly afterwards, some Ensign employees visited Spath to see how the conversions, devised by Ronald Alderson, were done; Ron told me that they had asked to see the plans, but he explained that it was all in his head! Subsequently they adopted Stevensons' method. Stevensons had pre-prepared stocks of parts ready for each conversion but the next to be done had the other body type and it

Here we see the process of converting twin doorway DMSs to single doorway, all carried out by Spath garage staff. Also, the lower-deck seating was increased from 24 to 29, the end result looking very neat, as indeed did the outside, as exemplified by **GHM 764N**, a **MCW**-bodied Daimler CRL6, as it stands in Rugeley Bus Station. (All EW)

In July 1979 the company made the most significant purchases in its history, namely nine Daimler Fleetlines, bodied by Park Royal or MCW (known as DMSs), which had been withdrawn from London Transport when only seven years old. This was the start of a long love affair with the type and Stevensons' engineers developed the 'invisible' method of converting the bodies from twin to single doorway, gaining additional seating capacity at the same time. The first to enter service in September 1979 was MCW-bodied JGU 284K (initially numbered 17, shortly altered to 41) which retained its twin doorways until rebuilt in May 1982, and it is seen in the original livery on 8th August 1980 at 'The Well', Doveridge, having arrived on the 12.15pm from Uttoxeter, driven by John Woodward. *(TJ)*

The third DMS to be converted to single doorway was MLH 315L, which entered service as no.44 in January 1980 with an improved livery which incorporated a white band between decks; the neatness of the doorway conversion is evident. On 3rd September 1980, Tom Ginnis is manoeuvring the bus round the usual gathering of parked cars at Park Place (known as The Wharf), Uttoxeter, when completing the 14.30 journey on the short Park Avenue circuit. The Wharf is so called because the old Uttoxeter Canal terminated a short way beyond the buildings to the left of this view. *(TJ)*

was found that there were differences between them under the skin, mainly concerning the windows. As a result, two different sets of kits were required thereafter.

Over a nine-year period 71 DMSs, 45 of which entered the fleet, would be purchased, this being the largest number bought by an independent operator, and four were converted and finished for other operators. Stevensons carried out a number of other modifications, vastly to improve their performance and reliability. This included the removal of the automatic gear change, and most of the later Leyland-engined examples had their units replaced with Gardner 6LXB engines. New wiring looms were produced, better heaters and demisters were fitted, and the electro-pneumatic unit, which controlled the gearbox, was re-positioned. Some seven-year-old vehicles purchased had been in store with LTE for three years and so had only worked for four years; others were acquired as scrappers for about £750, and a good number of those vehicles were easily and cheaply returned to service; latterly some were bought from other operators. Most of the DMSs covered about 1,000 miles each week. One important factor regarding vehicles' reliability was found to be the practice of allocating one driver to one bus, wherever possible. This led to a significant reduction in the number of defects, and a greater likelihood of any defects which did occur being reported. The re-building of Gardner engines and gearboxes was expertly carried out in the Spath workshops, spare units being readily available in order to reduce any down time resulting from a failure.

Traditionally, new or replacement vehicles had taken a vacant fleet number, but henceforth 'A' suffixes occasionally appeared beside vehicle fleet numbers, which usually signified that the vehicle was about to be re-numbered or replaced. From the 1980s various fleet re-numberings took place to keep abreast of an increasingly expanding fleet, vehicle types or sizes being grouped together. By this time the main body colours were being applied by roller and Len Blurton's work resulted in first-class finishes. Len started at Stevensons in August 1948 and worked with the founder John

JGF 196K (45), a Fleetline with Park Royal body, entered service in August 1980. It was the first double-decker to receive the new striped livery, a similar one having been applied previously to some single-deckers. On a fine summer's day it was passing Pasturefields, whilst working a Stafford to Uttoxeter journey on service 404. *(EW)*

Len Blurton, seen prior to his retirement in the summer of 1998. Len passed away in March 2016. *(TJC)*

Stevenson on bus bodywork. He passed his PSV test when he was 21 and regularly drove the Marchington Woodlands school bus, eventually having taken three generations of families to school! On one winter's day the bus was marooned in a drift, where it lay for three days before being rescued. Len also became responsible for the morning vehicle checks and always arrived on time at 5.30am (7.00am on Sundays, 5.30am when it was busy). It was George Stevenson's idea to apply to open an MOT Testing Station at Spath (for cars) and it was the first to be authorised in the Midlands area in 1960. Len was one of the original MOT testers with George Stevenson, working in the converted garage where John Stevenson used to carry out the body repairs (called 'the long garage'), and which at the time of writing is still a sound building. However, Len's main activity was on bodywork and painting, and in 1983 a new two-bay body and paint shop was built behind the main garage at Spath, where the old railway line had been. When Len retired in August 1998 he had amassed 50 years' service, thereby eclipsing Sam Barlow's record.

George Stevenson is seen working in the MOT bay at Spath. *(EW)*

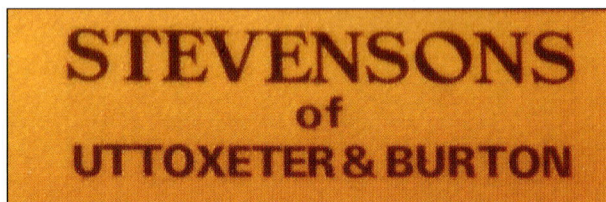

4. A New Traffic Manager and Expansion of Operations

After working for Alder Valley and City of Oxford bus companies, in 1978 Julian Peddle joined Staffordshire County Council in the Public Transport Planning Department as a Traffic Department Trainee. One day he answered a telephone call from a rather irate George Stevenson, who had an on-going complaint concerning routes or contracts. Although Stevensons' operation was not in Julian's area, he listened to George's complaint and, much to his satisfaction, Julian resolved it. Thereafter, he found that when George had cause to 'phone the Council, the calls were directed to him! After fifteen months with the Council, Julian was looking for a change and, wanting to return to the 'sharp end' of public transport, he applied for and was given the position of Traffic Manager with Maynes of Manchester. By 1980 George Stevenson was over normal retiring age and, looking to the future, it was believed that the company required a Traffic Manager. George and David knew Julian, and of course they knew that he was very familiar with Stevensons' operations, so Julian was approached, and he was persuaded to join the company from Maynes in March 1980. The timing could not have been better, both for Stevensons and for Julian, since there was scope for him to develop the company, particularly in the stage carriage field, and extend its operating area considerably. Having worked part-time at Burton depot, in 1980 Tim Jeffcoat started at Spath, where he ran the depot for some years prior to joining the Bus Network Office at Burton.

Four new coaches comprising three Ford R1114s and a Leyland Leopard arrived in 1980, three being to bus grant specification, including the Leopard which had a Duple Dominant II Express body. Compared with earlier Leylands which had minimal instrumentation, being in the driver's seat was like sitting in front of a Wurlitzer organ, with banks of switches and dials to either side of the steering wheel; it was a lovely vehicle and was often used for late turns and the Sunday service. New striped versions of the livery were introduced on single-deckers with these vehicles, double-deckers being so treated thereafter as previously mentioned. Two ex-Midland Red Ford service buses, bought shortly afterwards from Paul Sykes dealers, were at the other end of the desirability scale!

There was another occasion when I was driving the Wednesday market day journey from Milwich to Uttoxeter which was normally the preserve of the regular driver Jill Allen. We were passing the farm workers' houses at Morrilow Heath when there was a sudden cry of 'stop' from the three or four passengers collected so far; I did as ordered and looked round to enquire what the problem was. They said that a passenger was waiting, but no-one was in view. I was then informed that a lady had left her basket by the gate, which meant that she was waiting in the house for the bus, and she duly arrived. Jill knew the routine of course; such were the joys and peculiarities of country operations! Even on the 'main road' service to Burton many passengers were known by name.

The Forest of Needwood network brought in on 17th February 1979 was modified on 3rd April 1980, resulting in Stevensons operating a return journey on Thursdays from Kings Bromley to Burton (am), to Rugeley (pm), and a Rugeley to Burton round trip on Saturdays. A variation of the X48 to Birmingham was introduced from 5th April; it ran on the second Saturday of the month, but was discontinued after 16th March 1981. Meanwhile Midland Red completed the Market Analysis Project (MAP) for their Cannock garage, and

Julian Peddle. *(STEV)*

Tim Jeffcoat. *(TJC)*

In February 1980 another vehicle purchased new was **LFA 872V (I)**, a Leyland Leopard PSU3E/4R which had a Duple Dominant Express body seating 53 passengers. Peter Birtles is driving it on 12th May 1980 as it passes by the Brickmaker's Arms near Anslow, whilst working the 12.05pm Burton-Hanbury-Uttoxeter service. The fleet number became 102 in February 1986 and in January the following year its registration was changed to AEH 607A. Later it was based at Ilkeston and was one of the vehicles lost to Nottingham Corporation (actually to Erewash Valley Services Ltd) with the sale of the Ilkeston operation, having been re-registered again in August 1989 to KCH 489V; the previous registration and the company name were retained by Stevensons. *(TJ)*

PMT's services were similarly examined; both of these affected the Uttoxeter area. Afterwards, they presented to Staffordshire County Council plans for revised networks, which would require subsidies. However, Stevensons put forward an alternative network which they could operate without subsidy, with inter-working of contracts, and which the Council, 'through gritted teeth', was obliged to accept. From 31st May 1980 Stevensons operated a weekday service between Uttoxeter and Abbots Bromley (extended to Lichfield on Saturdays) with a round trip between Rugeley and Uttoxeter on Wednesdays; some extra trips were added to service 402, and service 403 benefited from an additional Saturday operation. In a bid to increase the number of passengers on the Burton to Ashbourne service, from 21st June 1980 it was re-routed via Church Broughton and Boylestone, instead of via Sudbury.

From 28th June Stevensons started a basically two-hourly service from Uttoxeter via Bramshall and Hixon to Stafford which was timed to afford connections with the main Burton service at Uttoxeter, and through fares were available. At the same time the Doveridge-Uttoxeter-Bramshall service was withdrawn; Doveridge village was served by occasional short runs from Uttoxeter and some diversion of through services to Burton, whilst Bramshall benefited from the re-routed Stafford service and from that to Milwich. The ex-PMT Uttoxeter-Newton Circular continued as a separate service for a while before being absorbed in the Abbots Bromley timetable. For some time the Uttoxeter Town Circular was operated jointly by PMT and Stevensons, the short Park Avenue loop being separated and operated by Stevensons. An Outer Circle service was introduced by Stevensons from 13th October to serve a new housing

In September 1980 two Neepsend-bodied AEC Regent Vs, 8859/60 VR, were hired from Maynes, Manchester, to whom they were new in 1964; the latter, which was subsequently purchased and became no.60, is seen at Spath. Behind are 204 BTP, CHG 551C and TTT 780, the latter then in use as a tree-lopper/recovery vehicle. 8859 VR was returned to Maynes in November, and no.60 was sold for preservation in December 1980. *(TJ)*

development. Stevensons' running costs were much lower than those of the NBC subsidiaries whose routes were taken over, allowing for up to 40% reductions in some fares, resulting in considerably increased loadings. Some country area market day journeys had to be duplicated! The company philosophy continued to be one of providing a viable network of necessary services at fares that the public could afford. The 1980 Transport Act, effective from 6th October, presented great opportunities for Stevensons. Prior to the Act companies had to prove that new or modified services would be of benefit to the public; anyone who wished could object, and the process was extremely lengthy. After the Act, although licences were still required, applications were assumed to be in the public's interest, and anyone who wished to object had to prove to the contrary.

In August 1980 Middleton's of Rugeley had their fleet reduced by the Traffic Commissioners, in view of maintenance issues, following which Staffordshire County Council asked Stevensons to take on some school contracts there from September 1980. To help with this work two AEC Regent Vs with Neepsend rear-entrance bodies (8859/60 VR) were hired from Maynes of Manchester in September, the latter vehicle being purchased subsequently, and I was fortunate in being allocated that one for a schools contract from Handsacre on 16th September. Both vehicles saw only a few months' service with Stevensons and were sold into preservation. Middleton's hired in some vehicles but they proved unreliable, and they decided to discontinue stage carriage operation. Stevensons took over most of the services from 13th October, running initially on hire to Middleton's who still had the licences, using buses from Spath and Burton depots, under the 'Yellowbus' name. Shortly afterwards, a Middleton's vehicle was involved in a fatal accident with a police motor cyclist, as a result of which more checks were made by the Traffic Commissioners. At a West Midlands Traffic Area (WMTA) hearing on 4th November the remainder of Middleton's vehicles were put off the road.

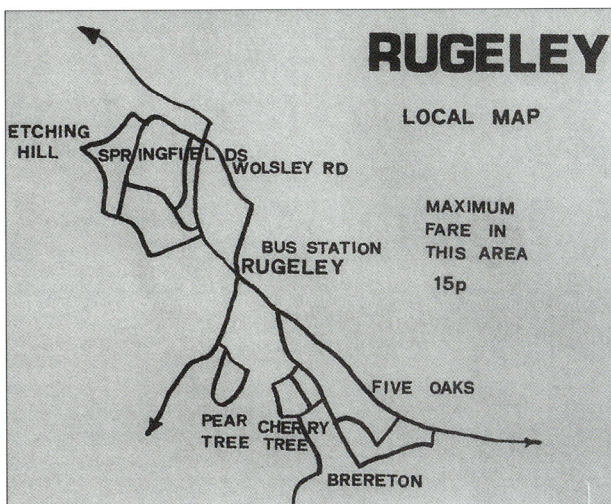

Both Stevensons and Warstones applied for Middleton's licences, but they voluntarily agreed to the following arrangement which started on 15th November. Warstones would operate the Rugeley to Lichfield and Handsacre to Wolverhampton services, whilst Stevensons would operate the X41 from Weston via Rugeley to Birmingham, and the Rugeley town services, the latter being operated between 8.00am and 8.00pm, and it was not long before passenger numbers had increased threefold. Thereafter, services were expanded into the surrounding area, including some between Abbots Bromley, Rugeley and Walsall at various times, between Walsall and Lichfield, and eventually a small number, centred on Sutton Coldfield, started. The ex-Middleton's X41 service from Weston to Birmingham was extended back to operate from Uttoxeter via Hixon and became the X49. From August 1983, 'Trent Valley' became the new local identity for Stevensons' Rugeley-based services. Some of Stevensons' vehicles for the Rugeley services were based in Middleton's yard in Armitage Road from September 1983; this practice ceased on March 2nd 1988 when a new garage, large enough to take double-deckers and with good maintenance facilities, was built in Power Station Road. It was necessary to undertake another fleet renumbering in January 1981, coaches and single-deckers being numbered 1 to 25, double-deckers 26 onwards. On 22nd July 1981 a shoppers' service (412) between Tutbury and Nottingham via Stretton, Burton and Swadlincote, started, which provided work for a vehicle in between morning and afternoon contracts; this was extended to start at Hatton on 11th November 1982.

RUGELEY

LOCAL MAP

ETCHING HILL
SPRINGFIELDS
WOLSLEY RD

MAXIMUM
FARE IN
THIS AREA
15p

BUS STATION
RUGELEY

FIVE OAKS

PEAR CHERRY
TREE TREE

BRERETON

MUS 103P, new in 1975, was one of two Leyland Leopards with 53-seat Duple Dominant bus bodies, bought from Garelochhead Coach Services in November 1980, this one entering service as no.21 in the following month. On 21st February 1981 I drove it for the first time, and it is seen in Ashbourne Bus Station prior to returning to Burton. *(EW)*

Both of the Garelochhead Leopards had coach-specification chassis, and in October 1983 no.21 was relieved of its Duple bus body at Spath, then the chassis was upgraded, including the fitting of a Leyland 0.680 engine. *(EW)*

The completed chassis is seen at Spath, with Russ Moore at the helm about to undertake the journey to Plaxton's Coachworks at Scarborough, where a Webasto heater was fitted in the new body. It then went to Jalna Coaches (Jalna Coach Conversions) where a toilet was fitted, following which it was completed at Spath as a 46-seater to Executive standard with tables and toilet. *(EW)*

In 1980 Garelochhead Coaches went out of business and was attempting to sell its fleet of vehicles, but being situated beyond Glasgow was having difficulty. Julian Peddle arranged to have the vehicles taken to Spath from where they could be sold more easily; I drove one of the Fords on that journey on 4th January 1981. Most of the vehicles were sold on, but two Leyland Leopards and a Ford R1014, all of which had Duple Dominant bus bodies, entered the fleet. After three years or so the bus bodies on the Leylands were scrapped and the chassis were up-graded, including the fitting of 0.680 engines, and then fitted with new Plaxton Paramount coach bodies, MUS 103P becoming an executive coach, being re-registered TFA 13. Some of the other up-graded chassis were similarly re-engined prior to being taken to the body-builders. On his return from one such journey driving a chassis to Plaxton's at Scarborough, Russ Moore said "That was wonderful; on the motorway I was overtaking Mercedes cars"! Henceforth, there would be increasing use made of 'cherished' vehicle registrations, some of which would be passed on in turn to other newly-acquired vehicles. The success of the Garelochhead exercise encouraged Stevensons to undertake more used vehicle dealing; some buses would see short periods of use in the operating fleet.

It re-entered service as no.12 in August 1984, carrying a striking black livery with red and white relief (fondly referred to as 'Black Beauty'). Re-registered TFA 13, subsequently the Leopard exchanged its spots for the stripes of a Tiger when a TL11 engine was fitted, which transformed its performance to one of legend. In December 1986 it passed on the executive mantle to a Volvo coach and was up-seated to 53; it is seen on 12th April 1987 after I had parked it at Penmaenpool, between Dolgellau and Fairbourne. *(EW)*

Seen fulfilling its private-hire role on 27th January 1981, in the splendid surroundings of Sudbury Hall, is PFA 50W (50), a Gardner-engined Bristol VRTSL3, with ECW body. The side advertisements announce that the vehicle is 'The Supercruiser', at the time the only double-decker in the Midlands with 70 coach seats. Henceforth, fleet numbers and registration numbers for new vehicles would be matched whenever possible. Sudbury Hall, now owned by The National Trust, was built between 1660 and 1680 by George Vernon, Earl of Shrewsbury. The area on the left of this block of outbuildings now houses the Museum of Childhood. *(TJ)*

A surprise purchase in January 1981 was RCN 699, an AEC Routemaster with Leyland 0.600 engine and a Park Royal forward-entrance body, which was new to Northern General, Gateshead, in 1964, but which was bought from Wombwell Diesels. Entering service as no.28 in July 1981, it was used mainly on contracts, but also attended many bus rallies, the first being in July to the National Showbus Rally at Purfleet where it won an award. It was immediately a popular choice for enthusiast tours, and the first was for the Omnibus Society on 19th September; the photo shows no.28 after I had parked it on Stevensons' stand at Pitcher Bank, Stafford. I enjoyed driving this bus, and had the pleasure of taking it on a number of other such tours, one being as far as Liverpool. It was also used on service, sometimes to Stafford, and for a while had its own duty on Saturdays. Re-numbered 52 in February 1983, it soldiered on until May 1986, and after use with Stagecoach and Magic Bus it was acquired for preservation and has regained Northern General livery. *(EW)*

Two Bristol Series 3 VRTSL3/6LXBs with high-speed rear axles, which cost around £60,000 each, were delivered in 1980/1, the first new double-deckers for over thirty years; they had ECW bodies to bus grant specification with 70 coach seats, the first being sign-written as 'The Supercruiser'. They were extremely reliable vehicles, used primarily on the Birmingham express services from Uttoxeter and Burton, and were popular vehicles for private-hire work. I took a very amiable party of 'ban the bomb' protesters and their placards to a protest march in London; we were all amazed at the vehicle's performance and I still have the complimentary letter which was forwarded to me by the company. The original order had been for Leyland Fleetlines with ECW coach bodies but Leyland ceased production of the chassis type and the Bristols were agreed on instead. January 1981 saw the purchase from Wombwell Diesels of ex-Northern General RCN 699, an AEC Routemaster which had a Leyland 0.600 engine and which carried a forward-entrance Park Royal body. Mainly used for contract work, it also saw service work on Saturdays and special occasions; it won awards at rallies and was a popular choice for enthusiasts' tours.

Rolleston Road depot was no longer suitable, and new, spacious premises were acquired in Wetmore Road, Burton early in 1981, the move being made on 9th and 10th May. The depot facilities included good

Andy Starbuck.

workshops and a paint bay. Also in that year, the garage opened as designated premises for car MOT testing, which became as popular as the facility at Spath. In anticipation of new PSV test regulations due to take effect in 1982, Wetmore Road depot was fully certified as a bus testing station during 1981, the first privately-owned one in the whole West Midlands Area to achieve that status. The Bristol VR no.50 was the first to be tested under the new arrangements. Andy Starbuck had started in 1979 as assistant to David Stevenson at Rolleston Road depot, and he became the Manager at Wetmore Road, where he helped also to develop further the private hire side of the business. Football excursions were operated to games involving Aston Villa, Derby County, Stoke City and Burton Albion. During 1981 Joan and George moved into a new house built on their land and 'Brooklands' thereafter was used as office accommodation. George had farming in his blood and continued with his smallholding and garden; he also had a number of fields nearby, connected by a strip of land which had carried the old railway track, part of which he had purchased earlier to give access to the fields, on which he kept a small herd of lovely Red Ruby Devon beef cattle.

Trent announced that they wished to withdraw from their Burton to Rolleston service via Horninglow from 17th August 1981. They would still operate their Burton to Derby service via Stretton and Rolleston but the public was outraged at the loss of the route via Horninglow. Stevensons proposed to replace it without subsidy, charging the same fares as Trent on the small common section of route in Rolleston, but lowering the fares on the remainder of the route. Because of opposition from the County Council, who feared the continuation of this service would abstract revenue from the Derby route, the application went to a West Midlands Traffic Area (WMTA) hearing on 28th August, but Stevensons started the service from 17th August, and for just over ten days until the licence came through no fares were charged. This was good publicity for the service, cost less than advertising, and the practice would be used again to good effect in the future. Stevensons' fares were more realistic than those of Trent, and patronage increased from about 70 to 300 per day.

From 12th October 1981 there was a regular Derby-Burton-Lichfield-Birmingham X38 City Link express service in operation. This service, co-ordinated with the X49 Uttoxeter-Rugeley-Lichfield-Birmingham service, was extremely popular from the outset, taking 1 hr 35 mins end to end, as opposed to the old Midland Red time of 2 hrs 18 mins. Some journeys operated between Birmingham and Burton only, and that timing was reduced by 30 mins; a few timetable adjustments had been made by December. The combined X38/X49 services required up to eight vehicles, and on Saturdays leading up to Christmas, I have driven the service bus from Uttoxeter and have been accompanied by two duplicates into Carrs Lane at Birmingham! For some time Midland Red continued to operate their express service between Lichfield and Birmingham, but Stevensons' fares were considerably less than those charged by Midland Red. The section between Burton and Derby received competition from Trent and Derby Corporation, but Stevensons had a fare advantage and their service was later amended to be a separate and more reliable one (renumbered 418) from 18th March 1985.

Three DMSs were bought from OK Motor Services, Bishop Auckland, in February 1982 and JGU 251K (35) is seen in Burnside, Rolleston-on-Dove on the service from Burton. All three vehicles had received early conversions to single door by Ensign Bus, Grays, as can be seen by the small replacement second window bay. (EW)

In March 1982 two new Leyland Tigers with 53-seat Plaxton Paramount Express bodies were bought, registered **UVT 13/4X (13/4)**. Keith Stanton is seen driving the latter down the bank from Foxt, near Cheadle (Staffs) on a tendered Ashbourne to Cheadle service which started in October 1986. The combination of manual gearbox and air operated clutch was not good for service work, particularly when starting on a gradient when loaded. *(EW)*

However, British Rail electrified their competing Lichfield to Birmingham service, making it quicker, and increased the frequency, whereafter patronage on the buses declined, resulting in Stevensons' Burton to Birmingham service being withdrawn on 14th April 1986. Simultaneously, the X49 was altered to run from Hixon via Rugeley, but that service was withdrawn completely in February 1987.

With the advent of motorways and the improvements made to many existing roads, day excursions and private hires could venture further afield in one day within the driving regulations, or passengers could be allowed

From Lancaster City Council came four Leyland Leopards with Alexander AY and AYS-type bodies of 1976, the first arriving in April 1982. All had a wide four-leaf doorway, Lancaster being the first concern to specify that feature. MFR 41P was a PSU4C with 45 bus seats, but these were changed for coach seats prior to entry to service as no.16 in May; having been re-numbered 25, it is seen at the Salt Box, Hatton on 13th March 1983, ready for a return journey to Burton. In April 1985 it became no.65. *(EW)*

The next two Leyland Tigers bought new had Plaxton Paramount Express bodies, but had semi-automatic gear change. The first, CBF 2Y (2), new in March 1983, is seen in company with no.22 in Carrs Lane, Birmingham, the terminus of the express services from Burton and Uttoxeter. A good queue of returning shoppers was waiting for them at the time. *(EW)*

One day I was waiting with a bus at the Salt Box Café car park, and was fortunate to capture this view of PAX 466F (30), turning towards Burton by the Kestrel Inn (previously The Salt Box), presumably on a private hire. This marvellous vehicle, the last traditional low-bridge vehicle built, was lovely to drive, and was further improved by the fitting of a Leyland 0.680 engine. *(EW)*

the other three remaining half-cab double-deckers, it ran on normal services during an enthusiasts' weekend on September 17th and 18th 1983, and occasionally was used on Burton town services. The company had tendered for three Bristol VRs they wished to purchase, and the PD3 was included in the tender. PAX 466F was owned by Julian Peddle personally and is now owned by the Cardiff Transport Preservation Group, re-painted in its original Bedwas and Machen livery.

more time in accustomed destinations. From the early 1980s, Stevensons' increasingly modern coaches were seen over a large part of England, Wales, and even Scotland, on day excursions and private hires.

On 20th March 1982 I collected a party from Derby Street, Burton, using one of the latest Ford coaches. Their destination was Neasden, where they would be attending an Indian wedding, and they all looked very well in their finery. I politely declined their invitation to join them afterwards for the meal, and left my coach at Vauxhall coach park in central London for the duration. At the appointed time the party re-joined the coach and asked me to open the boot so that presents could be loaded. It was then that I saw a large lidded vat being carried along the pavement by two of the men, and its destination was also the boot; apparently, it was tradition that any food left over be taken away by the guests. It was a very careful drive back to Burton, since at the back of my mind was a vision of catastrophic proportions should I have to brake suddenly, resulting in a rare mixture of presents and curry!

Leyland Leopard coaches and buses, many acquired from other operators, became the 'workhorses' of the fleet during the 1980s, and continued to arrive from various sources. Four new Plaxton-bodied Leyland Tiger coaches were bought between 1982 and 1984 using the bus grant. One Tiger was UVT 13X and for the first time ever, fleet number 13 was used. On a return journey to Stone on a contract for a private Friday market at Uttoxeter, it was forced into the hedge on the narrow road resulting in some injuries and considerable near-side damage to the vehicle. The day was Friday 13th! An interesting purchase in 1982 from Rhymney Valley District Council was PAX 466F, a Leyland PD3 of 1968, which had a Massey low-bridge body with rear entrance, and was also the last of its kind with an upper-deck sunken side gangway to be built; a Leyland 0.680 engine was fitted later. Together with

During the above-mentioned 'half-cab weekend' some of the DMS Fleetline double-deckers were also in use. A regular passenger who lived in Hatton normally travelled on the bus for the short journey to Tutbury, where he enjoyed a few pints at lunchtime. He would be set down at the Dog and Partridge and would sometimes make his way after a while to the Castle Inn in Bridge Street. On the Saturday of the event I was driving a rear-entrance PD3 on a Burton to Uttoxeter journey and, as I approached the corner of Bridge Street, the said gentlemen rushed out from The Castle Inn to the nearby bus stop. I pulled up with the rear entrance by the bus stop but, as he was now accustomed to front-loading buses, he came to the front of the bus to board. He tried without success in a rather befuddled state to climb over the front wheel and mudguard; I opened the side cab window and eventually persuaded him to try at the rear of the bus!

Tim Jeffcoat took this lovely photo of driver Des Ward and conductress Edna Bryan in Uttoxeter Bus Station on 3rd September 1980. *(TJ)*

Seasonal summer services were operated in summer 1984 to the Alton Towers Pleasure Park from Burton and South Derbyshire, and there were three routes from Derby in a joint exercise with Trent and Derby City Transport. For a while the first Saturday journey from Stafford on service 404 was extended to Alton Towers with all-inclusive fares, and with a corresponding late afternoon return journey. Heavy loadings on many 401 Uttoxeter-Tutbury-Burton journeys resulted in conductors and conductresses continuing to be employed in the day-time, long after the introduction of driver-only operation. Indeed, three-bell loads from Tutbury to Burton were not uncommon, particularly approaching Christmas; eventually, as the regular platform staff retired during the 1980s, one-person operation became standard. On one occasion an Atlantean which I was driving into Burton failed almost outside the Rolleston Road depot. The only vehicle available was an ex-Burnley Leyland PD2 and, although my conductor Tom Smith preferred the Atlantean, the service was able to continue into Burton. The South Derbyshire Shopper service 13 commenced on 23rd July 1982, initially on three days a week, but on five days a week from 15th August 1983. This provided a direct link to Derby for residents of numerous South Derbyshire villages and suburbs, obviating a change of buses in either Swadlincote or Burton.

Whilst travelling past Loxley on the A518 towards Uttoxeter in September 1982 on service 404 from Stafford, Stefan Senkow had to take evasive action when a lorry descending the bank jack-knifed in front of the bus, THM 708M (31), which was forced off the road. It came to rest at an acute angle at the edge of an embankment, but fortunately the passengers escaped with minor injuries, although Stefan's back troubled him thereafter. The bus was not lucky either, the twisted body resulting in its withdrawal. Its replacement was built around THM 689M which had its chassis rebuilt incorporating parts from two similar vehicles and was converted to single doorway. With a new chassis number SBS/FEL/001, it was registered CBF 31Y and entered service as no.31 in February 1983. It is understood that only one other DMS in the country received a new registration with a year suffix letter.

From the 1950s buses had occasionally carried advertising, either for the company's own activities or for local traders. The 1980s saw the development of all-over-advertising and, later on, rear-end advertising, all of which provided very useful additional revenue; in the case of the former, the lower front panel usually carried fleet livery to assist potential passengers. Both double- and single-deck vehicles were used for this purpose.

JGF 196K (45) is wearing the later simplified livery and is fitted with a Burton area destination blind in this view at the Butter Cross, Abbots Bromley; at the time it was based at Uttoxeter, to where it would return shortly. (EW)

Prior to 1981, all the DMSs that entered service were Gardner-engined. THM 708M, a Park Royal-bodied example which entered service as no.31 in May 1981 was a Daimler CRL6/30 (Leyland-engined), as were many that followed, although most, if not all, of the Leyland-engined DMSs would receive replacement Gardner units. The first photograph shows 31 at Dapple Heath en route to Abbots Bromley having recently entered service. As mentioned in the text, in September 1982 it was forced off the road at Loxley, near Uttoxeter, where it can be seen in the second photograph. *(EW)*

Following the premature withdrawal of no.31 THM 708M, its replacement was built around MCW-bodied THM 689M, but parts were incorporated in its re-build from other vehicles; it received a new registration, CBF 31Y, and entered service in February 1983. Shortly afterwards, it is seen about to leave Uttoxeter Bus Station on a Town Circular with Stefan Senkow driving. *(EW)*

Fleetline chassis produced after the takeover by Leyland received new designations. KUC 973P, an FE30ALR (Leyland-engined) with MCW body was purchased in September 1981. After running initially in London Transport livery, in November 1981 it was converted to single doorway and entered service as no.33 in February 1982 in an all-white livery. It was referred to as 'the ghost', prior to receiving the all-over advert for Toons Carpet Warehouse in April 1982, as seen in this view as it passes by Chartley Castle on a Stafford to Uttoxeter journey. Driver Bill Chell was well known for his 'approximate' destination blind settings but, not for the first time, here he seems to have forgotten to change it completely. In August that year No.33 received a Gardner 6LXB engine. *(EW)*

MLK 449L received an all-over livery promoting the company's Trent Valley operation in Rugeley. As so often happens with such-liveried vehicles, it is seen well away from the desired location, and in this case is working a local service in Burton, swinging round the corner from Calais Road into Belvedere Road. *(EW)*

MLH 303L (46) is seen at Derby Street depot wearing an advertising livery for Flow Spray (The Burton Body Repair Centre). The top-hinged upper-deck emergency door betrays that this is an MCW body. *(EW)*

5. Management Changes and Further Growth

Although George Stevenson had been physically strong, an illness in his mid-forties, exacerbated by cigarettes and the rather careless use of cellulose paint, left him vulnerable to sickness. In 1983 Joan and George Stevenson retired; David Stevenson became Company Chairman and Julian Peddle bought George's share of the business, becoming Managing Director. An un-registered test-bed for Leyland's Olympian (prototype No. B45-01) was bought from Paul Sykes (dealers) in June 1983. The engine was a Gardner 6LXB and it had a Voith 3-speed fully automatic gearbox; it carried an ECW body, with a Bristol VR type lower front panel, but internally was incomplete, having no seats, panels or electrics. Over the next eighteen months this vehicle was prepared for service using seats from scrapped DMSs; it entered service in January 1985, registered Q246 FVT (99), the prefix being used for kit cars etc, and to indicate a vehicle of indeterminate age. Interestingly, the registration document referred to it as a 'Morgan'. In future years a number of acquired coaches would be down-graded to buses using DMS seats, and the blue LTE moquette was adopted for seating on future new buses, a very large quantity of that moquette being bought from Houldsworth of Halifax. On 10th October 1983 a Monday to Friday service from Uttoxeter to Derby was started which was jointly operated with Trent. PMT operated the Saturday service, which was all that remained of their long-standing Hanley-Derby route, but from 26th October 1986 it became a tendered service operated by Stevensons, two journeys connecting at Uttoxeter with PMT's service to and from the Potteries.

Around 1984 there was a spate of vehicle thefts from Spath. The first coach was discovered by Bathpool Park in Kidsgrove; two boys aged 15 and 16 were responsible and in court it was found that they had carried out vehicle thefts elsewhere. When the same Ford coach was again taken from Spath, it was discovered once more at Bathpool Park. The next theft was different, but a 'phone call from the owner of a café on the A34 near Bathpool Park, asking when the company was going to remove its vehicle from outside his premises, resolved the matter. Barriers were then erected at Spath depot for use at night time but, despite this, some time later a coach was driven through the barriers, and was found at Rocester for a change. Three used Bristol VRs entered the fleet for short durations, and an ex-Reading VRTLL6G was purchased which was used on school contracts prior to spending a short period on hire to Berresfords of Cheddleton before being sold. One Leyland Leopard had most of its body removed and was used as a test-bed for the possible fitment of Gardner engines in Leopard chassis, but this idea was abandoned following tests.

In September 1984, Crystal Coaches Ltd of Marsh Trees Garage, Hassall Street, Newcastle-under-Lyme, was acquired. This company operated private hires and Keele Motorway Services staff contracts, and an elderly Leyland Leopard together with five Ford minibuses entered Stevensons' fleet. The Crystal Coaches Ltd company name was retained (whilst normally trading

Stevensons wanted to see whether or not a Leyland Leopard chassis could be modified to take a Gardner engine, and **WYX 320G** was used for the test-bed. As a result of this exercise the idea was dropped. *(EW)*

The Leyland Olympian prototype which had been completed to PSV standard by the company and registered Q246 FVT (99), is seen in Rugeley Bus Station, together with numbers 1 and 134. *(EW)*

With MLK 445L in Crystal Coaches' small yard in Newcastle is seen SDK 98S, a Ford A0609 with Dormobile 25 seat coach body which was new in 1978 to Les Bywater and Son Ltd, Rochdale, and was bought by Crystal Coaches in December 1981. Referred to as the 'chip van', it became 76 with Stevensons (176 from February 1987) and it received a partial re-paint, yellow replacing the red. The arrival of more new minibuses saw it withdrawn in January 1988. Behind stands St Paul's Parish Church. *(EW)*

as Stevensons Coaches), the concern being operated as a subsidiary, but with regular exchanges of vehicles from Spath as required, and it was managed for many years by Bill Stanton, the former owner of Tean-based BC Travel. A few vehicles received special liveries comprising yellow, deep orange and white, sign-written accordingly for either the Potteries 'Yellows' or the Rugeley 'Trent Valley' operations; these special liveries were deemed to be un-necessary after a few years. An ex-Greater Manchester PTE 'Mancunian' MCW-bodied Daimler Fleetline (ONF 893H) was bought around this time; it was used on contracts before it went on a short-term loan to Astill and Jordan prior to re-sale. By 1984 forty contracts were operated to schools in Uttoxeter, Rugeley, Hatton, Newhall and Rolleston-on-Dove; there were 25 full-time and over 60 part-time drivers, including seven female drivers, quite a rare phenomenon at the time. One such was Elaine Mayne who had been the outings organiser for the Anslow Women's Institute;

STEVENSONS of UTTOXETER L?
THE GARAGE, SPATH
UTTOXETER, STAFFS., ST14 5AC

during a conversation with a member of the company she commented that, as she had mastered the large family car, she believed she could even manage to drive a bus. Six weeks later she was contacted and told that the company needed more part-time drivers for school contracts. Elaine was interested, passed her Class 1 PSV test at the first opportunity, and shortly afterwards was driving single- and double-deck buses for over thirty hours per week!

The Engineering Department was having some disenchantment with Leyland's Tiger TL11 engine, as a result of which some Volvo chassis appeared in the fleet for the first time in 1985. These comprised two Plaxton-bodied B58-56s and a Duple-bodied B58-61, the latter bought from Coliseum Coaches Ltd, Southampton, having sustained accident damage. Its body was removed and the front part of the chassis was re-aligned by Hartsthorne Motors; the Volvo K19 gearbox was replaced by a standard 6-speed ZF box and the chassis was re-bodied by Plaxton; henceforth Volvo chassis would be the norm for coaches.

Erewash Travel Ltd of Ilkeston was acquired on 1st October 1985, together with services from Beeston to Eastwood,

The two vehicles painted in 'The Yellows' livery for the Potteries operation, XNE 882L and JGF 241K are seen at Spath. By March 1986, these special liveries for the Rugeley and Potteries operations were discontinued. *(EW)*

The only full-size vehicle acquired with the Crystal Coaches business in September 1984 was HNK 145G, a Leyland Leopard PSU3A with 51-seat Plaxton Elite body of 1969, and it became no.55. Re-numbered 24 in April 1985, then to 105 in October that year, it is seen at the Ilkeston depot when I was helping out there on a baths contract. Withdrawal came in August 1986, after which it was sold to Hollis Coaches, Queensferry. (EW)

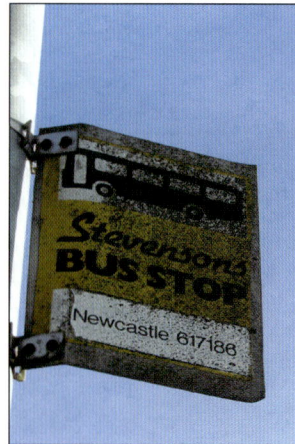

This Potteries area Stevensons' bus stop flag was still on its pole in November 2015, and still showed the original contact details for Newcastle garage. Many such flags were made in the 1980s and 1990s for use around the company's rapidly-expanding area of operation, using panels from scrapped DMSs, which was very good re-cycling. (EW)

New to Wallace Arnold Tours in 1975, HWU 73N was a Duple Dominant-bodied Leyland Leopard which was bought by Erewash Travel in April 1983. It is seen wearing a Plaxton lower front panel shortly after that business had been acquired by Stevensons in October 1985 at Denstone College, an independent day and boarding school. Built in the Neo-Gothic style, it opened in 1873 as St Chad's College. The late c13th Gothic-style chapel behind the coach was completed in 1887. From Stevensons' early years the company was the major provider of coach transport for the college. (EW)

and to Stapleford; these became tendered services in October 1986, at which time additional services, from Beeston to Cotgrave, Ilkeston to Cotmanhay, and local services in Hucknall, Beeston and Ilkeston were gained. However, the business, garage and some vehicles passed to City of Nottingham Transport on 13th November 1988. In the early 1980s two double-deckers were out-stationed at Cosy Coaches in Donisthorpe for use on William Allitt School (Newhall) contracts, these being driven by teachers with PSV licenses. Similarly, from some time in 1985 two double-deckers were out-stationed at the garage of Berresfords Motors of Cheddleton, from where two school contracts were operated to Leek schools, this finishing in September 1986.

East Staffordshire District Council operated 34 buses in Burton-upon-Trent on a network reflecting the tramway routes of old and reportedly had lost £245,000 in 1984/85, which ESDC expected Staffordshire County Council to cover in subsidy payment. Julian Peddle asked ESDC what they thought may happen in respect of its bus operations in view of possible competition following deregulation of the bus industry envisaged in the 1985 Transport Act. They agreed that the future did not look good for them, and they did not want competition from other companies which could move into the area; a merger with other concerns had been debated but finally a merger with Stevensons was agreed. The Council would hold 49% of the shares, with Julian Peddle and David Stevenson controlling 50% plus one share equally between them, and everything had to be completed by at least twelve months and one day before deregulation day as required by the deregulation legislation. The merger took effect on 1st October 1985, and a three-year lease on a new bus depot in Derby Street (built in February 1984) was included in the deal. Stevensons also became responsible for maintaining the council-owned refuse vehicles, lawnmowers and

Following the merger with East Staffordshire District Council's bus operation in October 1985, all the vehicles excluding the Dennis Dominators were retained initially. GFA 11L, a Daimler CRG6LX of 1973 with Willowbrook 77-seat body in the Nottingham style, is seen at Derby Street depot, sufficiently re-painted to indicate its new ownership. After one year it was sold to a dealer, and was acquired afterwards by Swanbrook Transport, Cheltenham. *(EW)*

To help with the speedy replacement of ESDC vehicles, some DMSs were pressed into service without being converted to single doorway initially, and also wore a simplified livery as seen on OJD 223R (87), which entered service in December 1985, and is seen in Burton. *(AJ)*

OUC 42R was the vehicle chosen to be re-painted in an experimental livery of yellow with blue and red stripes, re-entering service as no.82 in November 1985, and it is seen in Borough Road on a Burton town service. With reference to the shop sign by the bus stop, I suppose it would be fair to say that there were 'great expectations' for the new company. *(DS)*

other vehicles. This was possibly unique in the annals of bus operation in this country, whereby a complete municipal undertaking was acquired by an independent operator. It also resulted in the removal of the remaining Burton Standard Conditions, which controlled picking up and setting down within the old County Borough.

The Wetmore Road premises were retained, used mainly for MOT work, and for the storage of acquired or redundant stock. The Burton bus routes were completely revised on 27th October, resulting in average frequencies of 10 minutes, and only eighteen vehicles were required. Trent shared with Stevensons the cross-Burton service between Winshill and Horninglow, this being a deliberate move to keep Trent on-side and to deter interference from Midland Fox. Some of the Council's Daimler Fleetlines (single- and double-deck), three Bristol RESLs and three Leyland Atlanteans were retained but, although some troublesome and costly Dennis Dominators were used for a very short time, they were sold to Maidstone and District Motor Services (5), and the Borough of Thamesdown Public Transport (6), for £30,000 each. They were replaced by some relatively cheap but good DMSs, some of which retained their dual doorways, at least initially. One vehicle carried an experimental livery of red, blue and yellow but this was not repeated. A few of the Dominators were on hire to Maidstone and Thamesdown for a while prior to being purchased. Major revisions were made to Burton's new bus network after less than a month, including improved cross-town services. Fare zoning was introduced, and by the late 1980s weekly and monthly travel cards were offered. Julian Peddle recently said that he had been pleasantly surprised that the Council directors always acted in the best interests of Stevensons as a company, and did not put their political interests before those of Stevensons.

Key Coachways Ltd was set up at Rugeley in December 1981 and rapidly moved into stage carriage operations, competing in part with Stevensons. It was renamed Blue Bus Services (Rugeley) Ltd at the end of 1983, but the company ran into financial difficulties and ceased operations on 3rd October 1985. From the next day Stevensons acquired some of its routes, including one from Rugeley to Handsacre, and two vehicles, but not the company. One of their vehicles was an ex-SELNEC Leyland Leopard PSU3 (AJA 360L) which was relieved of its ECW body and the chassis was up-graded to Tiger status, including the fitting of a TL11 engine, after which it was sent to be fitted with a 53-seat Duple 320 body. The yellow, black and red livery was applied to a new style sweeping up towards the rear similar to the then livery of 'Roman City' and it entered service in May 1987; subsequently it was re-registered 479 BOC (18), and at the time was my favourite coach to drive. Keith Myatt, who had been a director of Blue Bus Services, joined Stevensons as Publicity Assistant at Burton, and Richard Hackett, Depot Manager at Rugeley, became Commercial Manager, also based at Burton depot. On

The origins of this lovely coach are with **AJA 360L**, a Leyland Leopard **PSU3B/4R** with **ECW** coach body, which was new to **SELNEC** in 1973. It was acquired with the business of Blue Bus Services, Rugeley in October 1985 becoming no.56 then, as recorded in the text, after chassis up-grading it received this Duple 320 body and entered service in May 1987 as no.18. It is seen in the picturesque surroundings of the RSPB's Dinas Reserve in South-Central Wales when I took some North Staffs Area members there on 20th May 1988. *(EW)*

DEN 247W (24) stands in the coach park at Symonds Yat, a beauty spot overlooking the River Wye, on 24th April 1988. It is one of three ex-Greater Manchester PTE Volvo B58s with 12-metre Plaxton bodies bought in November 1985. Sister vehicle **DEN 245W** was converted to become an executive coach in February 1987, whilst in November 1988 **DEN 246W** had a wheelchair lift fitted as part of its refurbishment as a mobility coach. *(EW)*

Two Leyland Leopards with Willowbrook 'Spacecar' coach bodies were acquired with the Midland Fox Swadlincote operation in August 1987, XCW 156R (125) being seen in Birmingham whilst on the service to Burton, and still wearing Midland Express livery. This, and sister vehicle XCW 154R, had been withdrawn by March 1988. Interestingly, another of this type of coach all of which originated with National Travel (North West) in 1977, but not belonging to Stevensons, is seen to the right. (DH)

Seen loading pupils at William Allitt School, Newhall, HSD 710N, is an Alexander-bodied Volvo B58, new to Western SMT in 1975 for motorway express work. It was bought in July 1986 from RAF Cosford and entered the fleet in May 1987 after being fitted out as a 53-seater coach. It always carried fleet number 25A since all the numbers allocated for coaches at the time had been taken. (CW)

28th October 1985 Trent Motor Traction cut back their Uttoxeter-Ashbourne-Derby service 107 to start at Mayfield. From the same date Stevensons commenced their service 409 between Uttoxeter and Ashbourne to replace the withdrawn section. Three 12-metre Plaxton-bodied Volvo B58-61 came from Greater Manchester Passenger Transport Executive in November 1985, one later becoming a 46-seat Executive coach, having been fitted out with the toilet from TFA 13 (12), which itself was re-seated to 53. In Uttoxeter, on 29th November PMT withdrew from the Town Circular leaving Stevensons as the sole operator on the local services.

On 19th April 1986 Midland Fox started to operate minibus 'Fox Cub' services, with a ten-minute headway between Swadlincote and Burton, diverting via estates served by Stevensons. In anticipation of this, on 13th April 1986 Stevensons' East Staffordshire and South Derbyshire timetables were revised again. Initially, passengers were abstracted by the Fox Cubs, which worried the company, but eventually the public turned against the minibuses. Midland Fox had axed a Swadlincote to Ashby-de-le-Zouch service stating that it was not required; Stevensons then introduced a direct service X52 on 15th September which ran between Ashby and Burton, competing with the Fox Cubs. The route became very successful, since it did not serve Swadlincote, and afforded a much faster journey into Burton for passengers from Ashby, Woodville and Midway. Significantly, this was Stevensons' first incursion into South Derbyshire with a regular service (as opposed to occasional shoppers' services). The company hoped to acquire Midland Fox when the National Bus Company started to privatise its subsidiaries. However, officials held the view that the acquisition would be

The first new Mercedes-Benz minibus was C78 WRE, a 608D with PMT body fitted with 19 coach seats, which entered service in February 1986 as no.78 (178 from 3/87). Stevensons successfully tendered for the Saturday journeys on the Cheadle to Leek service which commenced in April 1988, and no.178 is seen at the Green Man Inn, Bottom House, whilst on a journey from Leek on 9th April 1988. My few passengers were very patient. (EW)

PMT Engineering bodied three Freight Rover 300s for Stevensons, the first being D179 CRE which carried a rather striking mainly black livery on the 'Bursley' body, and was new in October 1986. It is seen in Newcastle Bus Station beside XNE 882L which has a special 'Yellows' livery, both vehicles having worked on tendered services. The Freight Rovers were not successful and all three had gone by the end of 1987. 179 went on loan to Cardiff City Transport from 21st October for two months before passing to its new owner Tentrek Expeditions Ltd, Sidcup. *(EW)*

New to Leicester Corporation in 1964 as 82 HBC, this East Lancs-bodied Leyland PD3 was bought from Astill and Jordan, Ratby in June 1983, entering service as no.54. It was re-registered RRF 109B in February 1985, at which time the original registration was transferred to coach 15. On 6th September 1986 it was photographed passing Sudbury village Post Office bound for Burton on the 401 service on a half-cab running day. Some local trees seem to have re-designed the front near-side dome, a not uncommon situation with Stevensons' double-deckers over the years. This was the least popular of the remaining Leyland Titan PDs. *(TJ)*

anti-competitive but, after initial frustrations and many discussions, Stevensons acquired a 30% holding in that company in August 1987, this later being increased to a 33% holding. Swadlincote depot and Lichfield outstation became wholly-owned by Stevensons and most of the routes were transferred. Forty-six vehicles were acquired which comprised thirty Ford Transits, seven Leyland Nationals, seven Leyland Leopards and two Daimler DMSs. These acquisitions resulted in yet another fleet re-numbering. Clive Whatling joined the company from Midland Fox as Swadlincote Depot Manager.

In July 1986 HSD 710N, a Volvo B58-6 with Alexander coach body, was bought from RAF Cosford. New to Western SMT in 1975 as a 42-seater with a toilet, for motorway express work, it had been bought without seats for spares, but on inspection was found to be in good order and was prepared for service, being fitted out with 53 Plaxton coach seats. To satisfy regulations in view of the increased seating, the rear window was modified to be an emergency exit, and it entered

service in May 1987. The first of very many Mercedes minibuses had arrived in 1985, these being two used converted 508Ds. A new Mercedes 608D, bodied by PMT Engineering and featuring bus-type doors and coach seating, was bought in February 1986, and PMT also built the bodies on three Freight Rovers, but these latter vehicles proved to be unsuccessful and were sold within a year. Two other events were held where the remaining half-cab double-deckers were used on service; special turns were arranged on Saturday 6th September 1986 between Burton and Uttoxeter, and one week later it was 'half-cab Saturday' in Rugeley.

The 1985 Transport Act, which deregulated bus services, was implemented on 26th October 1986. In anticipation of that, Stevensons had introduced a new commercial network for Burton in April that year and so was able to announce that there would be no changes to it at deregulation. Henceforth, it became quite normal for a route to be operated commercially by one company, whilst the unremunerative journeys, subsidised by the local authorities, might be awarded to the existing operator or to a different one. The company successfully tendered for many such contracts, although often they had quite limited durations. In any case, routes gained by tender could be lost at the next tender date or subsequently; some contracts were awarded either for peak-hour or off-peak journeys, or just for odd journeys. Some became more or less permanent services at depots, and occasionally became commercial operations. In general, the examples of tendered contracts given hereunder are of services for which the company was the main or sole provider. The details of such services shown henceforth in the book can only be regarded as a snapshot of the operations of any particular depot at any particular time.

Burton depot gained tendered work between Burton and Swadlincote via Coton-in-the-Elms, and on Sundays from Burton to Derby on services 103/104 via Willington or Hatton. Crystal Coaches had taken over a service from Happy Days Coaches on 30th June 1986 between Woodseaves, Eccleshall, Newcastle and Hanley, and from 26th October it became a tendered service, the starting point becoming Eccleshall; many more tendered services were gained in the Potteries area at that time. Others ran between Kidsgrove and Biddulph Moor, Rode Heath and Congleton, and on Saturdays two services linked Uttoxeter and Hanley, one via Alton and Cheadle,

and one via The Leighs and Hilderstone. Spath depot gained the Saturday Uttoxeter-Derby service and ones from Etwall to Ashbourne and Cheadle to Ashbourne on Thursdays.

Some of Stevensons' evening journeys on service 401 were lost to Zamir Coaches of Burton, and over the next few years this contract would be won by Trent, later returning to Stevensons. Zamir Coaches had started off as a private hire operator with a solitary pink-liveried Bristol coach kept at Stevensons' Wetmore Road yard, and had subsequently moved into bus service work. On 1st November 1986 the Transport Minister, David Mitchell, visited the Wetmore Road depot to unveil a plaque commemorating Stevensons' Diamond Jubilee, and was suitably impressed by the company's expansion since deregulation. Mr Mitchell referred to Stevensons as a shining example of free enterprise and praised the use of minibuses in maintaining some services at a lower running cost. December 1986 saw Richard Sherratt, from Trent, appointed to the new position of Bus Network Manager, enabling Richard Hackett to concentrate on the expanding coaching activities. At that time Stevensons operated 110 vehicles from five depots (Spath, Burton, Ilkeston, Rugeley and Newcastle). In March 1987 the Sunday service on route 401 was re-routed via Rolleston, as had originally been planned in 1976!

Two more of the popular Leyland Leopards arrived in December 1983 when LMA 60/61P, with Plaxton Elite coach bodies of 1975, were bought from Selwyn's Travel (Yates Tours), Runcorn and numbered 10/11. I was helping out on service with Crystal Coaches one day and photographed no.11 in Eccleshall having worked the tendered service from Hanley via Newcastle and Cranberry. *(EW)*

6. 'New Generation' Vehicles

The first MCW Mk1 Metrobus double-deckers were bought in December 1986, these being seven-year-old examples from Greater Manchester Buses; they were allocated to Burton, mainly for town services. Four more similar vehicles, but with Alexander bodies, and a solitary Roe-bodied Leyland Olympian, all being only five years old, came from West Yorkshire PTE early in 1987, together with some Plaxton-bodied Leyland Leopard PSU4 buses. Two Gardner-engined Leyland National 2s, sold prematurely by Provincial Bus Company, Fareham, joined the fleet in May 1987; five short Leyland National 2s with the 'rationalised' 0.680 engines were bought from Yorkshire Rider in October that year and were used mainly from Burton and Rugeley depots. Consequent upon Midland Red North pulling their minibuses out of Lichfield on 13th April 1987, both Stevensons (using conventional buses and minibuses) and Midland Fox (using Fox Cubs) registered replacement services. Following Stevensons' takeover of Midland Fox's Swadlincote garage and Lichfield outstation on 19th August as described, Stevensons removed the Fox Cubs, ending the competition. Also, at that time, Stevensons became responsible for the operation of the ex-Midland Fox Sutton Coldfield to Walmley service 165 (a Centro tender), which became Stevensons' first service wholly within the West Midlands, and eventually it would become a commercial operation.

The ex-Midland Fox services continued more or less without change for about ten weeks; the main services were from Swadlincote to a) Burton via Linton, b) Ashby, c) Overseal, d) Burton via Coton, and from Coalville via Swadlincote to Burton Hospital. However, service 118 Burton to Leicester was truncated almost immediately to operate from Swadlincote to Leicester, this being a joint operation with Midland Fox, which provided two buses to Stevensons' one. At the same time, Service X12 Swadlincote to Burton and Birmingham became Burton to Birmingham; on 8th November it was re-numbered 112, the terminus being Colmore Circus, but from 14th November this was altered so that buses made a circuit of Birmingham City Centre. The route used there was changed regularly over the next few years in view of congestion or pedestrianisation. Day Explorer tickets became available for use on all Stevensons or Midland Fox services, and there was acceptance of West Midlands Passenger Transport Executive (WMPTE) passes where and when valid. Also on 8th November, some quite substantial changes were made in the Swadlincote area, integrating the ex-Midland Fox routes with the Burton network, to continue to provide a comprehensive service at reduced costs, this new network being refined in the following June. The new direct links from Burton to Ashby, and Measham, proved popular with passengers. When new routes were started, initially much use was made of temporary destination boards displayed in the front windows of vehicles, although new destination blinds were provided in each of the operating areas as soon as possible. The company had always been good in providing up-to-date timetables, and from the mid-1980s onwards area timetables were issued and updated regularly.

On 1st November 1987 Stevensons acquired the assets of long-established coach operator Viking Motors (Burton) Limited and its sister company Victoria Motorways Ltd which ran a bus service between Burton and Measham. The owner, John Lloyd, remained in control of those two companies and on the same day Stevensons registered a new company 'Viking Tours and Travel Limited' to continue the business. Stevensons

The first 'new generation' double-deckers for the fleet were MCW Metrobuses, GBU 3/7/10V, bought from Greater Manchester Buses Ltd in December 1986 when just over seven years old. GBU 3V entered service in March 1987 (77) and is seen in Station Street, Burton, loading for the short service to Anglesey Road. *(EWC)*

C104 UHO was one of two Leyland National 2s bought from Provincial Bus Company, Fareham in May 1987, entering service as 71 in the following month, and it looked very smart in this version of the livery as it stood in Uttoxeter Bus Station. Surprisingly, both buses were sold to West Riding, Wakefield, in October 1989. *(EW)*

LUA 325V is one of five Leyland National 2s purchased from Yorkshire Rider in October 1987, this one entering service in March the following year. Based in Rugeley, it is seen in Hatherton Road, Walsall, having arrived on service 445 from Rugeley via Brownhills. (LRC)

The first new Leyland Lynx arrived in February 1988, registered E72 KBF, with a matching fleet number; although it had 51 seats when new, this was subsequently reduced to 49. It is seen in Corporation Street, Birmingham, and is bound for Burton-upon-Trent on service 112. (DH)

used the garage at Woodville, but the small garage at Burton was not included. In about 1962 John Lloyd had replaced the previous brown and red livery with a distinctive one of two-tone grey, after he had bought a Rover car which had those colours; the livery, together with the yellow boot lid which was a safety feature, was retained. The vehicles acquired comprised eight Ford, one DAF, two Leyland Tiger and two Leyland Leopard coaches (the last two becoming buses), and two Daimler Fleetlines. Victoria's bus service, the X22, was absorbed into the new service 27 which started on 8th November. An ex-Midland Fox National 2, which had been fitted with a wheelchair lift by Midland Fox as a mobility vehicle, was painted into Viking livery; subsequently, this was replaced by a Volvo/Plaxton coach, similarly treated. Express services for the 1988 season were to Blackpool, North Wales, Skegness, Scarborough, Yarmouth, Bournemouth, Torquay and Newquay, Portsmouth and the Isle of Wight, and were marketed under the Viking name. Stevensons' front-line coaches were repainted progressively into the Viking livery.

Chris Hawley, a coach driver at Spath, told me of a humorous moment when he was on tour at the south coast; his coach by then carried the Viking livery, the fleetname and Viking warrior's head appearing boldly on the vehicle. The policeman who was controlling traffic motioned to Chris to move forward, and then nearly collapsed in laughter as he noticed, and realised the significance of, the plastic Viking helmet complete with horns (no doubt acquired in Blackpool) that Chris was wearing!

Shortly after the takeover of Viking Coaches in November 1987, Plaxton Paramount 3200-bodied Leyland Tiger, A834 PPP, gravitated to Spath depot. Originally, when with Armchair Passenger Transport, it was a 55-seater, reduced to 44 by Viking, but this was altered later to 53. The scene is Buxton, early one misty autumn morning, whilst I was waiting for a party from the Old Hall Hotel which would be returning to Derby Station. (EW)

63

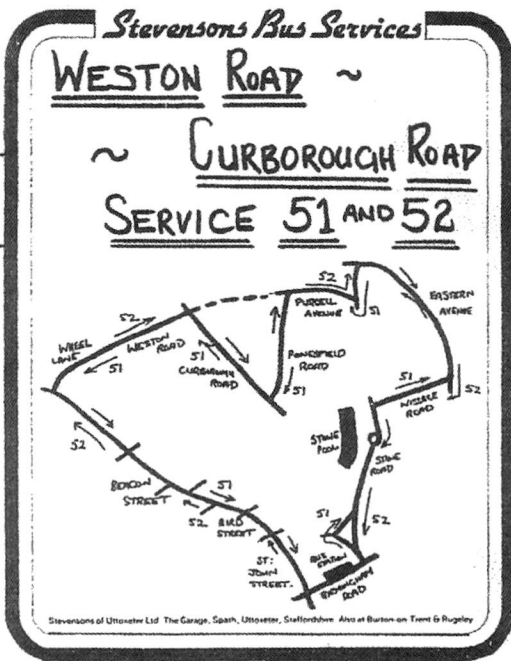

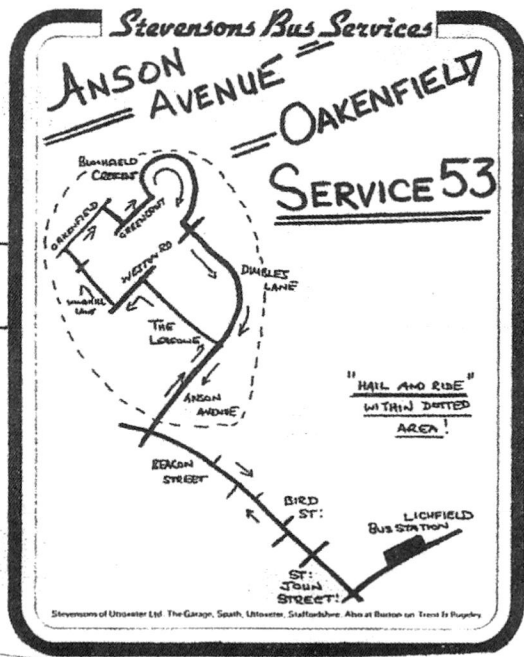

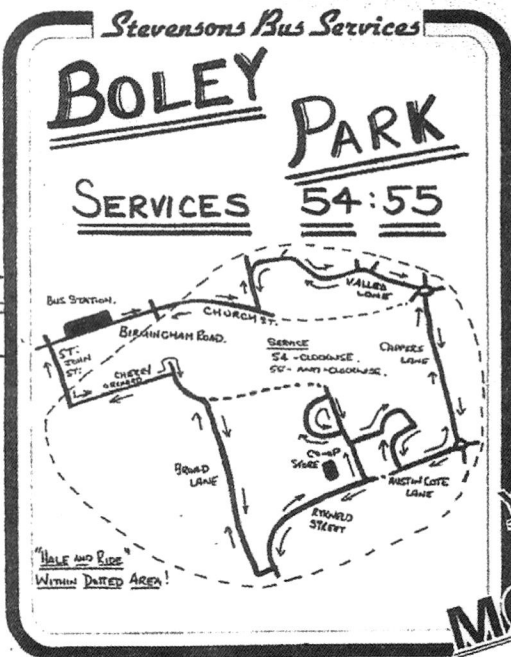

It is interesting to compare the size of the company and its operations over a seven year period:

Date	Fleet size	Stage service work	Tours & private hire	Schools and excursions & Works contracts
Dec 1980	49	20%	30%	50%
Jan 1982	52	45%	30%	25%
Dec 1984	74	45%	25%	30%
Dec 1987	176	75%	15%	10%

The first of many Scottish Bus Group Seddon Pennine 7s with Alexander bus bodies arrived in 1988. They proved to be good, reliable vehicles, had economical Gardner engines, and eventually replaced all the Leyland Nationals which found new owners eager for such vehicles following deregulation of bus services. At the same time the first new Leyland Lynx was bought following an earlier trial and more new and second-hand ones would follow in time. Two second-hand Bova coaches were tried and, surprisingly, four Leyland National 2s were bought from South Wales Transport, but they had coach-type seating and were more suitable for the longer-distance services. MCW Metrobuses continued to arrive and in September three East Lancs-bodied Leyland Olympians, which had the trusted Gardner engines, came from Plymouth Citybus. November saw the trial of an Alexander-bodied Scania K92; two new K93s, also bodied by Alexander, were bought in the following year and were evaluated against the Lynxes. A Scania N113 followed later but, being too complex and not as successful as the others, mainly due to rear axle and gearbox problems, it was disposed of early.

Crystal Coaches gained some Staffordshire CC tendered work from PMT on 3rd September 1988, for an off-peak Boothen (Stoke) to Bentilee circular service, and for certain Saturday journeys on the Longton to Leek services 106/107, the tendered Monday to Friday journeys being won the following year. From 3rd November Crystal also gained a tender for an ex-PMT minibus service which ran between Hanley, Sneyd Green, Burslem and Middleport (commercially Mondays to Fridays from August 1991). A Long Eaton town circular service, operated by Swadlincote depot and using two ex-Fox Cub Transits, commenced on 13th November 1987, a free service being operated for the first two days; after a year it was transferred to Ilkeston depot. Crystal Coaches tendered successfully for various Thursday routes around Sandbach in December 1987, followed in January 1988 by service K76, Congleton Town Services, all being Cheshire County Council tendered services. In April 1988, a Friday and Sunday tendered service X41 between Keele University and Leicester (primarily for students), together with the Sunday operation of X64 Hanley to Shrewsbury was added; the latter was withdrawn in 1989, and the X41 finished at the end of 1990. Rugeley depot gained another WMPTE tender in March 1988, from Walsall to Herberts Park but it was

Seen in the leafy surroundings of Sutton Coldfield Parade is CCY 817V, whilst on the way from Birmingham to Burton. It is one of four coach-seated Leyland National 2s of 1979, bought from South Wales Transport in March 1988. *(AP)*

Five eight-year-old Metrobuses with dual doorways, including JWF 490W (86), which is seen in New Street, Burton, were bought in March 1988 from South Yorkshire Transport, and no.86 entered service in May of that year. It appears that Inspector Billy Ireland is about to have a word with the driver. Behind is E183 BNN, one of two Iveco models with Robin Hood bodywork, bought as replacements for the Sherpas, and one of the ex-Fox Cub Transits. *(EWC)*

Three East Lancs-bodied Leyland Olympians of 1982, TTT 172-4X, were bought from Plymouth Citybus in September 1988, and were numbered 93-95. TTT 173X is seen when fresh into service in Duke Street, Tutbury on a Uttoxeter-bound journey from Burton, and driver Paul Dionne is slowing the bus to set down some passengers at the bus stop. *(DS)*

The first Scania in the fleet, which entered service in February 1989, was F110 SRF, a type K93 which had an Alexander PS 51-seat body. It is seen entering Erdington on service 112 from Burton to Birmingham. *(DH)*

Seen in Leek Bus Station is F186 PRE, a Reeve Burgess-bodied Mercedes-Benz 709D, new in August 1988 (186). Allocated to the Potteries operation, it was about to return to Longton on the 106 service with, I believe, Paul Rowley driving. Leek is the administrative centre for the Staffordshire Moorlands. On one occasion I had worked the first part of the Cheadle service using a minibus with a Toons all-over advert. When I turned up later with a vehicle in fleet livery, a lady with a return ticket needed some persuading to board, since she maintained that she had arrived on a Toons' vehicle! As the ticket in her hand had 'Stevensons' on it, that convinced her to board. *(EW)*

lost the following year. From April 1988 Spath depot operated the Saturdays only tendered service between Cheadle and Leek, normally worked by a minibus. At about this time Murray Shepherd joined the company as Operations Manager.

In June 1988 the Burton and South Derbyshire network was revised considerably in the light of experience. It also dealt with the difficulties caused to routes in Burton after the pedestrianisation of part of Station Street, and the enforced transfer of services to New Street, which entailed traversing more junctions for through routes, and had caused late running. From 12th June 1988 services 401, 402, 403, and 407 ceased to use Wetmore Bus Park, and Bargates became the timing point instead. The first Leicester County Council tendered service (97) commenced on 3rd October, between Tamworth, Ashby and Coalville (Monday to Saturday), operated by Swadlincote depot.

After considerable alterations and improvements had been made at Wetmore Road depot, the company relocated its Burton operations there from Derby Street on 24th October at the end of the lease on those premises. Following the re-building, the company became the first in the Midlands where Class 5 and 6 MOT inspections could be carried out for their own vehicles and commercially, this being done by Dept of Transport staff. The Bus Network Office, now managed by Clive Whatling, was moved to Wetmore Road depot's offices at the same time. Following successful operation of Leyland Olympians, two new ones with Alexander low-bridge bodies came in December 1988; they saw service from Swadlincote, also from Rugeley and Burton on the Birmingham services, and later moved to Spath. The vehicles out-stationed near Lichfield were moved to another site at Brownhills from 20th December 1988 and on 2nd May 1989 that operation was transferred to the new Rugeley depot, to where one of the Scania saloons was also transferred. By the end of 1988 Stevensons had 7 depots from which 156 vehicles operated in Staffordshire, Derbyshire, Nottinghamshire, Leicestershire, Cheshire and the West Midlands, and 42 of the 107 services operated were sponsored by local councils. The reduction in fleet size from the previous year was due in the main to replacement of

F96 PRE, one of two new Leyland Olympians with Alexander RL type bodies new in December 1988, was based at Swadlincote, and is seen in Memorial Square, Coalville, en route to Leicester on service 118. The Midland Red Fox Cub is ready to depart for Whitwick. *(DH)*

Fox Cub minibuses by full-sized vehicles. In addition to the seasonal express services operated to coastal resorts, there remained extensive excursion, private hire and contract work as well as quite frequent rail-replacement operation.

In January 1989 two long Olympians with coach seating were acquired from Eastbourne Borough Transport when only four years old; their rear luggage compartments were removed and windows were inserted, then the lower-deck seats were replaced by ex-DMS bus seats. Rugeley depot won three more WMPTE tendered routes in April, from Walsall to Coppice Farm, and from Sutton Coldfield to Erdington, and to Walmley. Crystal Coaches' ability to bid for work had been constrained by the small premises in Newcastle. However, this changed from May 1989 when they moved to a new garage, built on land acquired at the Hot Lane Industrial Estate, near Burslem; this became the base for the Potteries' area operations which comprised mainly tendered service work in Staffordshire and Cheshire, as well as contracts and private hire, requiring minibuses, a few saloons and coaches, together with one or two double-deckers. An hourly tendered service (ex-Pooles) between Newcastle, Knutton and Wilmot Drive, commenced on 10th July, two extensions to Audley being added from November. From late 1993 Crystal was managed by Dennis Williams, previously a driver, then Traffic Assistant at Spath depot.

The MCW Metrobuses continued to be the double-deck vehicle of choice; following thirteen examples of the Mk I type an order

Shortly after completion as no.80, TOJ 592S is seen in Lichfield Bus Station on the way to a Bus Rally. (EW)

This posed view in Spath workshops shows Mark Bowd to the left, overlooking (l to r) David Penlington, Paul Simnett, and Peter Wright in the pit, as they work on a Leyland Tiger coach. *(EW)*

for four new ones was placed with Metro-Cammell. However, there was considerable delay, and it was found that the company was closing down. MCW offered Stevensons a Metrobus Mk 2 ex-demonstrator, F181 YDA, which was bought. Whilst at Metro-Cammell, Julian Peddle saw the prototype MCW Metrobus Mk I, TOJ 592S, standing in a corner looking rather forlorn. It was purchased in June 1989 as a non-runner for spares, but eventually it was decided to prepare it for service; this involved a large amount of body re-building, and seats had to be fitted. The Gardner 5-cylinder engine had to be returned to MCW, as it was owned by Gardner, and a small bustle was fabricated at the rear to accommodate a larger, replacement 6-cylinder Gardner unit. This all cost over £10,000 but resulted in a good new-generation double-decker for the fleet, and it entered service in 1991. The Engineering Department Staff at Spath, under Fleet Engineer Mark Bowd, was extremely competent with body transformations, chassis and engine upgrades, as well as accident repairs and the usual routine work, and their war cry of "we can re-build" was well justified. Stories concerning garage staff are normally best avoided for sanity reasons, but one mechanic, Dave Cartlidge (Chewy), had additional skills. With Julian's blessing, during lunch breaks Dave would produce some marvellous models from bits of scrap metal, nuts, bolts etc. I recall a rather wonderful motorbike and a biplane hanging from the beams.

Four East Lancs-bodied Leopard saloons came from Inter Valley Link in May 1989, and another East Lancs-bodied Olympian with coach seats, which had been new to Ipswich Borough Transport, was bought from Eastbourne in October that year. The coach fleet benefited from two new Volvo B10Ms, with Plaxton and Van Hool bodies, which had arrived in August in the grey Viking livery. Another new Van Hool-bodied Volvo B10M was bought shortly afterwards, and second-hand coach

G21YVT was the company's first Volvo B10M and it carried a Van Hool Alizee body with seating for 51/55, and which had a demountable toilet fitted. Delivered in August 1989, it was still quite new when it attended the Showbus rally. *(EWC)*

acquisitions featured the same combination, although there was one with a Jonckheere body, and some carried bodies by Plaxton.

In September 1989 Drawlane Transport Group purchased the share capital of Midland Fox Limited, including Stevensons' shares in that company; this did not affect Stevensons' Swadlincote operation. At that time the company operated over 100 services, and further expansion came from 23rd October 1989 when Stevensons opened their first operating centre in the West Midlands, based in Darlaston, initially with nine vehicles, from a rented depot which was converted from a potato warehouse. The depot operated several tendered services (some being Centro experimental routes), in the area between Walsall and Wolverhampton, won in Centro's autumn re-tendering. These included services from Wolverhampton to Bilston, to Willenhall and to Northwood Park, and between Walsall and West Bromwich; some were converted to commercial operations. The four ex-Inter Valley Link Leopards were

The first ex-West Midlands Travel MCW Metrobuses appeared in Stevensons' fleet in 1989, but KJW 320W was bought in 1990 receiving fleet number 71, and is seen here on Dove Bank, Uttoxeter, near the end of a journey from Burton on the 401 service. (EW)

based at Darlaston, and their front panels were painted West Midlands blue to indicate that WMPTE passes were accepted. Rugeley depot remained responsible for some services to Walsall and Wolverhampton from the Rugeley/Lichfield area, and for those services around Sutton Coldfield. Dave Reeves joined the company around this time as Rugeley depot manager.

In December 1989 Bagnalls Coaches of Swadlincote was acquired for £450,000; this comprised seven coaches and a depot in Ryder Close at Cadley Hill, Swadlincote. This purchase also brought National Express work, the company operating one diagram on the 352 Norwich to Blackpool service which was retained; Shearings covered the other diagram. The ex-Bagnalls vehicles painted in National Express livery

retained that livery until Stevensons withdrew from the service. The depot was modernised to take 12-metre length coaches and the offices were re-built at a total cost of £70,000, whereupon the Viking operation was moved there from Woodville on 1st May 1990. In 1989 Stevensons bought two ex-West Midlands Travel Metrobuses from Stuart Johnson (dealer); over a period a total of sixteen were purchased. From December 1989 Stevensons had a 50% shareholding in Glynn Pegg's small Rotherham & District operation, where potential was seen in the Sheffield area; DMSs and other vehicles were loaned from time to time and Pegg's vehicles occasionally visited Spath garage for attention. In December 1990 no.41 was blown off the road on the moors above Sheffield and was written-off; unconnected

Seen in Sheffield on loan to Rotherham and District is MLH 315L (44), well away from the normal readership of the Burton Trader. It is followed by a Metrobus of South Yorkshire Transport, some of which were later purchased by Stevensons. The backdrop is Sheffield railway station, and beyond is the Park Hill housing estate, built in 1961, and which received Grade II listing in 1998. (EWC)

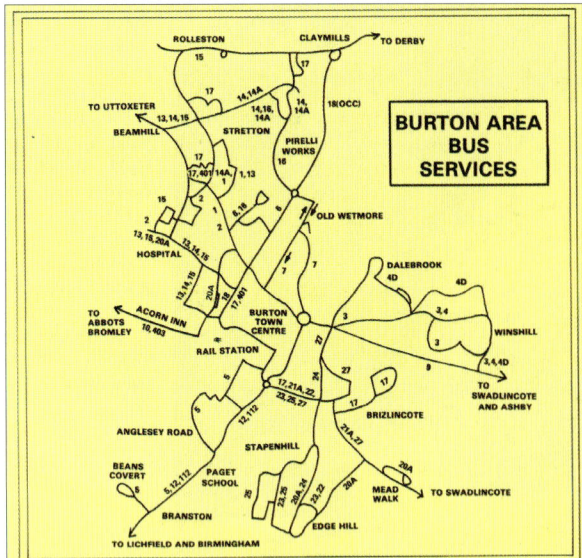

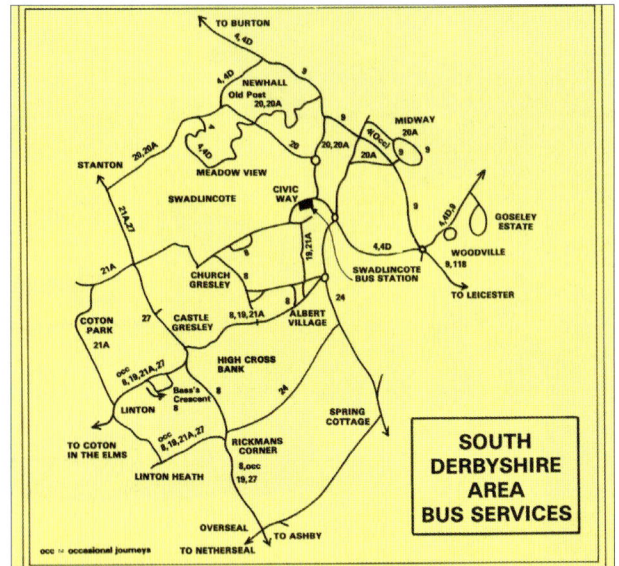

For Further Information on...............
STEVENSONS BUS SERVICES, TRAVEL CARDS, FARES AND SALES OUTLETS.

Tel: Burton-on-Trent   **44662**
or
217071

TRAVEL CARDS - There's one to suit you!
DISCOUNT BUS TRAVEL - IN THE FOLLOWING AREAS:

BURTON TOWNCARD
Adult 7 day - £3.20 — Adult 28 day - £11.00
Child 7 day - £2.25

COUNTRYCARD
7 day - £6.50
28 day - £25.00

ALL TRAVEL CARDS ALLOW UNLIMITED TRAVEL
ASK FOR A LEAFLET GIVING FULL DETAILS!!

with this event, Stevensons withdrew from the arrangement shortly afterwards.

January 1990 saw Swadlincote depot start to operate service 179 from Hinckley to Coalville, another Leicestershire CC tender. Darlaston depot's services now included tendered services from Walsall to Hough Road, the Dudley-Tividale circular, and Aldridge to Great Barr, the last two being Centro experimental services. Later in the year two commercial services commenced, between Halesowen and Bromsgrove via Frankley, and from Walsall to Palfrey and Delves. The first was notable in that it took Stevensons' buses into Worcestershire for the first time, and had previously been a Hereford and Worcester CC tendered service operated by Midland Red West. The second had been a tendered service operated by PMT from their Willenhall depot. In view of impending development work for the new Octagon shopping complex in Burton, the bus shelters on the south side of New Street had to be removed in June 1990. On each rainy day an ex-Fox Cub Transit minibus was parked in a vacant space as a temporary waiting room, and umbrellas (from lost property stock) were available on loan if required whilst passengers waited for their buses; that really was customer care! As part of this

Stevensons believed that the Wrights Nimbus bodies were the best of the minibus bodies produced for them on Mercedes-Benz chassis, and a 33-seat example on an 814D chassis, H197 JVT of 1990, is seen arriving in Dudley on 6th April 1991, on the 224 service from Bilston. Having turned left out of Castle Street into Fisher Street, it is about to turn into Dudley Bus Station. The M & B public house is no more, the premises being used for a British Heart Foundation shop. *(EWC)*

422 AKN, a Volvo B10M-60 Mk III with Plaxton Paramount 3200 53-seat body, was new in August 1989 as G25 YVT (25). Chris Hawley had been the regular driver of this coach which latterly had carried signage for the Afton Holidays operated by Chris using this vehicle. When Chris was given permission to have the coach re-painted in his own livery it was also re-registered. *(EW)*

development, new bus shelters, an enquiry office, and facilities for bus staff were provided.

In view of continuing expansion, large numbers of new and second-hand mini and midibuses would enter the fleet over the next few years, Mercedes-Benz 608D, 709D, and 811D chassis being the most-favoured types. They carried bodies by many different builders, although those with Alusuisse bodywork by Wright were regarded as being the best. The twelve months ending November 1990 had seen the largest influx of vehicles in the company's history in one year, including 24 Metrobuses (9 from South Yorkshire Transport having Rolls-Royce engines), and 24 new Mercedes mini/midibuses. Around this time Wayfarer ticket machines were introduced at Burton, Rugeley and Spath, then progressively elsewhere.

Richard Hackett left Viking in 1991, and early in the following year he started his own company, Swiftsure Travel, based at Stanton, near Swadlincote. Richard is married to Kathy (nee Watts) who had started with Stevensons in the Rolleston Road Office in the 1970s,

and worked for the company until 1992. Graham Allen became Depot Manager at Viking after Richard's departure. Stevensons had decided to discontinue selling excursions and holidays from Uttoxeter and Rugeley, and Chris Hawley, the leading coach driver at Spath, talked to Julian Peddle with a view to starting his own company to fill that gap in the market. This resulted in Chris setting up Afton Holidays, and he emphasised that this would not have been possible without the enormous support given by Julian, who allowed Chris to hire a good quality Volvo coach whenever he wanted it, and at a good hire rate. The coach carried the Afton Holidays name and, after a while, Chris was allowed to have it painted in Afton Holidays' own colours. When Arriva took over, the arrangement could have been continued, but the costs would have been much higher, so Chris bought his own coach and carried on with the very successful programme of holidays, excursions and private hires that he had developed. On his retirement in January 2013, Chris passed on the business to Swiftsure Travel.

7. Widening Horizons

In March 1991 a network was set up in and around Stockport, initially from temporary premises in Bredbury, then at Rooth Street, Stockport, close to the M63, where a small yard soon housed sixteen vehicles. They comprised Dodge S56, Mercedes-Benz and Ford Transit minibuses, as well as four of the eight Optare-bodied Dennis Dominos which had been bought from South Yorkshire PTE. They ran under the Pacer fleet name in a yellow and green livery; services were operated in Stockport and Macclesfield, and into Manchester, with Glossop and Ashton-under-Lyne being added later. Across the fleet as a whole, the Leyland Swift found favour for some time; seven new ones with bodies by Wadham Stringer and Wright were bought in 1991/2, the latter being the only Wright Handybuses built on Leyland Swift chassis. These preceded two Reeve Burgess Harriers purchased from Pennine of Gargrave when only one year old; various other second-hand Swifts which carried yet more variety of body types also appeared over the next few years, including three 7ft 6ins-wide examples bought from Armchair, Brentford.

In 1991 eleven Carlyle-bodied Ford Transits were bought from City of Oxford Motor Services. Some continued further north to the Pacer operation in Stockport and C727 JJO is seen in the town's Bus Station as the lady driver takes four fares for service 310, Heald Green circular. The Pacer operation only lasted for two years before the exchange with PMT for their Willenhall operation. *(EWC)*

The first Leyland Swift to appear in the fleet was F956 XCK with a Wadham Stringer Vanguard II 37-seat body, new in 1989 as a demonstrator, but bought from Jim Stones of Glazebury in May 1991 becoming fleet number 67. I stopped in Hazelwood on the Belper to Ashbourne service to record this winter's view on 31st January 1996. When the service was altered to be a through one from Uttoxeter, service number 409 was used throughout. *(EW)*

In my opinion the best Leyland Swifts operated were the two bought from Pennine of Gargrave in 1992, H313/4 WUA, with Reeve Burgess Harrier bodywork fitted with 39 dual-purpose seats, which became nos.33/5. The latter vehicle is seen with Oliver Ball in charge in Belper, having arrived there on the service from Ashbourne via Hulland Ward. *(EW)*

On 4th May 1991, Stevensons acquired Colletts Tours of West Bromwich with some express services, tours, excursion and contract work. This was followed by the purchase on 15th May of nearby Sealandair Coaches, West Bromwich, which also had contract work and operated a few tours. Two days later Classic Coaches of Wombourne was acquired; it operated some contracts and private hires, and two stage services, Dudley to Swindon, and Lower Penn to Wombourne. All the coaches acquired were concentrated at Sealandair's depot at Oak Road, West Bromwich, and Colletts'

The purchase of Sealandair also resulted in the re-introduction of Fords into the fleet after a long absence. Bearing the so-called 'Mister Softee' version of pink in its livery is PFK 174W, a Ford R1114 with a Plaxton Supreme IV 53-seat body new in 1980, fleet number 236. *(TM)*

depot at Hill Top was prepared for use as a bus depot, since Darlaston depot was full to capacity. The Hill Top depot opened on 2nd September and soon there were eleven vehicles, including double-deckers, operating from there. Some coaches were re-painted at Sealandair's depot into their pink and dark red livery; some vehicles received a rather gaudy pink resulting in their livery being irreverently referred to as the 'Mister Softee' livery.

Viking acquired an ex-Green Line Royal Tiger Doyen which was painted for National Express work, and was re-registered PCW 946, using the registration from the last Leyland PD2, which latterly had carried the striped livery, and which had been withdrawn. A rather different coach for the Viking fleet was ECT 912, a 1950 Bedford OB with Duple Vista body which was bought for specialised private-hire and nostalgia tours, although it did have its own school contract. I had the pleasure of driving it on two occasions to bus rallies. Julian Peddle was very enthusiastic and supportive, allowing vehicles to be taken to such events; Keith Myatt made suggestions as to which to attend and did the organising. They were very popular occasions for many employees, and vehicles won many awards and trophies. Also well supported were the Stevensons Sports and Social Club outings organised at Burton by driver Percy Laud.

Murray Shepherd left the company in August 1991 to start his own bus company in Edinburgh, Lothian Transit. Bill Peach had managed the Darlaston depot from its inception until September 1991, at which time he became Operations Manager (West) covering the West Midlands and Rugeley. At the same time Dave Reeves moved from Rugeley, where he had been Depot Manager, to be Operations Manager (East), covering Burton, Swadlincote, Spath and Crystal (the Potteries). The West Midlands depots were then supervised by Richard Cranmer (Oak Road), Colin Russell (Darlaston), and Dilbagh Singh (Hill Top). The vehicle allocation on 13th August 1991 was: Uttoxeter 27, Burton 42, Swadlincote 30, Rugeley 18, Burslem 13, Darlaston 22, Other West Midlands 23, Pacer 16, Viking 17, De-licensed 5, Total 213. In December 1991 the turnover was £7m. The respective fleet size and turnover for the competitors at the time were: PMT 400 and £17m, Derby City 130 and £6m, Leicester City 200 and

This Leyland Royal Tiger Doyen, new to London Country as A655 EMY, was bought in February 1990 for the Norfolk to Blackpool National Express contract inherited from Bagnall's, Swadlincote. The registration was changed to PCW 946 (previously on PD2 no.29) and it took fleet number 14. It is seen leaving Hanley Bus Station en route to Blackpool. *(TG)*

A really surprising purchase in May 1991 from Kime, Folkingham, was ECT 912, a Bedford OB with Duple Vista 29-seat body; I was photographed driving it at a rally in the West Midlands on 30th June that year. On withdrawal the vehicle was sold for continued preservation and now resides on the Isle of Anglesey. *(EWC)*

Keith Myatt and driver Andy Cooper hold the three trophies awarded to Stevensons' Mercedes-Benz 0405 Wright Cityranger L100 SBS (100), at the Sheffield Meadowhall Rally on 12th September 1993. The trophies were for: Best overall bus, Concours d'elegance, and the award for the Best new bus into service. *(EW)*

£8m, West Midlands Travel (WMT) 1,700 and £131m. From 2nd September 1991 Spath depot gained the tendered X86, Baswich-Stafford-Birmingham service, and the Ashbourne to Belper tendered service 113 (Mondays-Saturdays) commenced on 7th October 1991, with work for a midibus, a saloon covering the journeys extended to and from Belper School. The latter contract was gained as a result of the sale of Webster's Coaches, which used to operate it; from 25th October 1993 the service was subsumed into service 409, which became a through route between Uttoxeter and Belper. Crystal Coaches gained the tendered service from Newcastle to Scholar Green, and two tendered circular services from Hanley. Three more commercial services were started in the West Midlands, from Sutton Coldfield, Halesowen and Dudley, and one between West Bromwich, Oldbury and Birmingham was mainly commercially-operated.

G785 PWL was one of two DAF SB220 Optare Deltas transferred to Stevensons from Edinburgh Transport after that company became a subsidiary in 1992. It was given fleet number 266, and is seen at Spath before I set out for Uttoxeter to take up a journey to Stafford on service 404. (EW)

Under the snow on the bus would be found the registration number E478 NSC and fleet number 241. It was a Mercedes-Benz L709D with an Alexander Sprint body which had 25 high-backed seats, and came from Jones, Oakley. I photographed it in Ellastone whilst returning with the last journey from Ashbourne one winter's day. (EW)

When I was starting my lunch break in Belper one winter's day, it started to snow. By the time my few passengers and I had reached Turnditch Bank the snow had settled considerably and many vehicles were in trouble. In spite of persuading one or two struggling pedestrians to board and join the other passengers seated over the rear axle of the Mercedes minibus, D133 NUS, we came to a halt by the kerb at the steepest part of the bank. Clearing some snow with a shovel did little to help, and then a 4x4 police car travelling down the bank pulled up beside me. "Can you make it with a tow?" the policeman asked. Well, what would you have said? Almost immediately he came in front, hitched up a tow rope, and helped me to the 'Cross o' Hands', after which I was away through Hulland Ward to Ashbourne and Uttoxeter. That part of North Derbyshire in winter can be a different world.

In 1992 Stevensons took a 75% shareholding in Edinburgh Transport, the bus division of Silver Coach Lines. Major engineering work for the company was undertaken at Spath and some Stevensons' vehicles travelled to and from Edinburgh from time to time, some Leyland Nationals later making a one-way journey northwards. In the other direction came two Optare-bodied DAF SB220s which, together with a Mercedes minibus, were transferred to Spath. Edinburgh Transport used about 13 vehicles by 1994 on a series of routes which were not directly in competition with the established operators, a practice which was often used elsewhere by Stevensons to good effect. Stevensons also had a 10% share from January 1992 in the consortium which took over the part of National Welsh which became Rhondda Buses, the other shareholders being PMT, Drawlane (later British Bus), Western Travel and Julian Peddle personally, who also headed the operation. Seven Leyland Lynxes, one being the prototype Leyland B60, with Alexander (Belfast) bodies were bought from Citybus, Belfast in January and February 1992, but some of the bodies sustained damage to the lower panels during the ferry crossing. They were the only Lynxes in the country not to have Leyland bodywork and some had to be converted from partial-standee layout into 53-seaters. Stevensons continued to look for expansion and submitted bids in turn for London Buses' subsidiary Westlink, Ensign of Purfleet, Cynon Valley, Southern National and United Counties, although none of these was successful. The company was even interested in tendering for the Crewe to Derby rail link, since originally privatisation was to be line by line. However, when it became clear that the tender would be for Central Trains as a whole, Stevensons lost interest.

HXI 3006 was one of seven Leyland Lynxes with Alexander (Belfast) N type bodies bought from Citybus, Belfast in 1992, and is seen on 5th April that year at the Abbey Arcade bus stop in High Street Burton, carrying fleet number 256. I found them to be very pleasant vehicles to drive, especially this one which was actually a B60 prototype and a Gardner-powered example. Russ Moore is the driver, and the passenger seen through the second window is Keith West, who managed the Travel Office in Burton for many years, and has been James Boddice's 'right-hand man' at Midland Classic since that company commenced operation. *(JB)*

Early in 1992 three Leyland Leopards with Alexander AYS type bodies from Fife Scottish replaced some older Leopards; more Leopards were to follow from other sources. Legislation had been introduced which would mean that from 1st April 1992 new coaches would be limited to 70 mph (later reduced to 65 and subsequently 62); this would also apply to existing coaches, except for those first registered on or before 1st April 1974, which would be exempted. In preparation for that, Julian asked David Penlington, at the time engaged in vehicle servicing and inspection, to test the capabilities of the Leopards on the newly-completed dual-carriageway to Blythe Bridge. Once they were 'warmed up' the results were remarkable and it proved that more speed limiters would have to be ordered and fitted! In April 1992

Stevensons established a low-cost unit in Burton, trading as Victoria Travel, which had a livery similar to that of Sealandair, to counter the threat of local coach operators like Zamir, Cresswell and Machin, and were successful in obtaining school contracts and private hire work. April also saw Crystal's Longton-Leek service become a Saturday-only operation; the Newcastle-Audley service became an off-peak commercial one, and some tendered routes were lost. Around that time five new services from Wolverhampton, three of which were commercial, were started. An experimental Centro tendered service 303 from Bilston Station via Willenhall to County Bridge was operated from 13th July; it proved to be very popular and was operated commercially after a year with an increased headway. Similar tendered services were started between Sutton Coldfield and Kingstanding (lost in October), Dudley and Greets Green, and from Birmingham to Yardley Wood. A commercial Sunday service between Birmingham and Kidderminster commenced on 29th August; previously it had been a tendered service operated by Midland Red West, which still operated the Monday to Saturday service commercially.

The Bus Network office, latterly under Clive Whatling, was always responding to changing circumstances, including gains and losses of tendered services. The most active area was the West Midlands, where many new commercial and tendered routes were operated, and by June 1992 Darlaston had 14 vehicles whilst Hill Top had 17. All services in the area had been well received by the public and, additionally, received praise from Centro's Head of Operations; Rugeley depot's new Cannock to Hednesford service 35 also proved

A Dormobile Routemaker 25-seat body is fitted to the Renault-Dodge S46 chassis of E642 DCK, which together with D647 DCK was new in 1987, and bought from Fife Scottish in 1992, becoming nos.292 and 291 respectively. Both received the livery for Victoria Travel/Burton Bus Company, a low cost unit set up by Stevensons, and I photographed no.292 on 23rd March 1994 at Wetmore Road depot before setting out on a local Burton service around Brizlincote, for which the blind has yet to be set. *(EW)*

On 20th November 1993 K154 BRF, a Mercedes-Benz with a Dormobile Routemaker 29-seat body, is seen at The Dale in Willenhall on the 303 service to Bilston Bus Station. Many new Mercedes-Benz minibuses, featuring a number of different makes of body, were required in the 1990s, in view of constant expansion, particularly in the West Midlands. *(TJ)*

In Cannock Bus Station is C46 HDT (228), an ex-South Yorkshire Transport Optare-bodied Dennis Domino; driver Phil Haytree is waiting for time to start another journey on the popular 35 Rose Hill service, which commenced in September 1992. No doubt Midland Red North expected to win the service on tender, as it was right on their doorstep, but instead Stevensons moved in to operate it commercially from 1st September 1990. Another of MRN's local Cannock services (32) was won on tender in August 1993. *(TJ)*

The final **DMS** to be owned was CBF 31Y when it had been modified for use as a tree-lopper, as seen at Wetmore Road depot. Did a wayward branch off a tree result in a near-side window vent unit having to be replaced, apparently by one from a Metrobus? Four different fleetname styles are seen on the vehicle. *(DS)*

In 1992 this accident-damaged Van Hool-bodied Volvo B10M of 1982 was bought from Cumberland Motor Services; it was originally registered UHH 575X, then VRR 477, and it arrived in their Coachline livery. Work can be seen in progression at Spath to return it to its former glory; Richard Wain is perched precariously on the scaffolding. *(EW)*

When completed the Volvo was painted in the Viking coach livery as no.19, and is seen bearing new registration 468 KPX at the Keynes Country Park, Wiltshire, on 25th April 1993. I regularly drove 'request' jobs for the RSPB North Staffs Members' Group over a fifteen year period. *(EW)*

SOA 676S, a Leyland Leopard with Plaxton Supreme body, was bought from Rhondda Buses and, as can be seen in this view at Spath, was completely re-built including stress panels. Fitted with re-upholstered seats, it entered service in Victoria Travel livery with registration 488 BDN, which had been much used beforehand. *(EW)*

Similar vehicle VOV 926S (which started as Stevensons' XRE 305S, later 422 AKN) was re-built in the same way as SOA 676S. The finished coach is seen bearing Victoria Travel livery at Leigh Crossing when in use on the Milwich Circular with Les Smith driving. Leigh Station, which used to be adjacent to the crossing, was once quite busy, but closed in 1966 as part of Dr Beeching's cuts. Tim Machin took this lovely photo from his then place of work, Leigh signal box, which survived until 1999, when an automated crossing was installed. *(TM)*

to be successful. On completion of its advertisement contract, the last DMS was retired from service in August 1992, although CBF 31Y (ex-31) remained, then operating as a tree-lopper. More severe re-building projects were undertaken at Spath, led by Ray Buckley, the first resulting in an ex-Coachline Van Hool-bodied Volvo having extensive front-end damage re-built prior to its entry into the Viking fleet as no 19. By October 1992 old coach 16, XRE 305S, by then re-registered 422 AKN, was completely stripped down to a skeleton and renovated, including replacement of stress panels. It was by then the oldest vehicle in the fleet and on completion it was painted in the maroon and pink livery of Victoria Travel. When eventually withdrawn it was the longest-serving coach ever in the fleet. A similar vehicle acquired from Rhondda Buses was also re-built.

On 28th September 1992 Stevensons' position in the West Midlands was strengthened further when they exchanged their Stockport Pacer operation with PMT for their Willenhall Red Rider operations, with no less than twenty routes, mainly in the area bordered by Wolverhampton, Walsall, Birmingham and Stourbridge. PMT's depot was used by Stevensons for a while, and the maintenance contract with AE Costins was continued for a short time. Some ex-Pacer Cheshire routes, in the Macclesfield and Congleton areas, were retained and operated from Burslem depot, which also benefited from more tendered work. Land next to Oak Road depot was purchased and redundant buildings were demolished to increase parking facilities there, whereupon an exchange was completed taking Sealandair's coaches to Hill Top depot with the latter's service buses moving to the enlarged Oak Road depot

The Pacer subsidiary in Stockport received D38 NDW (134), a Dodge S56 with East Lancashire body which came from Newport Corporation Transport. After the exchange with PMT for their Willenhall operation, it was renumbered 289 and is seen in Wolverhampton Bus Station on service 574 to Willenhall. *(AP)*

At the Willenhall depot is seen F326 PPO, a Mercedes-Benz 811D with Robin Hood 29-seat body which was new in 1989 as a demonstrator and was bought in 1990, becoming no.193. *(EW)*

Keith Stanton and David Stevenson consult the map of Europe before David sets out for Romania, which is a long way from Uttoxeter Bus Station! *(TJC)*

on 1st November. Services 901 and 912 between Lichfield and Birmingham, replacements for similar withdrawn West Midlands Travel (WMT) services, were started in November, operated by Rugeley and Oak Road depots, and they became very popular.

A new depot, built almost opposite the old PMT depot at Willenhall, was opened in 1993; it was fitted out to be the engineering centre for the West Midlands operation, complete with two pits, and which enabled the servicing of double-deckers. This allowed Darlaston's depot to be closed, its vehicles and 40 drivers moving to Willenhall depot on 20th February 1993, by which time the West Midland's vehicle allocation stood at 70 vehicles; more services were started in the Dudley and Wolverhampton areas and some more tendered services became commercially-operated ones. A new commercial service 94B between Birmingham and Chelmsley Wood started in May 1993, using three buses from Willenhall depot. This service was well away from Stevensons' West Midlands heartland, and competed with both WMT and Claribel Coaches. Keith Myatt transferred from Burton to run the Oak Road operation (42 vehicles) in August 1993. A very noteworthy service was that between Kidderminster, Stourport and Worcester, as Worcester was the furthest south reached by Stevensons' buses; the service operated two-hourly, six days a week. Commercial services competing with West Midlands Travel between Dudley and Cradley Heath and between Birmingham and Wednesbury were added in November 1993, and by the end of the year the West Midlands operation was scheduled to have 100 vehicles, some based at a still-to-open depot at Smethwick. The first Warwickshire tender, the Tuesday and Friday service 107 from Appleby Magna to Nuneaton, was won from MacPherson's of Donisthorpe, and started on 23rd February 1993 operated by Victoria Travel. Other places where Stevensons' buses were to be found included Coventry (from June 1993) and Loughborough (from August 1993).

The longest journey by road (and ferry) for a Stevensons' vehicle took place in April 1993, when David Stevenson drove Mercedes minibus D906 MVU

(182) to Romania on a post-Ceausescu mercy mission. Nearly all the seats were removed and it carried medical supplies, clothes, old spectacles and anything else vaguely useful, which had been collected by passengers and employees. Additionally, it carried enough blue water pipe to enable water to be supplied to the host village. When David was in Bucharest and talking to some people, one of them noticed a nail head protruding from one of the rear tyres. It was then that he discovered that he had been despatched on that journey without a spare wheel. Being normally used on local service work it was not carrying a spare, and no-one had realised! In spite of the best efforts the problem could not be resolved for various reasons, and the journey was completed carefully and successfully with the nail still in situ. The journey covered 3,600 miles and, having driven on many severely pot-holed roads in the old Eastern Bloc, I understand that David was pleased to be back on ours, even though they may not be perfect. Another foreign traveller was one of Stevensons' ex-Burnley PD2s, PCW 944, which after withdrawal in 1980 was exported to Red Deer, Alberta, Canada for tourist work; a Leyland PD3 joined it in 1994. Leopard coach 961 PEH was sold to an operator in Malta, and Ford coach VRF 338L, finished its life in Cyprus.

Zamir Coaches in Burton had their licence revoked in mid-1993, but Zamir's son, Andre Al-Hamid, set up a new company using the title Burton Bus Company, a name already used by Stevensons on two Victoria Travel minibuses. Al-Hamid won the Staffordshire CC-tendered Sunday operation of Burton Town Services from 29th August 1993 but, just as a legal row was about to start over the disputed trading name, Al-Hamid's licence was revoked on grounds of inadequate maintenance facilities and insufficient cash for insurance. The Sunday services were returned to Stevensons from 12th December. Stevensons won the new X40 tendered service from 29th August 1993, which operated on Sundays and Bank Holidays from Burton via Uttoxeter, Alton Towers, Cheadle, Longton to Hanley, incorporating the Uttoxeter to Burton 401 service. This contract was lost to Frontline Buses of Lichfield from 10th April 1994.

1993 was a year in which new vehicle makes were trialled. The design and production rights for the MCW Metrobus had been acquired by Optare and DAF Bus; the two companies substantially re-worked the design and produced a new vehicle, the DAF DB250-based Optare Spectra double-decker, which had been launched in 1991. Stevensons was interested in this vehicle, and purchased two in 1993 for £112,000 each; initially these state-of-the-art vehicles were based at Rugeley. In September, after operation of a demonstrator, a new Mercedes-Benz 0.405N with Wright City-Ranger 51-seat body (L100 SBS) was also allocated to Rugeley to work the ex-WMT 901/912 services between Lichfield and Birmingham which had started in November 1992. Whilst helping out at Rugeley depot for a while I was fortunate to drive this vehicle for a day and I also drove the lovely Optare Spectras on the Burton-Birmingham 112 service.

Changes to Staffordshire County Council's student season ticket arrangements in 1993 affected revenue, particularly on the 112 and 401 services which carried students for Burton Technical College, and the 404 which served Stafford College; this led directly to fare increases in the Burton and Uttoxeter areas from November 1993, although they were the first increases for two years. Tendered service gains and losses at Burslem resulted in only mini and midivehicles being based there, one of the latter being a Swift for the X86 Baswich to Birmingham service, previously operated by Spath depot, but this route would be lost to Midland Red North in September 1994.

In February 1994 five low-height MCW Metrobuses with Alexander RL bodies, four of which had coach seating, were acquired from Kelvin Central.

A new Volvo B6 (L102 MEH) and a MAN 11-190 Optare Vecta (L43 MEH) were trialled in Burton, the

Six Dennis Dart 9.8 SDLs with Plaxton Pointer 40-seat bodies were purchased in 1994, and the first, which would be based at Spath, also received a select registration number, L300 SBS. Most enjoyable to drive, it is seen at Hatton at the end of a short working from Burton. *(EW)*

Five more Metrobuses arrived in 1994, but they had Alexander RL bodies, most of which had 78 dual-purpose seats. New in 1986, they were bought from Kelvin Central, and D676 MHS (89) is seen arriving in Burton from Uttoxeter on service 401 in Burton. *(EWC)*

latter would be joined in July 1994 by two second-hand examples which had worked on Glasgow Airport express services. Seven more of the very reliable Mercedes L709Ds were bought and six new Dennis Dart 9.8 SDLs with Plaxton Pointer bodies joined the fleet, the first being registered L300 SBS and based at Spath; many second-hand Dennis Darts also arrived. By this time the entire service bus fleet comprised modern vehicle types, older vehicles covering contract work.

One important person at Stevensons was Rhoda Heathcote who, at the age of twelve, went into service with Mary Stevenson at Fole Farm and remained with the family for her whole life. She had helped to bring up the seven children, although it is known that 'young' George was her favourite. Also, she assisted the family with very many tasks, in the house, and the office, as well as serving petrol; even in her later life I remember her providing tea for the office staff and cleaning inside the vehicles which were across the road in the parking area. Rhoda was a lovely lady, who sadly died on 8th March 1994, aged 94.

Rhoda Heathcote. *(TJ)*

8. Competition – 'Your Bus' to British Bus

Stevensons had realised earlier the potential in the West Midlands, particularly the revenue from Centro passes. The new services which had been built up, mainly around Sutton Coldfield, Walsall, Dudley and Wolverhampton, often used mini and midibuses to operate on streets in estates which were not served directly by WMT. However, after reasonable co-existence with WMT, eventually the relationship deteriorated significantly. The management and employees of WMT had been successful in a buy-out of that company in December 1991 following deregulation. Stevensons was due to move into the former depot of the Birmingham Coach Company at Smethwick in October 1993 on a joint venture with WMT which was to have been called Buslink (Midlands) Ltd, but WMT suddenly pulled out of the arrangement and the premises were let to City Buslines for three months from around the end of 1993 before opening as a Stevensons' depot on 5th April 1994. Commercial services commenced on 24th January 1994, in direct competition with WMT, between Bilston and Dudley (227), Dudley and Stourbridge (257), and service 974 Birmingham to Wednesbury was extended to Dudley.

Possibly the popularity of Stevensons' services had become too much for WMT, and they realised that the best form of defence was attack. The front page of the Burton Mail on 30th March announced that a company called 'Your Bus' was to commence services in May in Stevensons' heartland, Burton-upon-Trent; Your Bus was the trading name of Smith's of Shenington, a company recently acquired by WMT, which had terminated the services of Your Bus, and then had vehicles available for this attack. Meanwhile, more services in competition with WMT started up. Stevensons moved onto WMT's route 126 between Dudley and Birmingham on 5th April, and a new service 353 between Walsall, Cheslyn Hay and Cannock commenced on 25th April. With the news of the forthcoming competition in Burton now out in the open, Stevensons moved quickly to register additional journeys in the Burton area in late April to start on 6th June, designed to run in front of Your Bus timings. Additionally, in retaliation Stevensons placed registrations to run on the busy WMT Wolverhampton routes 511 to Underhill, and 529 to Willenhall from 13th June.

On 9th May, Your Bus started their operation from a yard near Burton Station, where they based eighteen vehicles, which comprised full-sized single-deckers and minibuses. The fares charged were half those of Stevensons, and free travel was offered on the first Saturday, 14th May. It was like the 1920s all over again with Your Bus vehicles running in front of Stevensons' buses on a number of important routes in Burton, even running as far as Tutbury. On the first day of Your Bus operation it was reported in the Burton Mail that 13 buses had occupied a 50 yard stretch of road by Burton's Octagon Centre! There was then a sudden retrenchment by Stevensons in the West Midlands area when the new Smethwick depot was closed from 14th May, vehicles being transferred to the West Bromwich and Willenhall depots. Stevensons' response to the Your Bus cheap fares in Burton was to offer a return for the price of a single fare on affected routes, but Stevensons' 7-day and 28-day travel cards were cheaper than the equivalent Your Bus cards. To cover the extra timings which started on 6th June, extra vehicles were brought in; these included a number of Metrorider minibuses, one of those and a Dennis Dart being hired from Rhondda Buses, but the Metroriders were disliked by the drivers in view of their fierce brakes. However, even before these buses started work, the outcome to the battle of Burton's buses had been settled.

Your Bus were constantly short of drivers and unable to operate all their services, but nevertheless Stevensons lost around 15% of their Burton passengers to them. The East Staffordshire District

This was a typical scene in New Street, Burton during the 'bus wars', with an Ikarus-bodied DAF SB220 of 'Your Bus' trying to muscle in to the stand for the Rolleston service. On the right is E801 UDT (263), one of thirteen MCW Metroriders acquired in 1993 from East Midland, many of which were used to counter the threat of the intruders. In the end it could be said that once again Ikarus flew too close to the rising sun and 'Your Bus' beat a retreat following the sale of Stevensons to British Bus. (EW)

Council (ESDC) directors were worried by these developments and decided to sell the Council's share. David Stevenson and Julian Peddle considered buying the Council out, but the price was too high, and there was too much risk involved as it was felt that competition law at the time was insufficiently protective for the smaller companies. Approaches were therefore made to sell the company to a third party – but not, Julian insisted, to WMT. An offer which was amenable to all the directors was received from British Bus (successor to Drawlane Transport Group) in May, the final ESDC approval was given on 26th May, and on 20th June 1994 British Bus acquired Stevensons' business

K320 FYG, an MCW Metrorider of Rhondda Buses, is seen at Park Place – also known as The Wharf, Uttoxeter on 5th May 1994, whilst on hire to Stevensons. *(EW)*

and all the shares en-bloc. During Julian Peddle's tenure Stevensons had become the largest independent operator in the West Midlands; the operating area had expanded enormously, fleet size had increased from 47 to 278 vehicles operating from 10 depots, and there were about 360 employees at the end. In the previous financial year Stevensons' profits had increased from £326,000 to £753,000. ESDC is recorded as having received £2.8m from the sale, as a result of which they hoped for match funding to boost jobs in the area. The last bus purchased prior to the sale was Mercedes-Benz 811D G900 TJA (221), and the first buses under British Bus ownership were MAN Vectas K140/1 RYS.

Julian Peddle left the company and undertook consultancy work for British Bus in addition to pursuing his other interests in the PSV industry. When Julian announced that he was leaving, he wrote the following to all employees: 'We pass on to British Bus a dedicated and skilful workforce, a fleet of buses which are second to none and a name which has been not only a watchword for reliability locally, but nationally, as one of the most dynamic members of the industry'. Stevenson's success story can be attributed in no small way to the vehicle purchase policy established in the very early years, whereby new vehicles were supplemented with good second-hand vehicles, thereby minimizing capital charges, a policy which continued to the end. Interestingly, the company had operated prototypes of the following successful chassis types: AEC Reliance, Leyland Leopard, Leyland Olympian, Leyland B60 (Lynx), and MCW Metrobus.

Peter Harvey, Managing Director of Midland Fox, was appointed as Stevensons' new Chairman and Mark Bowd remained General Manager. British Bus now did a deal to dispose of Stevensons' West Midlands operations, except for the services operated by Rugeley depot. This

This Mellor-bodied Mercedes-Benz 811D of 1990, G900 TJA, was the last vehicle purchased by Stevensons. Originally numbered 221, this was later changed to 450 with the Midland Red North renumbering. *(EW)*

was effected quickly, the Sealandair coaching concern (but not the premises) being sold to the Birmingham Coach Company on 12th August 1994, and two days later the bus depots at Willenhall, Hill Top and West Bromwich, together with the services operated from them, were transferred to WMT, thereby making about a third of the Stevensons' fleet redundant. Sixty-three routes were transferred to WMT, as shown in Appendix 3. Photographs and Omnibus Society records reveal that WMT used some of the premises purchased for a short time, many of Stevensons' vehicles being retained 'on hire', but WMT also brought in some of their own vehicles. However, it was not long before WMT covered the ex-Stevensons' services from existing WMT depots using their own vehicles. In his press release, Mark Bowd, as Stevensons' General Manager, was in the uncomfortable position of having to pretend that the company's West Midland's operation was losing money ("The huge investment in the West Midlands on vehicles and property has been a serious drain on the group's profits"). In Burton, Your Bus increased their fares to Stevensons' standard levels on 5th July and Stevensons withdrew their cheap return offer. Notice of withdrawal was given on all the Your Bus services and they finished running on 4th September 1994, exactly four months from the start of their operation. Julian Peddle immediately bought the shares in Rhondda Buses previously held by Stevensons; after various participants in the Rhondda consortium had been taken over by other companies, in December 1997 Rhondda Buses was acquired by Stagecoach. In 1994 Matt Evans, who had succeeded Mark Bowd as Stevensons' Fleet Engineer, travelled to Edinburgh to close Edinburgh Transport's depot and to sell the business, which was acquired by the GRT group, most of the vehicles used there returning to Stevensons.

TDC 854X, a 12-metre Leyland Leopard with Duple Dominant IV body, has fleet number 1654 in the combined Stevenson/Midland Red North numbering system. The livery is pure MRN, but very shortly Stevensons' yellow would be used on new vehicles and re-paints; the new 'ball of string' logo was common to both companies, but with the appropriate company names. By its side is AAL 303A (12), which has a similar chassis, but married with a Plaxton Paramount 3200 body, bought from Rhondda Buses in 1992 and painted in Viking coach livery, but with Stevensons' fleet names. (EW)

The new order. Metrobus LOA 388X (72) shows off the new fleet name style in Uttoxeter Bus Station following the British Bus take-over. The adoption of a new style rising sun motif was a popular move, reflecting the history of the company. (EW)

British Bus now merged Stevensons' administration with that of Midland Red North (MRN), based at Cannock, although the separate identity for the vehicles was retained. A similar red and yellow livery, as carried by MRN's vehicles, started to replace the cherished yellow, black and white of Stevensons, although it did incorporate the Stevensons' shade of yellow and a red rising sun motif. Later this livery was relieved by a white line, replaced after a while by a row of small white circles, which schoolchildren loved to peel off whilst waiting to board! Stevensons' vehicles were then re-numbered into MRN's fleet number sequence. Bill Peach initially remained with Stevensons, then became Managing Director at Rhondda Bus, but eventually returned to his native Lancashire.

What had been the North Western, and then Crosville, operation in Macclesfield had passed through a number of owners in recent years and by 1994 was in the hands of MRN. It was decided to transfer the Macclesfield operation to Stevensons' control and in November that year many of Stevensons' vehicles were moved to Macclesfield and showed 'on hire to Midland Red North' until the service registrations were completed on 1st January 1995. The main service operated was the half-hourly 130 to Manchester, which required a minimum of seven vehicles, mainly double-deckers, and there were town and rural routes based on Macclesfield. Since the garage at Macclesfield had been built with low-bridge vehicles in mind, some of Stevensons' own low-bridge double-deckers, including four of the low-height

DOC 29V (829) was one of three 50-seater National 2s of 1980 (new to West Midlands Travel) which were cascaded from Midland Red North. It was re-painted by British Bus subsidiary Pickerings of Leicestershire, the route branding being applied at Wetmore Road depot, Burton, and it is seen standing at the Abbey Arcade, Burton whilst on service 14 to Stretton on 21st August, 1998. (RM)

Seen in High Street, Cheadle (Cheshire) working on the busy service 130 between Manchester and Macclesfield is A152 UDM (1952), a Leyland Olympian with ECW bodywork, which was new to Crosville in 1984. (EWC)

Standing in Manchester's Piccadilly Bus Station is G727 RGA, a Leyland Swift with a Reeve-Burgess Harrier 39-seat body of 1990, which was bought from Kelvin Central in 1993 becoming 39 in the fleet, but re-numbered 1139 by the time of the photo when it was wearing the revised livery. It would soon be setting out on the 130 route to Macclesfield. Manchester Piccadilly's tram station makes an interesting backdrop. (EWC)

GDZ 795 (125) was one of two Leyland Leopards purchased from Loch Lomond Coaches which had Willowbrook Warrior (re-)bodies, both of which had seats for 62 (3x2 arrangement). When new in 1975 with its original Willowbrook body it was registered LPT 903P, a sister vehicle to one previously owned by Stevensons, and it became no.125, as can be seen in this view taken on 31st December 1994 in New Street, Burton. At the time, the use of Northern Irish registrations was in vogue with operators, so as to conceal a vehicle's age. (JB)

Carrying route branding for the service 15 in Burton is ex-West Midlands Metrobus KJW 296W. It has been renumbered 2051 into the new combined fleet list, and is standing by the Octagon Centre in New Street, Burton, ready to continue its journey to Rolleston. (EW)

Metrobuses and the prototype Olympian 99, were transferred there; they were supplemented by four ECW-bodied Leyland Olympians which MRN had operated out of Macclesfield previously. Also, on 20th November 1994, MRN's small operation based at Etruria in Stoke-on-Trent was transferred to Stevensons, eighteen services passing to Crystal Coaches, but Crystal's Macclesfield-based routes then passed to the depot there. In 1995 Frontline Buses, another British Bus subsidiary, based at Tamworth Road Lichfield, was transferred to Stevensons' control, bringing five Leyland National IIs, three double-deckers, two Mercedes minis, a selection of Leopard and Tiger coaches, and two Leopards with Willowbrook Warrior bus bodies; these latter vehicles joined three similar ones in the fleet. May 1995 saw all five Volvo coaches of Derby City Transport (also owned by British Bus) transferred to the Viking fleet.

From November 1995 a new livery of yellow and red was adopted for certain services in Burton, including use of the BURTONbus name; route 15 was the first

The 'ball of string' roundel.

to be branded, the 14 following on 29th July 1996. Consolidation of the two fleets was now highlighted by a new roundel logo applied to the vehicles, representing the Stafford Knot, MRN's deer antlers, and Stevensons' sunrise. However, staff usually referred to it as the 'ball of string'. In the middle of these changes, British Bus was sold to the Cowie Group of companies on 18th June.

With the delivery of some super-low-floor Dennis Darts which had retractable ramps the Ashby-Swadlincote-Burton-Horninglow service 8 was upgraded to the company's new high-quality 'XL' status. Other vehicles acquired at that time included some more Leopard, Tiger and Volvo coaches which in the main came from Green Line, Luton & District, National

In 1997 seven new Dennis Dart SLFs with 37-seat Plaxton Pointer bodies were allocated to Stevensons; six of them were branded for the introduction of a new 'XL'-branded route between Ashby, Burton and Horninglow. P321 HOJ (1321) is seen in New Street, Burton, with Tom Walker at the wheel, about to leave on a short-working to Castle Gresley. (PS)

TOU 962 (27), a Van Hool Alizee-bodied Volvo B10M of 1983, was acquired with the Sealandair business as MSU 573Y in May 1991. Under British Bus it received this drab coach livery, which was used henceforth instead of the smart two-tone grey livery previously used by Viking. The parking of the coach is not dangerous as may be presumed, since the old road to Rocester by the side of the garage had become a hardly-used cul-de-sac following the opening of a new by-pass in 1986. (EW)

422 AKN, a Volvo B10M new in 1989, has been seen earlier in Afton Holidays' livery and this new livery was applied circa February 1998. It is seen at Spath ready to undertake a private hire. (EW)

Sitting in Uttoxeter Bus Station are B148-50 ALG, Duple Laser-bodied Leyland Tigers which were new to Crosville in 1984, later passing to North Western, from where they were acquired in August 1995. B150 ALG is branded for the Ivanhoe express service recently started between Uttoxeter and Leicester. *(EW)*

On 11th September 1996, to mark the company's 70th anniversary, on the original Uttoxeter-Tutbury-Burton service the company charged the equivalent of the 1926 value fares for the whole day, and a ticket issued by me on the day is shown above. A '70 years reliable service' roundel was affixed to Spath-based buses.

Sitting at the bus stop in Stowe-by-Chartley whilst on the 404 from Uttoxeter to Stafford, is C40 CWT (1640), a Plaxton-bodied Leyland Tiger which was new in 1986 to West Riding. Later acquired by Arriva Midlands North, it was transferred to Spath depot in 1998. Opposite the vehicle is the Cock Inn, from where Sarah Williams operated bus services to Uttoxeter and Stafford between 1927 and 1936. The small corrugated iron bus shed and rotting petrol pump still stood nearby in the late 1990s. *(EW)*

Welsh and Crosville, although some, including a few Olympians, were cascaded from MRN. Many of the vehicles acquired under British Bus' and Cowie's control were of debatable quality and required a not inconsiderable amount of work to make them presentable. The Volvo coaches went to Viking, whose smart livery then in use for coaches was replaced by a disastrous and dull dark grey and red one during autumn 1996, whereas the livery then used on Stevensons' branded coaches was a very smart one of white with yellow and red relief. One of the ex-Crosville Duple Laser-bodied Leyland Tigers carried signage for the new Uttoxeter to Leicester 'Ivanhoe' shoppers' express.

The Stevensons' Travel shop in Uttoxeter High Street closed in November 1996. Finally, in November of the following year the Cowie Group decided to get rid of all the traditional names and liveries, and brand all its vehicles and operations under a single name, Arriva, with a standard livery of aquamarine and stone.

The headquarters of Stevensons had been at Spath since 1926, but in 1999 it was announced that Spath was to be closed from January 2000, all Uttoxeter-based bus services then to be operated by Burton or Stafford depots. Dunn Line Coaches of Nottingham acquired Stevensons' coach operation based at Spath, from where they then operated their Uttoxeter area contracts. Employees were offered the option of transferring to other Arriva depots or joining Dunn Line's Spath operation, which over the next few years would pass progressively to a number of other coach operators with very mixed results. Nevertheless, it was the end of an era, and an extremely loyal, friendly and dedicated group of employees, many having long service, was disbanded. All the property at Spath is still owned by David Stevenson; the successful car MOT bay at Spath is rented by Arriva and Ray Worbey still works there, with thirty years' service to his credit at the time of writing. An ex-Stevensons' employee, Phil Smith, had started a small coach company, Paragon Travel, which he later sold. The new owners used part of Spath garage for their Paragon Buses company, which for a few years operated service 428 to Lichfield,

G399 FSF, a Mercedes-Benz 811D with a PMT 33-seat Bursley body, was new to Henderson, Hamilton in 1990; it was bought by Stevensons in March 1994 (244), and passed to Arriva becoming no. 449. Whilst en route from Belper to Ashbourne on 11th May 1999, I stopped at Belper Lane End to take this photo. (EW)

F181 YDA was a Metrobus Mk 2 DR132 demonstrator, new in 1988. After a period of service with Dublin Buses it was sold by MCW to Stevensons in 1989, becoming no.81. It became 2081 with Arriva and is seen at Wetmore Road depot. (EW)

until they were taken off the road. The garage was then in non-PSV use, until 2014 when part was used by D & G Buses in connection with their Uttoxeter-based services, although that ceased when their new Staffordshire base was opened in Longton in December that year. The Viking coach operation at Swadlincote passed to Travelstyle of Tamworth.

George's brother John Stevenson, who had managed the company for many years, had also been a councillor for the Doveridge, Sudbury and Somersal seat for West Derbyshire District Council from 1945, and became an Alderman of Derbyshire County Council for two years. John was a member of Doveridge Parish Council, being the Chairman for many years; he died in 1992. Joan Stevenson was a very pleasant and patient lady and was the boss financially, giving truth to the old adage that 'behind every successful man there is a good woman'. For many years she had regularly driven a school contract taxi. In addition to her work with the company, she had been involved with the Royal British Legion, and the Inner Wheel, being President of the latter. Sadly, in 1995 Joan had a stroke, thereafter requiring specialist assistance, and George did everything possible to ensure that she had the best of care and was comfortable. Joan Stevenson passed away in April 1999, aged 79.

After his retirement George Stevenson survived cancer and afterwards lived for a further seven years, but passed away on 6th November 2003, aged 88. His body was taken to the funeral at Uttoxeter Parish Church inside a preserved single-decker, owned by Dunn Line, which carried Stevensons' old livery. George was a Councillor on Uttoxeter UDC from 1955, serving as Chairman from May 1962 to May 1963, then Vice Chairman from May 1963 to May 1964. He was a Rotarian, was President of the Uttoxeter branch of the Ex-Serviceman's Club, fundraising tirelessly in its support, and had received the Royal British Legion's Gold Badge. His will-power had enabled him to battle his way through the difficult task of keeping a family business going in challenging times, particularly when the industry was losing out to the motor car. Marjorie Nelson, a sister of George, celebrated her 100th birthday in 2010. Her nephew Basil Stevenson (son of Bernard) returned from Canada for the occasion and arranged for Marjorie to have a ride around her home village of Doveridge on board an ex-Stevenson's double-decker, preserved in the company's livery by Tim Stubbs of Burton. Basil also donated a seat to Uttoxeter in the family's name, and it now stands in Uttoxeter Bus Station. Marjorie achieved the grand age of 101, and her younger sister Gertrude was 98 when she died.

During the late 1990s and early 2000s Julian Peddle ran the Status group of bus and coach companies. His current interests include Centrebus, D & G Buses, High Peak Buses, Midland Classic and Swiftsure Travel, as well as other companies. Many of Stevensons' management team have since held important positions within Arriva and elsewhere. Mark Bowd, who had started as an apprentice mechanic at Spath, became Garage Foreman, and rose to the position of General Manager at Stevensons. With British Bus he was appointed Managing Director of Stevensons and ultimately became Group Engineering Director for Arriva plc. Similarly, Matt Evans progressed from Management Trainee at Burton to become Fleet Engineer; after various appointments within Arriva he became Regional Engineering Director, Arriva Midlands and held other positions in the group. He is now Managing Director of Centrebus. Richard Yoxall, who had introduced the electronic Wayfarer ticketing

Marjorie Nelson, on the occasion of her 100th birthday, with her nephew Basil Stevenson, having had a ride on preserved Stevensons' vehicle KLB 908 round her home village of Doveridge. (TS)

The Stevensons' memorial seat at Uttoxeter Bus Station. (TJC)

Marjorie's conductor's badge and one of a series of promotional mugs made in Stoke-on-Trent for the company. (TS)

system across the Company, progressed to be Fleet and Risk Manager for Stevensons and rose to become Procurement Category Manager Directs, Arriva UK Bus. Clive Whatling had managed the Bus Network Office from October 1988, and became Bus Services Manager at Centro, whilst Keith Myatt is currently Head of Communications at Arriva Midlands. Keith Stanton, who had managed the Spath depot for some time from 1986, ran Wardle Transport when it was still a private company, and now has his own bus and coach business, Stanton's of Stoke.

Richard Hackett had managed the Rugeley depot from August 1983, then became Commercial Manager at Burton, before becoming responsible for the Viking coach fleet early in 1988, but left the company in 1991. Early in 1992, together with Brian Kershaw, an ex-Stevensons/Viking coach driver, he set up Swiftsure Travel, which operates from Stanton, near Burton. It is ironic that, having taken on work from Felix Coaches and Afton Holidays following the owners' retirements, Swiftsure Coaches' current catchment area is not dissimilar from that of the Stevensons/Viking/Erewash empire in the late 1980s (i.e. Burton and South Derbyshire, Rugeley, Uttoxeter, Ilkeston and Heanor). Having been made redundant from the role of Operations Manager in 1993, David Reeves had a spell with West Midlands Ambulance Service, then in April 1998 teamed up with Gerald Henderson to form D&G Buses, which developed services in Stoke-on-Trent and Cheshire. After acquiring other businesses D&G Buses is now a significant company covering a wide area. Tim Jeffcoat started in 1980 and ran Spath depot for some years, then joined the Bus Network team at Burton. He continued in that capacity with British Bus and Arriva, then from 2004 became Bus Network Manager for D&G Buses. Richard Emery joined Stevensons in October 1988, and had positions as Depot Manager (Rugeley, then Burton), Commercial Manager (Spath, then Cannock) and, following a number of appointments within Arriva Midlands, is currently their Commercial Manager. Mark Bowd, Matt Evans, Richard Emery and Richard Yoxall had all started with Stevensons straight from school.

Interestingly, the year 2000 was not to be the end for Stevensons. The company name remained in being, and when Arriva took control, the legal lettering on Burton-based buses was 'Stevensons of Uttoxeter Ltd', with the Cannock address of MRN initially, then the Leicester address later on. More recently that ceased, but when Arriva acquired Wardle Transport in the Potteries, their legal lettering became 'Stevensons of Uttoxeter Ltd, T/A Wardle Transport, 4, Westmoreland Avenue, Thurmaston, Leicester, LE4 8PH', and their buses ran along many roads previously served by Stevensons' vehicles from its garage in Burslem! However, from 9th May 2015 Wardle Transport was acquired by D&G Buses, which marked the end of Stevensons of Uttoxeter Ltd as an operating entity.

For me personally it is not quite the end, however, since I have been a member of the Model Bus Federation for over forty-five years and have numerous scale models of Stevensons' vehicles which I have built, many representing vehicles that I have driven. The models are often seen at exhibitions around the country.

When the 80th anniversary of Stevensons was celebrated in 2006 with a gathering in Burton of appropriate buses, some of which were ex-Stevensons' vehicles, Arriva kindly re-painted Plaxton-bodied Dennis Dart L303 NFA in the traditional Stevensons' livery. I thought that may have been the last time that Stevensons' livery would be seen on a bus in service. However, nine years later another bus has been so treated. James Boddice, who in 2005 set up Midland Classic, had started in the PSV industry at Stevensons' Swadlincote garage. That company is fondly remembered by James, and he kindly arranged to have a Scania double-decker painted into Stevensons' yellow, black and white livery, as worn by their DMSs, to celebrate the 90th anniversary in August 2016, and as a promotion for this book. Julian Peddle arranged for ex-Stevensons' registration TFA 13 (now owned by him) to be transferred to this vehicle, and I thank them both for their generosity.

The 90th anniversary of the first journey is to be celebrated on 11th September 2016, with a time-tabled operation of some appropriate vehicles between Burton and Uttoxeter, and a small gathering of vehicles in Burton. Midland Classic started from premises near Swadlincote, and is now based at Stanton, from where it operates many routes around South Derbyshire and in the Burton and Uttoxeter area, which had been the heartland of Stevensons' operations from 1926. The vehicles carry a smart red and yellow livery, virtually identical to that introduced by British Bus after the takeover.

Good leadership is essential for any company to flourish. Stevensons was fortunate in that regard and, as re-iterated by Julian Peddle and David Stevenson, it was always recognised that good employees were at the heart of the company; I hope that they, their contributions and achievements will live on through the pages of this publication.

Eric A Wain
Stone, August, 2015

Pictorial Survey

John Stevenson (Uttoxeter) Ltd (from November 1941)

VT 7640 was a TSM B49A with a 35-seat Beadle bus body, new in 1932 to Grice and Greaves (Gem) of Cobridge, Stoke-on-Trent. It passed to Associated Bus Companies Ltd, Hanley, in 1933, thence to Stevensons in 1938 as no.7, and is seen in Wetmore Bus Park, Burton in the late 1940s, having arrived there from Uttoxeter via Hanbury. Before the arrival of double-deckers, this vehicle and the Maudslay SF40 were the preferred vehicles for the main service via Tutbury, possibly because they had the highest seating capacities. Withdrawal came in June 1950. Note that on the vehicle to the right, GE 7222, a piece of wood has been used as a temporary repair for a broken window. *(JC/OS)*

John Stevenson jnr had his training as a mechanic at Williamsons Garage Ltd, Heanor, and RA 4517, a Roe-bodied Bristol B, had been new to them in 1927, but passed to Midland General in 1931. It was with Stevensons by March 1944 (16), and worked until June 1951. Basil Stevenson recalled that there was a single seat facing sideways behind the driver. Latterly, this and VT 4482 (14) were the only vehicles which had to be started by handle. The fuel pump beside Parker's Wheatsheaf Inn was at the entrance to the Green Bus Company's yard, and the Bristol is by Stevenson's stand in the Market Place at Uttoxeter around 1949. Parker's Brewery started in the 1860s, becoming Parker's Burslem Brewery Co Ltd in 1889 at which time it had 110 public houses; when it was absorbed by Ind Coope & Samuel Allsopp in 1949 the number had risen to 468. *(CW)*

RB 6093, a Morris Dictator with a Reeve & Kenning body which was built in Clay Cross, was bought from Truman, Shirebrook, in September 1944. It later received this Leyland radiator and is seen on the A50 by-pass at Uttoxeter in the late 1940s. Reeve & Kenning eventually became Reeve Burgess Coachbuilders. *(TJC)*

WG 37, a 26-seat Cowieson-bodied Leyland Tiger TS3, new to W. Alexander & Sons, Falkirk in 1931, was used by the War Department between August 1940 and June 1943. It passed to Millburn Motors and was bought for £450 by Stevensons about June 1944. The body was repaired and modified by Lawton Coachbuilders and it entered service as C30F (no.10) in March 1945. A Cov-Rad radiator conversion was fitted at an unknown date. The grand building behind was Spath House, which for many years was the home of George and Joan Stevenson and family. (TJC)

In September 1945 VD 3432, a Leyland Lion LT5A of 1934 with Leyland rear-entrance bus body, was bought from Central SMT Company Ltd, Motherwell for £1,250, and received fleet number 12A; perhaps the use of no.13 did not appeal! In 1949 it received the 39-seat Willowbrook dual-purpose body seen here, which dated from 1939; this had been purchased from Tailby and George (Blue Bus Services), Willington, having previously been removed from their ERB 92 when it was re-bodied. VD 3432 was then re-numbered 23. It is believed that the waist band was painted maroon, a few other vehicles receiving a similar livery for a short time. The driver is Basil Stevenson, the son of Bernard, and the view dates from about 1953/4, at which time Basil worked for Rolls-Royce and drove for the family company at the weekends. (TJC)

It would now appear that the body of RA 4996 (see photo on page 10) was removed from its chassis, and that it was mounted onto the 1930 chassis of Milton Bus Co's VT 4202, which was five inches longer than that of RA 4996. The body then seems to have been lengthened around the first window bay, so that it matched the other bays in length; this could have allowed for some increased seating. Rebuilt in a dual-purpose style, it is seen recently repainted in Uttoxeter in the early 1950s. Withdrawal came in December 1952. (GM)

George Bullock recorded this view on the recently-acquired parking ground opposite Spath garage in 1948. The vehicles are (l to r) **VD 3432** (the only known view with its original Leyland body), **GO 4307**, **RA 4517**, **RA 4996** (with rebuilt body), **RF 7091**, and **GE 7222**. The latter vehicle, a Leyland Titan TD1, was new with a Cowieson body in 1930 to Glasgow Corporation. In 1940 it passed to Young's Bus Services Ltd, Paisley, and received this unusual Croft low-bridge utility body around 1942. Stevensons purchased it for £1,500 in March 1947 (19), and later fitted a fully-floating rear axle, Gardner 5LW engine and a Leyland Retriever radiator; it worked until July 1954. *(GHB/RM)*

WJ 9970, a Leyland LT5A, was new with a Cravens coach body in 1934 to A. Kitson, Sheffield, and passed to Sheffield United Tours in 1935. Stevensons purchased it in 1949 (24) and fitted a Cov-Rad radiator, after which it received this new Burlingham 35-seat coach body in 1950, the total cost being £1,984. It is seen at Spath, still bearing trade plates, having just returned from the coachbuilders at Blackpool; however, it only saw a further six years' service as it was withdrawn in May 1956. *(CW)*

Another vehicle to originate with **W. Alexander** of Falkirk was **WG 3256**, a Leyland LT5A of 1935 which carried an Alexander body seating 38 passengers, and it was bought from a dealer in 1946 for £1,350 (6). In 1951 it received a replacement Gardner 4LW engine, a larger 5LW one being fitted in 1954; the body received significant attention, including the fitting of rubber-mounted glazing, and it re-entered service as no.9. The vehicle looks very tidy in this view at Spath, and it lasted until June 1960. *(EWC)*

One of the next purchases was **GVT 508**, a Willowbrook-bodied Leyland TS8 of 1939 which came from Davies Transport (Stoke) Ltd in May 1952. Pictured in April 1954, it saw over five years' service, being withdrawn in November 1957. It contrasted sharply with the new Royal Tiger coach seen on page 95. *(RM/OS)*

In April 1949 the company paid £3,850 for RRF 330 (22), a new Guy Arab III with Meadows engine and 33-seat Burlingham coach body. Driver Tom Ginnis told me that he was amazed with the vehicle's sprightly performance when he collected it from Blackpool; however, Meadows engines were rather thirsty and the one in no.22 was later replaced with a Gardner 5LW unit. The coach gave over 16 years' service before withdrawal in November 1965. Behind is ERB 92, a Willowbrook-bodied Daimler COG5, which came from Blue Bus Services, Willington, in November 1957. (EWC)

The 1950s

The first Dennis to be owned was AVW 453, a Lancet I with 5LW engine and 35-seat ECOC body with rear entrance, which was new to Eastern National Omnibus Co Ltd as a dual-purpose vehicle in 1934. In 1940 it passed to the Ministry of Works, later being operated by Enterprise Bus Service, Newport, Isle of Wight, from where it was bought by Stevensons, with whom it entered service as no.14 in July 1950. It is seen in Uttoxeter by Orme's shop, and withdrawal came in February 1957. (RM/OS)

Four Daimler COG5s of 1935/6 were bought from Birmingham City Transport in 1951/52; three had 34-seat bodies by MCCW but that on AOP 70, which was new in 1935, was by Strachans. It became no.6 and is seen near St Mary's Church in Uttoxeter, where passengers have boarded even though the destination has not been divulged. This was the longest-serving of the four vehicles, being withdrawn in March 1960. (RM/OS)

The first underfloor-engined vehicle was VRF 139 (16), a Leyland PSU1/15 Royal Tiger with a Burlingham Seagull 39-seat body, new in June 1951. It is seen at Rolleston Cross Roads near Lodge Hill on Friday, 28th June 1968 at 2.40pm when operating the 2.00pm Uttoxeter to Burton service. *(TJ)*

With underfloor-engined coaches now being built, half-cab coaches began to appear quite dated. Therefore, one of those coaches, PRE 607 (8) received a replacement 8ft-wide Burlingham 'Sun Saloon' body on the 7ft 6ins-wide chassis in 1953, and the extra width is noticeable at the rear wheel arch. Drivers disliked it for its tendency to sway somewhat following its re-bodying, but it lasted until December 1969. *(HP)*

Driver Tom Ginnis and conductor Ken Charlesworth engage in conversation at Stevensons' bus stand in front of Geo. Orme's shop in Uttoxeter; both vehicles are on the cross-town Bramshall to Doveridge service. Bound for Doveridge is EOG 237 (1), a Leyland Titan TD6c with Manchester-style English Electric body, new to Birmingham City Transport in 1939. Acquired in December 1952, it worked for twelve years with Stevensons. The Guy single-decker, FA 8532, is described on the next page. *(AC)*

Two all-Leyland TD7s, FON 326/630 (19/10), were purchased in 1954 from Birmingham City Transport, to where they had been new in 1942. The former is seen departing Uttoxeter via Church Street on 26th March 1958 for the short journey to Doveridge. The adverts on the front of the bus remind us that Elkes' Biscuit factory (now Fox's Biscuits) has been a major employer in the town for over 100 years. For some time that company operated its own double-deckers for staff transport. The advertisements on this vehicle, and on EOG 237 above, are typical of the work of Harold Foster. *(RM/OS)*

FA 8532, a Guy Arab III with Guy rear-entrance 35-seat body was new to Burton Corporation in 1947. It was bought by Stevensons in February 1954 (21), and is seen back in its original home town at the Wetmore Bus Park on 17th February 1962, sixteen months before its withdrawal. *(TJ)*

On 11th June 1970 it was necessary to hire a vehicle from the Green Bus Company, and Len Blurton is seen driving JOW 922 as it arrives at Hatton, to run the Hatton to Scropton school contract. The vehicle was a Guy Arab UF with 39-seat Park Royal body, new to Southampton Corporation in 1952, and acquired by GBC in March 1965. *(TJ)*

599 LRE, a Bedford SBG with Duple 41-seat body, was new in May 1956 as no.24. Driver Bill Chell is in charge as it pulls out of Hoon Road, Hatton at 4.12pm on 10th June 1970 when engaged on the Hatton Schools to Church Broughton contract. This coach gave over sixteen years' service. *(TJ)*

Bob Crawford was driving KGK 725 following George Stevenson in the Bedford recovery vehicle, but George's attention was taken by his cattle in the field to the left and he slowed down. Bob pulled out to overtake but the Bedford veered towards the centre of the road, forcing the bus through the hedge into pastures new (Reg Bailey's field). After the vehicle was righted it was checked in the workshops, where it was found that minimal damage had been sustained, and it was soon returned to service. The Bedford can be seen in the background, and George Stevenson is directing operations on the right. *(TS)*

Seen at Spath is GUS 293, a Daimler CVD6 with Plaxton M1/49 body which had been new to Northern Roadways Ltd, Glasgow in 1949. It later passed to J F Findlow, Biddulph, prior to being bought by Stevensons in June 1958 (25), with whom it served for just over eight years. *(PB)*

The final Guy Arab III to be bought was EP 9503 which had a Duple 'A' type body, and was new in 1947 to Mid Wales Motorways Ltd, Newtown. It was purchased through a dealer in November 1958, and it entered service one month later as fleet no.15. Seen at Beaudesert scout camp on Cannock Chase, it only operated for four years before withdrawal. (TJC/R Haynes)

CNU 872 (2), a Daimler COG5/40 with 39-seat Willowbrook coach body, was new to Tailby and George (Blue Bus Service) in 1936, and was one of two acquired by Stevensons from the company in 1959. It is seen on the parking ground of the Salt Box Café at Hatton, and it was retired in May 1964 when twenty-eight years of age. *(RM/OS)*

On 8th February 1969, KGU 216 was being driven very carefully along Wakefield Avenue, Tutbury at 10.51am on the 10.30 Burton to Uttoxeter service. From 1960 all the buses bound for Uttoxeter and for Burton travelled in a clockwise direction through the narrow roads in the estate, and since occasionally they arrived there around the same time, the difficulty of establishing which was which in winter can be appreciated. It will be noted that platform doors have now been fitted. *(TJ)*

The 1960s

The AEC Regent IIIs were well liked, and in March 1961 KWB 86 entered the fleet as no.6; it was new in 1947 to Sheffield Corporation ('A' fleet) with a Northern Coachbuilders 56-seat body. On 8th December 1965, whilst working the 5.00pm journey from Burton to Uttoxeter, the bus was travelling along Bridge Street Tutbury following a lorry, from which some bags of gypsum plaster fell onto the roadway in front of the bus. This caused the bus to mount the pavement and crash through a ten-foot-high wall adjoining Staton's Mill; fortunately, the mill building stopped the vehicle from falling down a ten-foot drop into the Mill Fleam, a water channel by the mill. Thirteen people, including driver Stefan Senkow and conductor Sam Barlow, required hospital treatment; the bus received extensive damage as a result of which it was prematurely withdrawn. *(EWC)*

Tom Ginnis seems to be talking to another driver who may be about to set off on a North Wales tour in the company's first underfloor-engined AEC Reliance, UBA 554, which had a modern-looking Yeates Fiesta body. It was new in August 1961 to W Hankinson, Salford, from where it was bought in March 1962 becoming no.5, and it served for just over fourteen years. *(EWC)*

Samuel Morgan Ltd (Blue Line), Armthorpe, was the first owner of RWT 613, a Guy Arab UF with Burlingham 44-seat body which was new in 1956. It entered service with Stevensons in January 1964 (1), and is seen being driven by Cyril Hollins on 12th June 1970, arriving empty at Boylestone on the Hatton School contract to Sutton, Long Lane, Longford and Dairyhouse Farm. On withdrawal in February 1972 it saw further use as a tree-lopper as shown elsewhere. *(TJ)*

DJP 841, a Leyland Tiger Cub with Plaxton 41-seat body, was new in 1958 to Smith of Wigan, and after passing between companies in the group was bought by Stevensons in May 1964 (2). It was withdrawn in March 1973 whereupon it started a new lease of life as George Stevenson's greenhouse! *(EWC)*

RVM 37 was new in 1955 to North Manchester Coaches, and was owned by various operators before reaching Stevensons in July 1964 (19). The Daimler D650 chassis carried a Duple Elizabethan centre-entrance coach body which had 41 seats, and it is seen at The Morledge, Derby. After working for five years it passed to Burwell and District Motor Services. *(RFM)*

DHE 352 (7) was one of four Leyland Royal Tigers purchased in 1965 which had been new to Yorkshire Traction in 1951, the 43-seat Brush bodies being equipped for one-man operation. It is seen being driven by Norman Tucker at 12.01pm on 3rd April 1969, having descended Castle Street, Tutbury whilst working the 11.30am Burton to Scropton service; Fishpond Lane branches off to the left and Tim Jeffcoat's trusty bike can be seen leaning on the fence. The view is hardly recognisable now, since the buildings to the right have long since been demolished. This vehicle operated for less than five years, but the others achieved slightly longer service. *(TJ)*

KLB 908 was the only eight foot-wide Leyland 6RT with Leyland body to be bought from London Transport. New in 1949, it entered service with Stevensons as no.11 in January 1966 and was fitted with platform doors during that year, possibly before entry to service. On Saturday 20th April 1968 it is seen at 3.15pm in Duke Street (originally Duck Street), Tutbury, whilst working the 2.45pm Uttoxeter to Burton journey; the near absence of traffic is very striking. Following withdrawal in October 1977, it was sold for preservation in January 1978 and is currently preserved by Tim Stubbs in Burton, still in Stevensons' livery. Thanks to Tim, I have had the pleasure of driving this lovely vehicle. Webb Corbett's glass factory (originally Tutbury Glass Works) stood at the road junction behind the bus. *(TJ)*

In May 1952 Allen's Motor Services of Mountsorrel took delivery of HJU 546, a Leyland Royal Tiger with Leyland 44-seat body. It passed to H Boyer and Sons of Rothley, then to Midland Red, and finally to Stevensons in April 1966 (25). On 1st June 1970 it was photographed at the B5017 cross roads in Hanbury Woodend at the start of the first experimental concrete road in Great Britain, appropriately named 'The Concrete Road' (now Pipey Lane). Brian Kershaw was the driver on the 4.00pm Burton to Uttoxeter journey and he would be aware that a reasonable speed would be required when traversing that stretch of road in order to cope with the surface undulation. The end of the road for no.25 came in November 1973. (TJ)

The only new vehicle for Stevensons in 1966 was VBF 118D, a Ford Thames R192 with Duple Empress 45-seat body which entered service in June that year as no.6, and it is seen in April 1974 at Rolleston Road garage, Burton. On withdrawal in April 1976, it was sold to Thomas, Llansamlet. (TBG)

This delightful view captures KGU 69 entering Anslow at 3.50pm on the 3.35pm Burton to Anslow journey on 18th April, 1968. The Leyland 7RT with MCCW body was new to London Transport in 1949 and was purchased from there in June 1967 (15). Six months after being photographed it was involved in a bad accident whereupon it was withdrawn and stripped for spares, the remains being sold for scrap in 1972. (TJ)

In 1956 Devon General purchased some AEC Regent Vs with MCCW bodies fitted with platform doors, of which TTT 780 was one. Stevensons entered it into service in September 1968 (3) and for a while it wore this experimental livery of mainly yellow; eventually it received the traditional livery incorporating a greater proportion of black. On 20th September 1969 it was photographed at The Beacon emerging from Beam Hill Road at 2.20pm, when operating the 1.30pm Uttoxeter-Hanbury-Burton service. On withdrawal in October 1977 it was converted into a tree-lopper/recovery vehicle numbered 05, which role it undertook from December 1977 to February 1981. The area in front of The Beacon Hotel was the turning circle for the Burton Corporation Service 1. *(TJ)*

JEE 123 was new in 1957 and was purchased from Starks Luxury Coaches in July 1969 becoming no.19 with Stevensons. The coach had a Leyland Tiger Cub chassis fitted with a Duple 41-seat body, and lasted until April 1973. It is seen at 2.44pm on 9th February 1970 when operating the 2.00pm Uttoxeter to Burton journey, and has climbed up Burton Street, Tutbury, whereupon Stefan Senkow eased the throttle for the Ironwalls Lane bus stop. *(TJ)*

The 1970s

The AEC Regent Vs delivered to City of Oxford Motor Services in May 1957 had exposed radiators unlike the later ones, and had 61-seat Park Royal bodies. 959 AJO was purchased in May 1970 (9) and is seen in Wetmore Bus Park, Burton, which has been improved by the addition of island platforms. Driver Brian Fern chats to conductress Coral Davies prior to the short journey to Anslow. Platform doors were fitted in August 1970 and withdrawal came in March 1978. Coral had worked previously from the Green Bus Service's garage in Uttoxeter before that company was acquired by Midland Red. *(EWC)*

Two Park Royal-bodied AEC Reliances, DHD 192/3, which were new to Yorkshire Woollen District in 1959, passed later to various operators before being bought by Stevensons in October 1970, becoming nos.26 and 7 respectively. The former was climbing Burton Street, Tutbury when seen on the 1.15pm from Ashbourne to Burton on 17th March 1973; the Trent double-decker in Duke Street is on their Tutbury to Derby service, and behind can be seen the remains of Tutbury Castle, where Mary, Queen of Scots was incarcerated at various times between 1569 and 1585. *(TJ)*

EHE 160, a Leyland Royal Tiger with 43-seat Roe body, was new to Yorkshire Traction in 1952, passing to Green Bus Co, Rugeley, in May 1966. It was not operated by them, and was bought by Stevensons who entered it into service as no.30 in February 1967. On Wednesday 28th May 1969 (market day) it was arriving in Balance Street, Uttoxeter, nearly ten minutes late, having operated the 11.0am Burton to Uttoxeter via Hanbury journey driven by Stefan Senkow. On Wednesdays every bus, with the exception of Whieldon's vehicles, had to use this street, which for buses was effectively a cul-de-sac. They had to reverse into a small side street to turn round, and one can appreciate the problems caused by the increasing number of private cars. These problems would be resolved with the opening of the town's Bus Station on 6th September 1970. *(TJ)*

DEK 106, a Leyland PD2/20 with Massey 58-seat body, new to Wigan Corporation in October 1957, was acquired in October 1970 and was fitted with platform doors prior to entry into service as no.16 in December that year. On 16th May 1978 it was photographed leaving Etwall on an Etwall Baths contract being driven by Robin Young and later that month it became no.16A, two months before being withdrawn, when it was sold for preservation. (TJ)

After arriving in Uttoxeter Bus Station on 14th October 1974, driver Bill Chell and conductor Tom Smith stand beside their vehicle, 564 FTF, an MCCW-bodied Leyland Titan PD3/4 which was new to Lancashire United Transport in September 1958. After purchase by Stevensons in March 1971, platform doors were fitted, and it entered service in May that year as no.10; the unusual low windows on the door will be noted. Withdrawal came in October 1978 when just over twenty years old, and after sale to Lister (dealer) it was bought for preservation;. however, restoration was not carried out, and the bus was cut-up in April 2015. Stevensons' allotted stand for the Burton services in the new Bus Station was in prime position near the shops. (TJ)

Pictured on 4th April 1974 with Peter Birtles driving, next to the now long-demolished Burton Baths is CLT 95H (22), a Plaxton Elite-bodied Ford Thames R226, new in 1970 to Linkline Coaches, London, from where it was bought in May the following year. Maroon re-appeared in the livery with this purchase, but only round the front screen and under the side windows, and this feature was not perpetuated. It was withdrawn and sold for further use in March 1978. Burton Corporation buses generally brought in pupils from the local schools, but Stevensons provided the transport from the surrounding area. (TJ)

Two Roe-bodied Leyland PD3/1s seating 73 (3908/14 WE) of 1959 were bought from Sheffield Corporation in July 1971 (23/17) and had platform doors fitted. The former is seen in Tutbury High Street at 1.35pm on 9th October that year having recently entered service, and is working the 1.00pm Uttoxeter to Burton journey. It became fleet number 23A in July 1977 and kept that number until withdrawal in December 1979. The splendid Dog and Partridge Inn dates back to the 15th century, and the fast 'Red Rover' night coach from London to Liverpool used to stop there when it was a coaching inn. *(TJ)*

WCD 72, a Weymann-bodied Leyland PD2/37, was new to Brighton Corporation in March 1959 and was bought in March 1972 (24) entering service two months later. It is seen under louring skies in Horninglow Street, Burton, presumably returning to Rolleston Road garage having operated a school contract; it became no.24A in June 1979 and was withdrawn during the following month. The vehicle's after-life was interesting; sold to the Birmingham and Midland Motor Omnibus Trust, Wythall in September 1981, it passed immediately to Wolverhampton Social Services for use as a play bus, thereby releasing a vehicle in which the Trust was interested. After ownership by a dealer and an engineering company, it was converted to open-top and fitted with scaffolding on the upper deck for use in the tunnel of the A1 north of Hatfield, and finished up with Hardwick (dealer) Carlton by December 1986. *(RM/OS)*

Two of the Leyland leopard L1s bought from Sheffield Corporation in 1972 (5907/9W) were new in 1960, and had Burlingham 41-seat dual-purpose bodies. The former became no.18 and is seen being driven by Keith Walters (Skippy) whilst passing Sudbury Hall top lodge (in use as a splendid bus shelter) on the 11.38am Sudbury to Ashbourne journey on 14th January 1978. In March it became no. 18A and it was withdrawn in July that year. *(TJ)*

1972 Stevensons of Uttoxeter Ltd

The last two vehicles to be bought from Sheffield Corporation were 6306/7 W (31/2), Leyland Leopard L1s with Weymann 44-seat bus bodies, new in July 1960. They arrived in November 1972 and entered service in April and March 1973 respectively. I have a soft spot for 6307 W, since it was the first bus that I drove having passed my PSV test in September 1978, seventeen months before it was withdrawn. It is captured at Blackbrook, between Anslow and Hanbury whilst en route to Uttoxeter from Burton. *(DPC)*

What interest there is in this view at the Salt Box, Hatton on 1st May, 1974! DFC 365D was the sole AEC Renown to be operated by Stevensons and it had a 65-seat forward-entrance body by Park Royal. New to City of Oxford in May 1966, it was acquired in November 1973, and entered service in March 1974 (34). It is seen working the 7.50am Uttoxeter to Burton journey driven by Stefan Senkow, and Tony Hopkins is about to bring DHD 192 from the Salt Box Café car park round to the shelter to follow as a duplicate. Turning the corner is Trent 389, VCH 839, a Willowbrook-bodied Leyland Tiger Cub travelling from Derby to Tutbury, whilst waiting on the car park of the Kestrel Inn (formerly the Salt Box Hotel) is another Trent vehicle, about to follow on the Hatton to Burton service via Tutbury and Rolleston. In due course the two Trent services would be merged to become a through service between Burton and Derby. The Café remains although the Salt Box Hotel (later The Kestrel) closed as a pub in 2009 and no longer sells the advertised Double Diamond beer. *(TJ)*

The second grant-aided purchase was **VRF 338L**, a Ford R1114 with Plaxton Elite Express body seating 49, which entered service in May 1973 (19). On 5th July 1979 Dave Royall, with Olive Stevenson as his conductress, was setting out from Rolleston Road garage to cover the 7.50am Scropton to Burton journey. It was up-seated to 53 and re-numbered 11 in April 1980, and was withdrawn in November 1983, then sold to Yeates (dealer) from where it was exported to Famagusta, Cyprus in September 1984. *(TJ)*

SFA 82 and **SFA 84**, Daimler CCG5s with Massey 61-seat bodies, were new in March 1963 to Burton Corporation, from where they were purchased in August 1973, and entered service in the following month as 32 and 33. Both are seen in the yard at Spath in February 1974; the rear of withdrawn DJP 841 is of interest, bearing the name 'John Stevenson' on the boot lid. Both Daimlers were withdrawn in March 1977. *(TBG)*

The first coach that I drove with Stevensons was **KRA 200D**, a Bedford SB5 with Plaxton 41-seat body which was new in 1966 to Bowers Coaches, Chapel-en-le-Frith, but which was bought from Stubbs, Manchester in June 1974 and was numbered 30. Lock to lock on the steering took many turns, and the small, curved gear lever lay somewhere behind the engine. The gear lever was brought by the side of the driver and back to select first gear, second was over to the left and forwards, straight back for third (whilst hanging on to the steering wheel so as not to leave the seat), then an inverted 'U' movement found fourth in the centre, and fifth was forward again. On 6th October 1978 I set out to collect a party from Abbots Bromley and the gear-change routine was practised many times before I arrived there. The vehicle was photographed by Tim Jeffcoat at Rolleston Road garage on 8th April 1977, about two years before its withdrawal. *(TJ)*

JRF 785N, a Bedford YRT with a Duple Dominant body seating 53, was a further grant-aided purchase, entering service in May 1975 (36). It only saw five years' service before sale to Chambers, Moneymore (NI). Prior to that, it is seen on 17th May 1978 at Hatton Heathfields on a Hatton School contract, with Keith Russell driving; behind, Ron Alderson is in charge of CTT 423C. *(TJ)*

The new coach for 1976 was OEH 512P (6), a Ford R1014 with 45-seat Duple Dominant body, which entered service on 5th May. In January 1981 it received the revised livery and fleet no.15, as seen in this view when parked at Milton Keynes whilst on a private hire on 23rd October 1982. In January 1983 it became no.18, to which the 'A' suffix was applied prior to withdrawal just over one year later. *(EW)*

In May 1977 Stevensons purchased a new Ford Transit with 16-seat Dormobile body, TRF 411R (40), which is seen at Staverton Airport, Gloucestershire, after I had taken passengers there who were bound for a holiday in Jersey. The rather basic facilities at the airport were being shared with fellow travellers from Monks' Duple-bodied Ford KBV 621N and those from PMT's URF 51S, a Leyland Leopard with Duple Dominant Express body. When withdrawn in September 1980, the Transit passed to Donovan's Taxis, Corby. *(EW)*

VHE 205 was new to Yorkshire Traction, Barnsley, in 1961, and was a Leyland PD3A/1 with Northern Counties 73-seat body. Stevensons purchased it from Middleton, Rugeley in November 1974 and it worked until January 1981. It is seen at Spath garage, and to the left are two of Stevensons' minibuses which stand in front of the earlier part of the garage. DRE 569E was a Bedford J1Z2H, new in 1967 as an ambulance, the Hawson body being converted to a 12-seater; it was withdrawn in May 1977. There are no details recorded for LAY 526E, but very likely it was one of the self-drive hire vehicles. *(EWC)*

Seven Leyland PD2A/27 double-deckers with forward-entrance bodies by East Lancs (2) and Northern Counties (5), new in 1964 and 1965 to Burnley, Colne and Nelson Joint Transport Committee, were bought from a dealer in September and October 1976, six of which entered service progressively during the next sixteen months. PCW 945 (8), a Northern Counties-bodied example, was the vehicle in which I did my PSV training and subsequently passed my test; it was a nice bus to drive and, obviously, I have fond memories of it. Here it is seen on 9th June 1980 at Sudbury, whilst being driven by Bob Horobin on the Hatton School to Cubley contract. *(TJ)*

Watched by John Sharpe, Brian Shaw is about to set off from Rolleston Road garage in PUP 123P (1), a Duple Dominant-bodied Bedford SB5, on a contract from Rosliston to William Allitt School on 10th May, 1978. The coach was new in February 1976 to Alexandra Coaches and Northern Motor Rentals, Sunderland, and passed to Stevensons in March 1978, where it served for two years. In the background can be seen ex-Burnley CHG 548C and an ex-Shearing Ford coach. *(TJ)*

JC Bamford Ltd of Rocester had used this Bedford VAS5 with Plaxton 29-seat body for transporting visitors to and from their factory and demonstration sites. It was acquired in July 1977 (38) when four years old, and was re-registered from JCB 234 to YVT 937M, but the JCB livery was retained for its duration. When I drove it to London down the M1 on 17th March 1979 there were several times when the small size of the wheels and the narrow track were not compatible with grooves in the road caused by the wheels of heavy lorries, which made steering interesting to say the least! In June 1980 it was re-numbered 23, and in April 1981 it was sold to Wright Bros, Nenthead. *(EW)*

Another ex-Burnley Leyland PD2, FHG 158E, with forward-entrance East Lancs body of 1967, was bought in May 1978; it entered service in September 1978 as no.24 and served for nearly five years. On 9th September 1981, I was working a service turn from Spath and my single-decker failed at Burton. The only spare available was this bus, now renumbered 30, to which I was transferred for my next run to Ashbourne. However, the low trees in Boylestone were potential hazards, and so having driven it 'omo' from Burton to Scropton, I was greeted there with Ford coach LRE 783K which had been brought from Spath, the photo recording the changeover. *(EW)*

FVO 428/434D, were Leyland Leopards with Weymann dual-purpose bodies, new to East Midland Motor Services in 1966, which were purchased in August 1978, entering service in November and December respectively as nos.10 and 28. Stefan Senkow is seen starting from Uttoxeter bound for Bramshall with a good load of passengers in no.10; when driving this vehicle, drivers had to remember when engaging reverse gear that a bolt head stood out proud from the cab side just at knuckle height! The Ford Transit minibus behind belongs to David Glover, Ashbourne. *(EWC)*

On 10th May 1978 Len Blurton is seen leaving Hatton School on a contract, driving DGE 339C, a Leyland PDR1/1 with Alexander 78-seat body which was new to Glasgow Corporation in 1965. It entered service with Stevensons in October 1977 (11) but only worked for two years. *(TJ)*

Stevensons of Uttoxeter Limited, Spath Garage, Uttoxeter, Staffs. ST14 5AE. Telephone Uttoxeter (STD 08893) 2131.

Staffordshire's largest private 'bus and coach operator.

Stevensons
OF UTTOXETER LIMITED

STEVENSONS

Five Massey-bodied Leyland Atlantean Mk IIs, new to Maidstone Corporation in 1967 and 1968, were bought early in 1979 and entered service progressively. JKE 335E is seen in Rugeley Bus Station in September 1982 in the care of Keith Russell, of Burton garage, ready to undertake a local service. The fleet number 53 was the third to be carried by the vehicle before it was withdrawn in December that year. *(TBG)*

The fifth **DMS** to be converted to single doorway, MLH 303L, entered service in October 1980 as no.46, and it carried adverts for Stevensons' Travel. It is leaving Hanbury village on the 402 service from Uttoxeter, bound for Burton; on the engine cover can be seen an advert for the company's car **MOT** activities. *(EW)*

Park Royal-bodied JGF 298K started with Stevensons in January 1981 as no.48, but by October 1982 this had been changed to 38, as seen in this view when under the control of Tom Ginnis, and loading at the bus stop in Holts Lane, Tutbury. It will be noted that the destination apertures had been re-arranged, and the top one was then used to show the company name, behind which was painted the rising sun emblem, which was a pleasing re-introduction. *(EW)*

NGD 971P, a Ford R1014 with 45-seat Plaxton body, was new in 1976 to Northern Roadways, Glasgow, but was bought from Salopia Saloon Coaches of Whitchurch in November 1979. It is seen on 24th April 1980 being driven by George Ward as it turns into Dunstall Road in Tatenhill whilst working the 12.10pm from Burton to Kings Bromley, contrary to the destination display. *(TJ)*

The 1980s

Bristol VRT PFA 50W sits in Carrs Lane, Birmingham, the terminus of the express services from Uttoxeter and Burton. I had driven the Bristol from Uttoxeter and would shortly return via Lichfield to Rugeley. Behind is Daimler Fleetline JGU 284K which has arrived from Burton. *(EW)*

LBF 454V, a Ford R1114 with Plaxton Supreme IV body was new in February 1980 (2) as a 53-seater, but occasionally had some seats removed and tables fitted to enable it to act as an 'executive' coach, as evidenced by the destination blind. Brian Kershaw acknowledges the photographer in Rolleston Road, Burton, as he sets off for a private hire on 13th February 1980; St John's Church is in the background. On 11th July 1981, circumstances dictated that I would have to use no.2, in executive mode with tables fitted, to complete a service turn which included a return journey between Burton and Ashbourne, and it was surely the classiest vehicle ever to be used on the service. The few passengers carried were quite impressed! In May 1982 it was sold to Pathfinder Luxury Coaches, Chadwell Heath. *(TJ)*

Two Ford R192s with Plaxton 45-seat bus bodies, HHA 163/173L, which were new in 1972 to BMMO, were bought via a dealer in July 1980. The first to enter service in October that year was HHA 173L (20), and it is seen in Church Leigh on 17th February 1982 when I had it for the Leigh Circular. Its sister vehicle saw service from September 1981, but both were withdrawn in November 1983. *(EW)*

An example of the company's coach holidays brochures, which shows Chris Hawley in charge of coach number 9, 961 PEH. This Plaxton Paramount body was fitted to the upgraded Leyland Leopard chassis of ex-Garelochhead Coach Services TGD 218R, as described in the text. *(STEV)*

113

Plaxton Derwent-bodied Leyland Leopard 6 MPT is seen in July 1980 as it pulls out of Bradley Street, Uttoxeter on the 12.50pm Uttoxeter to Abbots Bromley journey, with George Ward driving. *(TJ)*

On 25th July 1980, Duple Dominant-bodied Leyland Leopard LFA 872V is seen on the approach road to Uttoxeter Railway Station as it rests between duties on the Town Circular, some journeys of which had been extended to and from the Station. *(TJ)*

On 5th September 1980 Tim Jeffcoat was using Northern Counties-bodied Leyland PD2A PCW 946 on the late turn. It is seen early that evening in Uttoxeter Bus Station in the company of two of the ex-Maidstone Atlanteans. *(TJ)*

The last Fords to be bought new were **NVT 451/2W**, **R1114s** with **Plaxton Supreme IV Express 53-seat** bodies to bus grant specification which arrived in August 1980 (4/5). When still quite new, the former is seen in Bradley Street, Uttoxeter, on 4th September that year. Shaw's Fish and Chip shop was often the provider of a substantial meal for drivers on break during the late turn. *(TJ)*

The chassis of the other ex-Garelochhead Leopard, TGD 218R (22), was upgraded at Spath, as that of no.21 had been, but it received a standard 53-seat Plaxton coach body. The resulting vehicle, re-registered **961 PEH** (then no.9), can be seen in this view on 27th June 1986 at Hartington on the occasion of the annual sponsored walk by pupils of Thomas Alleyne's High School, Uttoxeter, when about fifteen coaches would be required. On this occasion the pupils had been taken to Waterhouses to start their walk along the Manifold Valley, and would re-join the coaches at Hartington. The drivers visiting the local café had to explain the reason for the absence of passengers; needless to say, the cafes were very busy in due course! *(EW)*

A new Plaxton-bodied Leyland coach, PFA 6W, the chassis of which was originally built for a horse-box body, arrived in February 1981. It is seen at the head of a line of coaches awaiting the returning, and somewhat tired, schoolchildren on the occasion of another of Thomas Alleyne's High School sponsored walks. TFA 13 is next in the line of coaches. *(EW)*

GUS 368N, a Ford R1014 with Duple Dominant bus body, was a prototype for this combination, and was new to Garelochhead Coach Services in November 1974 and, like the Leopards, was bought by Stevensons in November 1980, entering service in May the following year as no.23. On 15th August 1981 I photographed the bus after parking it in Ashbourne Bus Station. *(EW)*

No doubt Tim Machin was working on the late turn when he took this fine view of KUC 974P (34) one evening in Uttoxeter Bus Station. It carries an advert for Stevensons' X38 Derby to Birmingham service. *(TM)*

OJD 89R was a Bristol LH6L with semi-automatic gear change and 7ft 6ins-wide ECW body, which was new to London Transport in April 1977 and purchased by Stevensons in October 1981 (24). I photographed it at the turning point near the Robin Hood Inn at Bramshall on 19th December that year, a snowy winter's day that was causing some late running on the longer routes. In between journeys on the Bramshall service I was on standby in Uttoxeter to cover local services as necessary, in view of buses arriving late from Burton. On withdrawal in February 1984 it was sold to Thomas Bros, Llangadog, but it returned to the area later when it was bought by Express Motors, Hulland Ward. *(EW)*

A second coach-seated Bristol VRT series 3, to the same specification as no.50, was bought new in October 1981 and was the last of this chassis type built; registered **UVT 49X (49)**, it is seen at Middleton's yard, Rugeley in coach-style livery in company with **JGU 284K**, which then had received the later livery and re-positioned spotlights. Behind stand some of the towers of Rugeley Power Station, which had the world's first large dry cooling towers. After passing to British Bus and Arriva, **UVT 49X** was bought for preservation. However, in mid-2013 it was stolen and never seen again! *(EW)*

One of the three buses bought from OK Motors was **MLK 445L (36)** which is seen near Bargates, Burton, with minimal application of yellow to indicate Stevensons' ownership. *(EWC)*

On Saturdays from the late 1980s a service was operated in the morning from Uttoxeter via Alton and Cheadle to Hanley, and after other duties the vehicle returned in the afternoon. Carrying the revised coach livery, Plaxton-bodied Leyland Tiger **UVT 13X** is seen being driven by Russ Moore on the outward journey whilst passing through the village of Alton, and in the background is a tower of Augustus Pugin-designed Alton Castle. The site had been fortified since before Saxon times; the original stone castle was built in the 12th Century for the Earl of Shrewsbury and Pugin was commissioned to restore the near-ruins in the Gothic revival style in the mid-19th Century. *(EW)*

MCW-bodied Daimler Fleetline JGU 251K passes through the pretty village of Newborough on a journey between Burton and Abbots Bromley. The two children await the arrival of the bus from Uttoxeter to Burton via Hanbury. *(EW)*

OJD 136R (26), an FE30AGR with Park Royal body of 1976, bought in August 1982, entered service in May 1983. It is seen at Blackbrook whilst travelling between Burton and Uttoxeter on the 402 service via Hanbury, that straggling village being less than a mile away. For a while some DMSs had their spotlights re-positioned as they were prepared for service, though most had the lower panels replaced at the same time, which looked better. I make no apology for the number of photos of DMSs, particularly since Stevensons had the largest number of the type of any independent operator, and they were important in the company's success story. *(EW)*

This Plaxton Supreme-bodied Leyland Leopard was new to Monks of Leigh in May 1979 registered WTE 351T, and was bought by Stevensons in October 1982 (18). Re-numbered 15 in January 1983 and re-registered 82 HBC in February 1985, it is seen at the RSPB's Ynys Hir Reserve, near Machynlleth on 21st April that year. In November 1988 it was one of the vehicles lost with the sale of the Ilkeston operation; Stevensons retained the registration when the coach was re-registered ERC 360T. *(EW)*

In December 1982 BTX 540J, a Bristol VRTSL6G with Northern Counties 77-seat body was bought from Rhymney Valley District Council, becoming no.48; it had been new to Gelligaer UDC in 1971. Although based at Burton garage, it was seen passing The Globe Inn, Rugeley, having departed from the Bus Station situated a little to the rear, and bound for the Springfields Estate. This slow and unpopular vehicle was sold in June 1984 to Green (dealer), Weymouth, and had passed to Red Rambler, North Bradley by August 1984. *(EW)*

LPT 902P, a Leyland Leopard with 55-seat Willowbrook body, new to Trimdon Motor Services in 1975, was bought in May 1983 from Everton Coaches Ltd, Droitwich. It was numbered 21, re-numbered 61 in April 1985, and is seen in Ashbourne Bus Station ready to return to Uttoxeter on the 409 service, which was a replacement for a withdrawn service of Trent Motor Co; also seen is Trent's Leyland National PRR 451R. The slip board in the Leopard's front window was for a short diversion on two journeys to serve Stramshall, near Spath, for schoolchildren which started in January 1985. This was one of the first of Stevensons vehicles to carry an all-over advertisement. The treatment of the lower front panel was a later addition to assist potential passengers to identify the bus as belonging to Stevensons. *(EW)*

The last ex-Burnley Leyland PD2 in service, PCW 946, then running as no.29, was repainted into the new striped livery, and is seen in Wakefield Avenue, Tutbury during the enthusiasts' weekend of 17/18 September, 1983. (EW)

Not all things go to plan, as coach driver Adrian Proctor found in 1989, when he started on a journey from Spath depot in Leyland Tiger CBF 2Y which turned into an un-planned mystery tour in the countryside! (EW)

XRD 23K, a Bristol VRTLL6G with Northern Counties dual-doorway bodywork, was new to Reading Corporation in 1975 and bought by Stevensons in July 1983. It operated on contract work prior to going on hire to Berresfords Motors, Cheddleton for a while and I was fortunate to see and record its return from there. It was not allocated a fleet number and was sold to Jones, Clydach, in September 1983. (EW)

This line-up was taken on 29th August 1982 at Trentham Gardens, when the vehicles were on a private hire. At the far end is no.50 which I was due to take to Nantwich, then to the left of it are nos. 45, 38 and 41, the latter being inspected by Tom Dawson and Bill Chell. The reason for their interest was the Nottingham-style deep front bumper which was being trialled on 41 in an attempt to protect lower front panels in certain locations. However, unlike Nottingham's rubber bumpers, this was solid metal; it solved the problem of the damaged panels, but had an adverse effect on road surfaces, so had to be removed. Instead, in future DMSs had their front offside corners cut back at an angle, which solved the problem. (EW)

XNE 886L was the first of three Plaxton Elite Express-bodied Leyland Leopard coaches with glider doors which were new in 1973 to South East Lancashire and North East Cheshire (SELNEC) PTE, which became Greater Manchester PTE, from where it was acquired in October 1983 (17). Re-numbered 23 in May 1985, it was changed again later to 69, as seen in this view as it passes through Alton village whilst heading towards Uttoxeter. (EW)

Two Bristol VRT SL6Gs with ECW bodies of 1973 (AJA 418/421L) were purchased from Greater Manchester PTE in February 1984 (48/51). No.48 was fitted with power steering by Alder Valley Engineering in December that year, but no.51 was not so treated. It received the all-over advertisement as shown but the sponsoring company went out of business before the end of the contract. After sale to a dealer, both were bought by Silcox, Pembroke Dock, that well-known user of Bristols, in August 1987. To the left in this view at Uttoxeter Bus Station is re-built and re-registered DMS, CBF 31Y. *(EW)*

MFR 18P was the only 11-metre Leyland Leopard PSU3 bought from Lancaster City Council. New in 1976, its Alexander AY-type body had 49 coach seats, and it arrived at Stevensons in April 1984. Appropriately, it was given fleet number 18, and received a livery which was standard at the time, but which incorporated an advert for the company's express services which was superimposed quite un-sympathetically on the side panels. Russ Moore is seen driving the vehicle through Withington on the Leigh Circular, with the usual handful of passengers returning from Uttoxeter. It was re-numbered 68 in February 1987, then in 1988 during a refurbishment it was downgraded and fitted with 53 bus seats. *(EW)*

In April 1984 Stevensons bought HWU 61N, a Leyland Leopard PSU5A/4R with 12-metre Plaxton 57-seat body, which was new to Wallace Arnold Tours, Leeds, in 1975, but came from Berline Coaches, Gloucester. It entered service in May carrying Trent Valley livery (61), was later given an updated front end, and was re-registered 488 BDN in June 1985. At some time in 1986 it was fitted for omo working and received fleet no.119 in December 1987; on 21st August 1988 it is seen on the Central Coach Park, Blackpool after I had driven it there on a private hire. *(EW)*

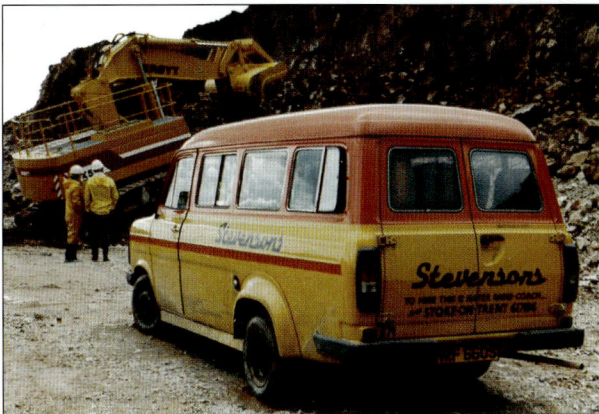

Four Ford Transits of Crystal Coaches joined Stevensons' fleet in September 1984, including VRF 660S (71), which was new in 1977 with a 12-seat Deansgate body. The running units were retained but Stevensons bought and fitted out a new body, and thereafter it was designated 'Stevensons C12F'. In March 1987 it became fleet no.171 and it is seen after I had taken a party of visitors to J C Bamford's testing and demonstration ground in the Weaver Hills near Ashbourne on 24th March 1989. *(EW)*

ONF 893H, a Daimler CRG6LXB with MCW 'Mancunian' body, new to SELNEC PTE in 1970, was bought from Graham Compton Coaches, Chorley, in September 1984 and is seen at Spath. It did see some use on school contracts, then went on loan to Astill and Jordan, Ratby, from some time in November to 22nd December 1984, but was sold in the following month. *(EW)*

Three Leyland Leopards with 51-seat Plaxton Supreme Express bodies which had been new in 1978/79 to Lancashire United Transport, Atherton, were bought from Greater Manchester PTE in September 1984, and re-seated to 53 two months later. TWH 687T of 1978 (17) is seen in Wetley Rocks whilst on the Leek to Longton service previously operated by the erstwhile Berresfords Motors of Cheddleton; at the time of the photo the route was a tendered one, operated by Stevensons' Newcastle depot (Crystal Coaches). All the coaches ran for some time in the GMPTE livery; this vehicle received the grey livery of Viking Coaches in January, 1989. (EW)

A further Leopard with Plaxton Elite Express bodywork, XNE 882L, was purchased from Greater Manchester PTE in October 1984 (22); it had only 45 coach seats but this was increased to 53 in December that year, and in view of its earlier use on Manchester Airport duties, acquired the nickname 'Concorde'. It received a special livery for the Potteries' area operation of Crystal Coaches, and is seen entering Hilderstone on a journey from Hanley. The fleet number became 62 in February 1986. (EW)

The final Leyland Leopard bought from Lancaster City Council in October 1984 was MFR 126P, a PSU4 with Alexander AYS bus body seating 45, which became no.23. This useful bus carried a special livery advertising the company's MOT facilities at Spath (sister vehicle MFR 125P had fleet livery); it is seen in Cheadle passing the garage of Stoddard's Coaches heading towards Butler's Hill, whilst engaged on a Saturdays-only service, returning from Hanley thence via Alton to Uttoxeter. This was service 239, not 401 as displayed. In April 1985 the fleet number became 63. (EW)

Three East Lancs-bodied Leyland Atlanteans of 1978 were acquired with the ESDC merger; numerically the first was XRF 24S, seen on Station Street in Burton whilst en route to the Acorn Inn. Spanning the road is a concrete pipeline bridge, which was built in the 1960s, and linked Bass's New Brewery on the right, and Middle Brewery on the left. Burton was in a unique position in the history of brewing. There were thirty brewers in the town in 1881, although that had declined to eight by 1927. In addition to Bass, famous names included Ind Coope & Samuel Allsopp, Worthington, and Marston, Thompson & Evershed. (EWC)

Three East Lancs-bodied Bristol RESL6Ls also came from ESDC; HTD 324K was transferred to the Ilkeston operation and is seen as no.67 in Beeston, prior to May 1987 at which time it became no.109. Withdrawal came in September 1988. (DS)

EWS 819D, a Leyland Atlantean with Alexander body, was new in 1966 to Edinburgh Corporation Transport, and was acquired by Stevensons in October 1985 with the business of Blue Bus Services, Rugeley. After operating on contracts for one month as no.57 it was withdrawn and sold. (EW)

At some time after 1987, no.18 received the Viking fleetname at the rear, as seen in this classic view in the Lake District. (TM)

KUC 933P, a Leyland CRL6 bought in October 1985, was operated in this commemorative London Transport livery as no.80 until July 1987, and is seen so adorned on Burton Station Bridge. A Gardner 6LXB engine was fitted in March 1986 and in July 1987 it was transferred to Swadlincote depot. The old Midland Railway warehouse provides the backdrop. *(DS)*

New to Aerial Travel, Edinburgh in 1981, CSC 818W was a Mercedes-Benz L508D with 21-seat Reeve Burgess body, bought from Nelson, Bellshill in November 1985 (77). PMT Engineering fitted the power door in April 1987, and it is seen in the Bentilee Estate on a service from Stoke. At the time of building in the 1950's, Bentilee Estate was one of the largest in Europe, with around 4,500 properties. *(EW)*

C78 WRE, a Mercedes-Benz L608D with a body by PMT Engineering, crests Ipstones Edge, heading down towards Ipstones village, after which it will continue to Froghall and Cheadle. On the skyline is The Morridge, which forms the southern boundary of the Peak District National Park. *(EW)*

XJA 551L (58) was one of two Park Royal-bodied Daimler CRG6LXBs to be bought from Greater Manchester PTE in October 1986; both entered the fleet immediately on contracts and service work, but withdrawal came in September 1987. *(EW)*

JWU 253N, a Plaxton Derwent-bodied Leyland Leopard PSU4, was new to West Yorkshire PTE in 1975, from where it was purchased in February 1987, entering service as no.105 two months later. I recorded the vehicle at Pitcher Bank, Stafford before starting the return journey to Uttoxeter on route 404. Before the buses took over, Pitcher Bank was the site of a general market, as well as horse and cattle fairs on Statutory Days. *(EW)*

The tendered Longton to Leek service included a double run between Weston Coyney and Caverswall on some journeys; D906 MVU, a Mercedes-Benz L609D with 'Made to Measure' body, is seen in Caverswall Square, about to set off past the island on which can be seen the village stocks. The village name is said to derive from the name Cafhere, a local Anglo-Saxon who discovered a waelle (well or spring) here, and thought it a good place to reside; in time this morphed into Caverswall. The building behind and to the left of the stocks is part of the Red House Inn, which used to be kept by my Great Grandfather. *(EW)*

125

Also from West Yorkshire PTE in 1987 came four Alexander-bodied Metrobuses, and **UWW 517X (76)** is seen in Derby Street, Burton; contrary to the information on the destination blind, the bus is heading for Uttoxeter on the 401 service. *(EWC)*

Seen in Derby Bus Station whilst on demonstration from Leyland Buses on 12th March 1987 is Leyland Lynx D573 LSJ, which belonged to AA Motor Services, Ayr. Sadly, the bus station is no more, and by now a similar fate may have befallen the Lynx. *(EWC)*

E183 BNN is one of two Fiat 49.10s with Robin Hood body bought new in 1987, and is seen leaving Lichfield Bus Station on city route 56 to Oakenfield. *(EWC)*

Stevensons' vehicles were often used on rail-replacement duties, particularly on Sundays, generally for the Derby to Crewe line. Josiah Wedgwood seems to be more interested in his Portland vase than in TTT 173 and 174X which are seen standing at Stoke Station, awaiting their passengers. *(EW)*

Some Vehicles Acquired from Midland Fox

From Midland Fox came PHH 613R, a 49-seat Duple-bodied Leyland Leopard PSU3D/4RT which was new in 1977 to Cumberland Motor Services and became no.67 with Stevensons. It is seen in Eccleshall on 25th June 1988 just before I set off for Hanley via Cranberry and Newcastle with a Crystal Coaches working. This was one of the first single-deck vehicles to receive the livery comprising white, black and red blocks on the sides. *(EW)*

Midland Fox had modified a Leyland National 2 EON 830V, for use as a mobility bus, complete with coach seats and a wheelchair lift, and that bus was also acquired in August 1987. It continued to be available in that capacity in Stevensons' fleet as no.129, being painted into Viking's coach livery. It also carried out service work, and in due course it received fleet livery, at which time it was replaced by a suitably-converted Volvo coach. *(DH)*

One of the thirty Rootes-bodied Ford Transit 'Fox Cub' minibuses, C551 TJF, is seen resting at Foxt, high in the Staffordshire Moorlands, where I had paused on a journey between Cheadle and Leek on 3rd February 1990. The vehicle was repainted at Ilkeston depot and was unusual for the type in having the striped livery applied. *(EW)*

127

HWY 719N was one of four Leyland Leopards with Alexander 'AY' Type dual-purpose bodies of 1975 that came from Midland Fox in August 1987. It is seen in Lichfield Bus Station en route from Birmingham to Burton. *(EWC)*

On 26th October 1986 the Uttoxeter to Leigh service was combined with that from Hanley to Hilderstone to give a through service, albeit a very sparse one, on Saturdays. New to Crosville Motor services in 1982, DDM 33X, a Leyland Leopard with a Willowbrook 003 body, had been in Victoria Motorway's fleet for four months before passing to Stevensons with the Viking operation in November 1987, becoming no.136. In December the following year it was re-painted into Stevensons' bus livery, as can be seen in this view in Lower Leigh, near the River Blythe, where on 25th February 1989 it was ready at 12.54 to continue to Hanley. The valley used to be a renowned milk-producing area, but the dairy at nearby Fole closed in March 2009. *(EW)*

For over three years Viking had operated two ex-West Riding Northern Counties-bodied Daimler Fleetlines on contracts; BHL 625K and BHL 621K, then numbered 58 and 57, are seen in Stevensons' Derby Street depot. Surprisingly these vehicles, still in Viking livery, were sometimes used on service work. *(EW)*

128

In July 1988 the company bought two 53-seat Bova Futuras which had been new to Shamrock and Rambler Coaches in 1984. They did not receive full Viking livery, and 125 EJU is seen being driven into Uttoxeter Bus Station by Dave Royall. *(EW)*

Stevensons
Bus Services

BSN 878V (89), a dual-door Metrobus, was new to Tayside Regional Council in 1979; it passed to Enterprise and Silver Dawn, Lincoln, from where it was acquired in April 1988, and operated in their livery for a while. It is seen at Wetmore Road depot in company with an ex-West Midlands Travel example. *(EW)*

Standing in Hassall Street, Newcastle-under-Lyme, near to Crystal Coaches' Marsh Trees Garage, is F187 REH, a Mercedes-Benz 609D with Whittaker Europa body which was new to Stevensons in 1988. *(EW)*

PMT Engineering built the body on F188 REH, a Mercedes-Benz 609D; it is seen at Holden Bridge (which carries the Hanley to Chell road) whilst working the Middleport-Sneyd Green-Hanley service. *(EW)*

A343 ASF, a Mercedes-Benz L608D new in 1983, was formerly an ambulance and was acquired in October 1988. Stevensons converted the doorway and fitted 25 bus seats, and on completion it entered service in April 1989. Whilst on a journey from Cheadle to Leek on 2nd January 1991, I stopped to record this view by the lonely bus shelter which is at the highest point on the route, between Whiston and Foxt. *(EW)*

Two Daimler CRG6LXs with 51-seat Marshall bodies, DSR 132/3V, were bought from Dodds of Troon (AA Motor Services) in March 1989. New to Dundee Corporation with Alexander dual-door bodies in 1970, Dundee's successors, Tayside Regional Council, had the new bodies built in April 1980. Only DSR 132V received a fleet number with Stevensons (120); it was given the moniker 'the Green Slug', and both vehicles were very short-lived in the fleet. *(EW)*

The two Leyland Olympians with Alexander RL type bodies new in December 1988, F96/7 PRE (96/7), are seen in Uttoxeter Bus Station, ready for local services which normally were inter-worked with the 401 Uttoxeter to Burton service. *(EW)*

Leon Richardson of Rugeley depot is seen at Sutton Coldfield in the summer of 1994, ready to take Leyland Lynx F258 GWJ on service 117 to Walmley and Erdington. The bus was one of two bought from The Wright Company in 1994. *(LRC)*

Following earlier purchases, eleven more Seddon Pennine 7s with Alexander AYS bodies were bought in October 1989 and YSG 652W (126) is typical of the type. This one came from Kelvin Central and is seen in Wharncliffe Road, Ilkeston on 24th August 1992. *(EWC)*

B45 NDX (90) was a Leyland Olympian with a 73 coach-seated East Lancs body, which was new in 1985 to Ipswich Borough Transport, but was bought in October 1989 from Eastbourne Borough Transport. It is seen in Uttoxeter Bus Station just about to start a journey to Burton on service 401; to the rear, Russ Moore prepares for a trip to Stafford in MFR 41P. When acquired it had coach-type seating, but this was later replaced with seats from spare DMS vehicles. *(EWC)*

Seen in New Street, Burton, G162 YRE was one of four Mercedes-Benz 709Ds with 29-seat bodies by LHE which were new in 1989. This body style with a more sloping windscreen was not popular, and subsequent deliveries featured a normal screen and bonnet arrangement. *(EW)*

G175 DRF of 1990 was the only new Mercedes-Benz 811D of Stevensons to have a LHE body, this having 33 seats and it is seen waiting at Hilderstone ready for a journey to Hanley. Hilderstone is a village of Saxon origin, situated to the north of Stafford. In 1086 the name was Heldulvestone, deriving from Hildewulf's ton, meaning a warrior wolf and a place or town. *(EW)*

Metrobuses virtually identical to this one were commonplace in the West Midlands, but JHE 138W was one of five South Yorkshire Transport examples which Stevensons purchased in 1990. It is seen in Coles Lane, Sutton Coldfield, whilst working the 17.15 service 117 from Sutton Coldfield to Erdington on 19th April 1991. *(RM)*

Another vehicle bought for comparison purposes in service was L102 MEH, a Volvo B6 with a Plaxton Pointer body. It is seen approaching Bargates in Burton, no doubt on its way to Wetmore Road depot. *(TM)*

Standing in front of Stoke-on-Trent Railway Station on 22nd January 1994 is L95 HRF, one of the two DAF DB 250s with Optare Spectra 77-seat bodies bought new in 1993. Together with other double-deckers, it was on hire to Regional Railways on Rail Replacement duties. This magnificent station building was designed by HA Hunt of London for the North Staffordshire Railway Company; building began in 1847 and it was opened the following year. It is reputed to be the finest example of Neo-Jacobean architecture and Victorian urban planning in Staffordshire; the railway company's board room was situated above the colonnade of eight arches which was later enclosed. The two Optare Spectras were also very stylish and were well liked by the drivers. *(EW)*

Three Mercedes-Benz L709Ds which had Wadham Stringer 29-seat bodies were bought in 1994, and L255 NFA is seen at the Forest of Needwood High School, Rolleston, that being the turning point for Stevensons' service 15 from Burton. However, on 6th June 1994 I was working a special turn in competition with 'Your Bus' which had started to operate on some of Stevensons' routes. *(EW)*

In May 1989 four East Lancs-bodied Leyland Leopards, new to Rhymney Valley District Council in 1979 and 1980, came from Inter Valley Link, Caerphilly. DUH 78V is seen in pleasant surroundings in Bretby ('dwelling place of the Britons') having arrived on a short Thursday only service from Burton. Coal mining was a feature locally for many years, and the Bretby Pottery was nearby. (TM)

Stevensons

Company Feedback

From 1988 a staff magazine was produced two or three times a year to enable the company to keep employees informed of news and things in general which affected them and the company. It also provided the opportunity for correspondents from the various depots to say what had been happening at their depots and in their areas. Metrobus KJW 296W stands in the Parade, Sutton Coldfield, awaiting departure on service 374 to Kingstanding on 5th May 1993, with driver Suginder Singh (TJ)

Edited by : Tim Jeffcoat

12th Edition
June 1993

Viking Coaches

565 LON (previously F114 UEH), an MCW MetroRider, was new in 1989 to PMT, from where it was purchased in 1991, and was allocated to the Viking coach fleet as no. 200. *(EWC)*

Viking's no.20 was a Volvo B10M with a Jonckheere Jubilee P50 body seating 53, new in 1987, which was bought from Telling-Golden Miller in 1993 and re-registered from D319 VVV to 784 RBF. It is seen in Hawkins Lane, Burton. *(EWC)*

In 1986 Viking of Woodville bought this DAF MB200 which had a Plaxton Paramount 3200 body as their no.25, and it bore a select registration of JGL 53 (owner John Lloyd's initials). In Stevenson's ownership it was re-registered 82 HBC and became no.2 in the fleet; I took the photo on arrival at the Cwm Clydach nature reserve near Neath on 22nd May 1994. *(EW)*

This Volvo B10M-61 with Plaxton Paramount 3500 body seating 53, new in 1983 as **YNN 29Y**, was acquired with the business of Bagnall's of Swadlincote in 1989. It received an updated lower front panel, and was re-registered **VOI 6874**, becoming no.15. On 24th April I drove it to Spurn Point near Hull, where it was photographed. *(EW)*

This Volvo B58-61 with relatively rare Plaxton Viewmaster Express C53F body was new to Flight's, Birmingham in 1981, and the coach was then altered to C48FT. Originally intended to be registered **FOP 707V**, is actually carried **GOP 708W** when it entered service. By the time it was acquired by Bagnalls of Cadley Hill near Swadlincote it had been re-registered **2488KB**. It passed with Bagnall's business to Stevensons who re-registered it **RUT 717W**, but David Stanier noticed that the registration plates fitted (RUT 171W) did not match the tax disc and pointed out the error. The coach received Viking livery in February 1990 but the vehicle's identity crisis was not yet over, for in April that year it was re-registered yet again to **POI 9786**. Withdrawal came in November 1993. *(EWC)*

In 1991 **G417 WFP**, a Bova FHD Futura was purchased from Boyden, Castle Donington, and became no.9 in the Viking fleet. It had been fitted out to executive specification with 36 seats, servery and a toilet, being used primarily on a Rolls-Royce contract, and it was not re-painted. It was normally parked at Derby overnight, and I saw it on just this one occasion on one of its rare visits to Spath. *(EW)*

More Advertising Buses

MLK 457L (43) boldly advertises Stevensons Travel as it sits in Rugeley Bus Station. Driver Dennis Williams prepares for a trip to less exotic places than advertised on his bus; in time, Dennis went on to manage the Potteries operation at Burslem Depot. At the time of this photograph no.43 was Dennis' regular bus. *(EW)*

Toons Carpet and Furniture Warehouses, at Church Gresley and Uttoxeter, were advertised on a large number of Stevensons' vehicles. Gardner-engined Leyland Fleetline OUC 47R (47) is seen at the Butter Cross in Abbots Bromley on the 408 service to Uttoxeter. The village dates from at least 942AD and the market used to be held in this location. The Butter Cross, named after the produce sold under it, is possibly the oldest building in the village, although some believe the present structure dates from the 1600s, replacing one from the 13th or 14th century. An annual event held in the area is the Abbots Bromley Horn Dance, which takes place 'on the Wakes Monday, the day following Wakes Sunday, which is the first Sunday after 4th September'. *(EW)*

Two Metrobuses are seen by The Octagon Shopping Centre in New Street, Burton. JHE 192W with the smart advertising livery for The Bed Company was bought from South Yorkshire Transport in 1990, whilst BOK 75V, in front, was new to West Midlands Travel. *(EWC)*

On 20th November 1993 Andy Cooper was photographed in Weston Road, Lichfield whilst on service 54 in K138 BRF, a Mercedes-Benz 811D with a Dormobile Routemaker body, which carries a livery for Justin Pinewood. The advert at the rear of sister vehicle 139 (shown below) could be open to misinterpretation! *(TJ)*

EWF 473V was one of five MCW Metrobuses of 1980 bought from South Yorkshire Transport in March 1988, and received this livery promoting Burton Round Table, as seen in this view in New Street, Burton. *(PS)*

Standing in Station Street, Burton bound for Winshill is OUC 34R (81), a Leyland Fleetline with MCW body, new to LTE in 1976. After purchase in November 1985 it received a Gardner 6LXB engine and was converted to single doorway; it entered service in February 1986 in this advertising livery for Peter Smith Sports Cars, which it carried until July 1989. *(PS)*

Seen climbing Burton Station Bridge, with St Pauls church and Burton Town Hall in the background, is C103 UHO (70), one of two Leyland National 2s of 1985, purchased from Provincial Bus Company, Fareham when not quite two years old in 1987. It entered service in Provincial livery, then in June 1987 it received this advertising livery for JT Leavesley, a car dealer in Alrewas. Both these Nationals were sold in October 1989 to West Riding Automobile Company, Wakefield. *(EW)*

Sitting in the new push-round bus wash area at Spath is VAJ 785S, a Leyland Leopard of 1977 which had been re-bodied in 1990 with this Willowbrook Warrior 48-seat body. It was bought from South Lancs Transport in 1994 and became no.111. The bus has obviously come up to Spath from the West Midlands, since service 581 was a Wolverhampton route. *(TM)*

Some Leyland Leopards with Alexander AYS type 53-seat bodies were also acquired. YSF 93S of 1977 was bought from Fife Scottish in 1992, becoming no.116. On 28th January 1994, I had just returned to Spath from a school contract in this vehicle, when I was asked to go to Uttoxeter Railway Station, where a diesel unit was in distress, as were the passengers! Fortunately, although this type had 53 seats, the legal lettering showed that 20 (I seem to recall) standing passengers were allowed. That was no bad thing, and having got everyone on board, I set off as an 'all stations to Crewe', and the photo records my eventual arrival there. *(EW)*

There were still more surprise purchases, such as when a Leyland PD3 with MCW body, LFR 532F, new in 1968 to Blackpool Corporation, was bought in 1993 from Eastbourne Buses, where it had been in use as a driver training vehicle. It was numbered 29 with Stevensons and I had the pleasure of driving it on 14th September 1993 on the Admaston school contract from Uttoxeter; on return to Spath, I parked it by the fuel pump and recorded the scene. Note the small piece of tape on the cover for the radiator filler cap, which stops the cover blowing up in the breeze. Across the road, Ray Buckley heads back to the garage, whilst driver Norman Crane makes his way to the bus park. After withdrawal, this bus was exported to Red Deer, Alberta, where it joined 'Burnley' PCW 944 which had been exported there in 1980. *(EW)*

One of the Optare-bodied Dennis Dominoes in the Pacer fleet is seen leaving Manchester centre via Oldham Street on service 188 to Gorton. C42 HDT was bought from South Yorkshire PTE in April 1991 and numbered 223. The Domino chassis was effectively a shortened Dominator double-decker chassis, but had a small Perkins engine, and was quite ponderous in operation, not good on fuel consumption, and generally unreliable. *(EWC)*

G645 EVN was a CVE Omni demonstrator, and was used on service in the Uttoxeter area, as can be seen by the signage and the wayfarer machine as it stood close to the office at Spath. There were no purchases of the type following its visit. *(EW)*

C823 SDY, a Mercedes-Benz L608D with Alexander 20-seat body of 1986, was bought from East Midland Motor Service in 1993 and numbered 224. I took advantage of a very quiet evening journey on the 401 service to take this photo opposite Sudbury Hall's imposing south lodge, which acts as the bus stop in the village for Uttoxeter-bound journeys. *(EW)*

In Newcastle Bus Station E219 SOL, an MCW Metrorider, is seen ready for a journey to Audley, and behind is PMT's A747 JRE, a Leyland Olympian ONLXB with ECW body of 1984. The Metrorider was bought from North Bedfordshire Health Authority in 1991. *(EW)*

KJW 318W (70), is seen turning from Bradley Street into Uttoxeter Bus Station where it will take on board a good number of passengers who are waiting for the bus to Burton at Stand One. Also seen is KRN 217W, a Ford Transit of R & D Motors, Abbots Bromley, which at the time operated the Uttoxeter Town Circular evening journeys, on tender to Staffordshire CC. *(EW)*

Three Leyland Swifts of 1988 with 7ft 6ins wide Wadham Stringer Vanguard II bodies seating 37 were purchased from Armchair, Brentford, and I collected **E990 NMK**, numerically the first, from there on 7th September 1993. On 4th July 1996 it is seen at Belper Lane End whilst on the Uttoxeter - Ashbourne - Belper tendered service; originally allocated fleet number 121, this had been changed to 321 by the date of my journey. *(EW)*

Roy Leason is seen driving Leyland Swift **H313 WUA** down Bradley Street, Uttoxeter, about to turn into the Bus Station. Roy use to work at Hilton CVD and also drove one of Stevensons' contract buses between Uttoxeter and Hilton each day. When the unit closed, he started to work full time at Stevensons. This bus and its sister **H314 WUA** retained the Pennine livery for some time. *(TJC)*

D401 MHS, a Leyland Lynx of 1986 which was purchased from Kelvin Central in 1991, is seen after arrival in Ashbourne Bus Station from Uttoxeter on service 409, which previously had been operated by Trent. The suspension on the Mersey-Coach Duple-bodied Leyland Tiger would have been so much better than the rock-hard one on the Stevensons' vehicle; when driving no.60 it was essential to check the road surface in front carefully for any potentially body-jarring ruts or objects! *(EW)*

The first Dennis Dart to be bought was J556 GTP, a 9SDL type which had a Wadham Stringer Portsdown body seating 35. New in 1991, it was acquired the following year from Irwell Valley, Boothstown, and was given fleet number 40. Allocated to Rugeley depot, it is seen in the town's Bus Station, the destination being set for the short, but well-used, local service 423 to Pear Tree Estate. Arriving on their service from Cannock via Cannock Chase is Warstone Motor's (Green Bus Service) no.20, RWT 58R, a Leyland Leopard with Plaxton Derwent body, bought from Parkinson, Allerton Bywater in 1993. The Pear Tree route was the scene of competition between Stevensons and Key Coachways in 1982. (TM)

New in 1984 to Crosville as A43 SMA, this Leyland Tiger with Duple Laser body carried registration 1205 FM for some time. After transfer to North Western it received accident damage which was repaired by East Lancs, when it was given this unusual front end and was later re-registered A195 KKF. Following acquisition by Stevensons in August 1995 the body was refurbished further and it was repainted in September, when it became no.126. It is seen in Burton about to set off on the X38 limited stop service to Derby, operated jointly with Trent. (EWC)

It seemed to be a shame to downgrade coach 18, but 479 BOC, seen at Derby Bus Station in its special livery, looks to be a much more appropriate vehicle for the half-hourly X38 express service than no.126 seen above in this late 1990s view. (AP)

143

E829 AWA, a Leyland Tiger with Plaxton Derwent 54-seat body, was new in 1988, and was purchased from Liverline, Liverpool, from where I collected it on 1st May 1993. It is seen in Swadlincote Bus Station on 3rd June 1994 having arrived there on service 118 from Leicester. *(JB)*

Seen here, having just transferred from Edinburgh Transport is G897 TGG, a Mercedes-Benz 811D with Reeve Burgess Beaver 33-seat body which was new in 1989, and is seen at Spath still wearing Edinburgh Transport livery, but carrying Stevensons' fleet number 145. *(TM)*

F170 DET, a Scania K93 with Plaxton Derwent 57-seat body of 1989, was bought in 1993 from Capital Citybus, in whose livery it is seen in New Street, Burton having arrived from Birmingham. It was numbered 107 and did receive fleet livery in due course. *(DS)*

LJA 641P (28) was an ex-SELNEC Leyland Atlantean with NCME body which came to Stevensons from Stagecoach Ribble in June 1993, and is seen at Wetmore Road depot. It was soon was on the move again, going to Cardiff Bluebird, which was connected to Tellings, with which Julian Peddle was involved at the time. (EW)

Sealandair Coaches

After many years without an AEC in the fleet, some Reliances were acquired with the Collett's Coaches business in 1991 including this one which had a Plaxton Elite body. New in 1973 to Jalna Coaches of Church Gresley as ENU 665L, it was later re-registered 468 KPX; Stevensons transferred that registration to a Viking coach which resulted in another new registration, FEA 55L (239). On 25th July 1993 I had the privilege of driving it back from the Sandtoft Rally, that being the last operation of the last AEC in the fleet. (TM)

From the Sealandair operation came XOR 841, a Volvo B10M with Van Hool Alizee body seating 53, new in 1983, which was previously registered MHS 665V. It is seen at Spath bearing the new combined fleet name, Sealandair/Colletts/Classic, and fleet number 26. (EW)

Minis and Midis

This is not 'trouble at t' Mill', since I had parked no.128 by Belper Mills in order to take the photo. D133 NUS was a Mercedes-Benz L608D with Alexander 21-seat body which was new in 1986 and came from Kelvin Central in 1992. The rather striking livery was for the Leek United Building Society, and no.128 had arrived in Belper on the service from Uttoxeter via Ashbourne. Strutt's North Mill, to the rear, was built in 1804 by William Strutt, replacing one destroyed by fire the previous year. It is one of the oldest-surviving examples of an iron-framed 'fire-proof' building in the world. To the right is the large 20th century brick-built East Mill of the English Sewing Company. *(EW)*

In 1990 Stevensons purchased a Robin Hood demonstrator, F272 OPX, which had a Mercedes-Benz 811D chassis and was new in 1988. It is seen in Gibfield Lane, Belper, where I had left it whilst on break, having worked in from Ashbourne. *(EW)*

F907 PFH (38) was a Leyland Swift with an unusual GC Smith (of Long Whatton) 'Whippet' body, new in 1988 for Gloucestershire County Council's welfare fleet. It was purchased from there in 1993, and Stevensons fitted it out as a 36-seater bus, but the centre rear exit door was retained. It is seen in Burton High Street, working on service 4 to The Acorn. *(EWC)*

H801 SKY (242), a Mercedes-Benz 709D with Reeve-Burgess body, was one of three bought from Kinch, Mountsorrel in April, 1994, and is seen in Dudley Bus Station ready for a journey on service 243 to Cradley Heath. They all retained the Kinch's livery for a while. *(EWC)*

G141 GOL was a Dennis Dart which carried a Duple Dartline 36-seat body. Carlyle Works Ltd acquired the design rights and the partially-built vehicle, and when completed it became a demonstrator for Carlyle; following the closure of Carlyle in 1992, the design rights passed to Marshall Bus. Registered in May 1990, it was bought by Star Line, Knutsford, from where it was acquired in 1992, becoming no.41, and is seen at Erdington Six Ways on Rugeley depot's route 109 to Kingstanding. *(DH)*

Oliver Ball is seen in charge of G702 NGR (152) whilst in Bell Lane, Doveridge on the way to Burton. This Mercedes-Benz 811D with a Scott body was new in 1990 to Rush, Newcastle-on-Tyne and came to Stevensons in 1993. *(EW)*

On 12th August 1994 at the height of the 'bus wars', I was photographed in New Street, Burton, ready for a journey to Rolleston in L229 HRF, a Mercedes-Benz 709D with Dormobile Routemaker body of 1993 which carried an advertising livery for Burton Cleaning Centre. *(EWC)*

147

British Bus – Service Buses

Leading driver Barry Hurst watches on whilst Len Blurton and Workshop Foreman David Eadie affix a new vinyl fleetname to a Metrobus on the garage forecourt at Spath, following the take-over by British Bus. *(EW)*

The new letter heading

K140/1 RYS, MAN Vectas with Optare body of 1992, were ordered by Bruce, Airdrie for use on the Citylink 502 service from Glasgow to Glasgow Airport. The company passed into British Bus ownership, but was quickly closed down. These vehicles passed to Express Travel, Perth, from where they were purchased in October 1994. The latter vehicle, re-registered UOI 772, is seen at Burton Depot having been painted for the new half-hourly X38 express service between Burton and Derby, which commenced on 6th March 1995 and was jointly-operated with Trent, one bus per operator. This vehicle was eventually replaced by the coach 479 BOC, seen on page 143.*(EW)*

It was not long before it was decided to add red to the fleet livery at the expense of black, and KJW 310W (55) is seen in New Street, Burton in the revised livery, also carrying an advert on the rear. The old fleetname above the cab window would be removed when the side advertisement was changed. *(EWC)*

Some vehicles were transferred to Stevensons following the absorption of Frontline, including 904 AXY (previously VOV 936X) a Leyland Leopard with Willowbrook Warrior body. I photographed it by the impressive ruins of Croxden Abbey having completed a school contract. The Cistercian Abbey was founded in the 12th century and was dissolved in 1538. *(EW)*

A number of vehicles carried route branding under the BURTON*bus* name, including Plaxton Pointer-bodied Dennis Dart L301 NFA (301), seen leaving New Street in Burton, bound for Swadlincote. This was one of the buses specifically branded for service 15, Rolleston - Burton - Swadlincote - Midway. One of the two Optare Spectras is seen in the distance. *(DS)*

A215 PEV, a Leyland Tiger with Duple Dominant bodywork of 1982, has fleet number 1615, which shows that the company was then administratively under Midland Red North's control; Stevensons' yellow replaced the lighter shade previously used by Midland Red North. The vehicle had been fitted with 53 bus seats for service work, and was waiting in Uttoxeter Bus Station before setting out for Abbots Bromley on service 408. Across the road is Bradley House Club, meeting place of the Uttoxeter British Legion, of which George Stevenson had been president. *(EW)*

GMS 295S (120), a Leyland Leopard PSU3 with Alexander AYS 53-seat body is seen arriving in Bank Square, Wilmslow, en route from Manchester on Macclesfield depot's service 130. It was new in 1978 and was acquired from Henley, Abertillery in 1991. *(EWC)*

Originally Stevensons' no.32, J32 SFA was one of four Leyland Swifts with Wright Handybus bodies bought in 1992. These were the only bodies of that type to be built on the Swift chassis. Now painted in the new British Bus-devised livery and carrying fleet number 1132, it is seen in the old Macclesfield Bus Station in Sunderland Street and may well go on the Upton Priory Circular when the driver has finished chatting to a Maxonian (and finished his cigarette). Macclesfield is a prosperous area and is known as the 'Silk Town', since it was once the largest producer of finished silk with 71 mills operating in 1832. All are now converted to other uses or demolished. *(EWC)*

In 1994 British Bus bought four used Leyland Nationals for the fleet, one of which was KOM 797P (352), a 46-seater of 1976 which came from Evag Cannon in 1994. However, having been painted in the livery of Edinburgh Transport (and with their legal lettering applied), once the near-side wiper was replaced, it would be venturing north across the border. *(EW)*

150

G4I HKY, a Scania K93 which has a 57-seat Plaxton Derwent body, was passed to Stevensons from MRN, and is seen at Erdington, ready for the Centro tendered service 24 to Shard End in the Birmingham suburbs. *(DH)*

New in 1989 to Kentish Bus, G507 SFT, a Northern Counties-bodied Leyland Olympian, passed to the Bee Line Buzz Company, then to MRN (Tamworth depot), from where it was cascaded with six others to Stevensons (2007) in August 1997. The livery includes branding for the 112 Birmingham service, but the bus is seen in New Street, Burton, departing on service 17 to Stretton. *(DS)*

B204 DTU, a coach-seated Leyland Olympian with ECW body which was new to Crosville in 1985, passed to Midland Red North and was cascaded to Stevensons. The destination is set ready for the return journey to Burton as it turns into Navigation Street on its circuit of Birmingham City Centre. *(DH)*

British Bus – Coaches

Side by side at Wetmore Road depot are two 12-metre Leyland felines. **FAZ 3194 (1694)** was a Leyland Tiger with 53-seat Duple 320 body new to London Country in March 1986 as **C250 SPC**. It passed via Luton & District to Crosville Wales in December 1994, and then received registration **FAZ 3194**. It arrived at Stevensons in January 1997, and is seen at Wetmore Road depot carrying bus livery. **AAL 404A (13)** was a 1980 Leopard with 53-seat Plaxton Paramount 3200 body of 1987 and wears the new Stevensons coach livery. It was one of two (the other being **AAL 403A**) bought from Rhondda Buses in 1992. *(EW)*

B148 ALG, a Leyland Tiger with Duple Laser body, was new to Crosville in 1984, and was acquired from North Western in 1995. It is seen on the ex-Frontline service **X79** from Hurley to Birmingham. *(EWC)*

Originally registered **C153 SFB**, **JSK 994** was a Leyland Tiger with Berkhof body new in 1985 to London Country; it passed to Crosville Wales from where it was acquired. By its side in MRN bus livery is **E26 UNE (1746)**, a Leyland Tiger with 53-seat Alexander (Belfast) N-type body of 1989, bought from Timeline, Leigh in 1993, and subsequently cascaded to Stevensons. *(EW)*

This delightful photo was taken by Tim Machin from his signal box at Leigh Crossing, and captures long-term employee Charlie Allen returning to Spath from Morrilow Heath. OKY 822X (1500), a 1982 Leyland Leopard PSU5 with 57-seat Plaxton Supreme VI body, entered the fleet with the transfer of Frontline to Stevensons' control. Charlie's father Jim operated a small coach business, Dove Valley Coaches of Roston, Derbyshire, from the early 1920s, and one service ran to Uttoxeter on Wednesdays. *(TM)*

FAZ 5279 (29), a Leyland Tiger with Plaxton Paramount Express body, was new in 1984 to London Country as A145 EPA and was subsequently operated by Crosville Wales. It was purchased from there in July 1995 and was repainted in the new Stevensons coach livery two months later. It was a good coach, and is seen on 24th April 1996 where I parked it at the Keynes Country Park (now the Cotswold Water Park) in Wiltshire. The park comprises one of the largest areas of man-made lakes in Britain, following many years of gravel extraction, and is a haven for wildlife. *(EW)*

Happy Birthday Stevensons Wednesday 11th September 1996

70 YEARS RELIABLE SERVICE

stevensons

1926-1996

TRAVEL AT 1926 FARES ON OUR 70th BIRTHDAY!

On service 401, the original Stevensons bus route, between Uttoxeter and Burton, on Wednesday 11th September 1996, we will be charging the equivalent of our original Uttoxeter to Burton fares for any journey made:

	1926	70th birthday
single	1/4d	7p
return	2/-	10p

stevensons

Coach Hire FROM THE PROFESSIONALS

stevensons

This coach hire leaflet of the late 1990s features a Leyland Tiger with Duple 320 body which was new in 1986 to London Country and came to the Stevensons' fleet via Crosville Wales in November 1996. Subsequently it was re-registered from C249 SPC to GDZ 795. (EWC)

Sister vehicle YYJ 955 was new to London Country as C248 SPC and also arrived at Stevensons from Crosville Wales in November 1996 as no.1620. The new registration came from an ex-Frontline Willowbrook-bodied Leyland Leopard. (EW)

In the Bleak Mid-Winter

Tim Jeffcoat recorded these views on 8th February 1969. At the top to the right we see KGK 725, an AEC RT with Cravens body, as it passes by The Beacon at 2.26pm whilst working the 1.30pm Uttoxeter-Hanbury-Burton journey. Top left is KXW 110, a Weymann-bodied AEC Regent RT driven by Dennis Fowle, seen at 2.58pm near the Salt Box, Hatton, with the 2.30pm Uttoxeter to Burton journey. In the picture below, KGU 216, a Leyland 7RT with a Park Royal body, passes Tutbury Station at 3.14pm with the 2.45pm Burton to Uttoxeter working. Tim Jeffcoat's bike is leaning on the fencing. (All TJ)

From Burton Mail, February 1979

Also on 8th February 1969, another Park Royal-bodied Leyland 7RT, LYF 65, is progressing carefully in Holts Lane, Tutbury, at 3.40pm on the 3.15 Burton to Uttoxeter journey (top). On the same day ECW-bodied Guy Special MXX 371 approaches Lodge Hill at 2.40pm on a journey from Tutbury to Burton. (*Both TJ*)

Early in 1994 Dormobile-bodied Mercedes-Benz K148 BRF is seen (just about) in Clifton, near Ashbourne. A few journeys diverted off the usual route of the 409 Uttoxeter to Ashbourne service to serve this village. *(TM)*
On a winter's day in the 1990s, one of the two Scania N113s with Alexander PS bodies sits in Swadlincote Bus Station. No doubt the driver will provide details of the destination for any intending passengers. At least the buses are still on the road, unlike what often seems to happen today at the first sign of snow. *(AP)*

Brief Encounters

On 22nd April 1975 Park Royal-bodied 959 AJO waits to cross the A50 at Rolleston Cross Roads on a Rolleston School contract. Meanwhile DFC 365D, an AEC Renown, also bodied by Park Royal, driven by Michael Morris and working the 7.50 Uttoxeter to Burton, picks up passengers. Both vehicles originated with City of Oxford Motor Services. (TJ)

On 27th May 1969 Brush-bodied Leyland Royal Tiger DHE 347, working the 11.00 am Uttoxeter to Burton via Hanbury journey, loads passengers at 11.48am at Outwoods Lane between Anslow and Beam Hill. Park Royal-bodied Leyland 7RT KGU 216, having previously worked the 11.35 journey from Burton to Anslow, is returning out of service to Wetmore Bus Park. (TJ)

UVT 13X, a Leyland Tiger with Plaxton Paramount body, waits at Foston Cross Roads with a return working on the Ashbourne to Burton service, whilst JGF 298K, a Park Royal-bodied Daimler Fleetline (DMS) passes quickly along the A50 on the Uttoxeter to Burton service. *(EW)*

The two coach-seated Bristol VRTs, (PFA 50W, UVT 49X), and MUS 103P, a Leyland Leopard with Duple Dominant bus body, wait on layover in Elkington Street, Birmingham, having arrived in the city on the express services from Uttoxeter and Burton. *(EW)*

VRF 338L, a Ford R1114 with Plaxton Elite Express body, meets up with Bristol VRT UVT 49X in Carrs Lane, Birmingham, the terminus of the express services from Uttoxeter and Burton. I had driven the Ford from Uttoxeter and would shortly return via Lichfield to Rugeley. A West Midlands PTE Daimler Fleetline passes both vehicles. *(EW)*

Downgraded

In the late 1980s a number of coaches were downgraded for use as service buses and bus seats from spare DMSs were used to re-seat them. Plaxton Elite-bodied Leyland Leopard LMA 60P has also been re-registered, with the much-used number 488 BDN, and is seen at Parwich School on an Ashbourne baths contract. *(TM)*

Similarly treated is MFR 18P, a Leyland Leopard with Alexander Y-type body, which has also lost its embellishments; it is seen at Rocester whilst working on the Uttoxeter to Ashbourne service 409. *(TM)*

XTF 827L, an ex-North Western Duple Dominant-bodied Leyland Leopard bought in May 1987, is seen at Spath as no.60 having been fitted with 53 bus seats. *(EW)*

Pressed into Service

Sometimes, as seen elsewhere in the book, circumstances dictated that buses had to be used in service as acquired before fleet livery could be applied, although a sticker indicating ownership would be exhibited somewhere at the front. Here are a few examples from the 1990s.

D141 NUS, a Mercedes-Benz L608D with Alexander 21-seat body, new in 1986, was acquired from Kelvin Central in 1992, becoming fleet number 130, and is seen on School Bus duties. *(AP)*

Henley's of Abertillery previously owned this vehicle, which retained their livery for a while with Stevensons. GMS 295S, a Leyland Leopard with Alexander AYS 53-seat body, new in 1978, was bought by Stevensons in April 1991. Initially given fleet number 67. It soon become no.120 and is seen in Rugeley Bus Station, preparing for a journey on the short but well-used route up the hill to Pear Tree Estate. *(AP)*

YSG 653W carries a similar body to that on no.120 but is mounted on a Seddon Pennine 7 chassis; the Gardner engines in these vehicles returned an extra two miles per gallon over the Leyland Leopards. New to Scottish Omnibuses (Eastern Scottish) in December 1980, it passed to Central Scottish and Kelvin Central before arrival at Stevensons with ten others, nine being used from this batch. Still carrying its earlier Central Scottish livery, it received this partial frontal repaint so that passengers were not completely confused, and it became no.127. It is seen in Burton town centre and will shortly take a good number of passengers on its journey to Coton-in-the-Elms. *(EWC)*

Also acquired from Kelvin Central was D680 MHS, an MCW Metrobus of 1986, with Alexander RL body fitted with dual-purpose seating for 78 passengers, one of five bought by Stevensons in March 1994, this one becoming no.91. John Robinson steps down from the vehicle so that the driver can pull on to the stand in Uttoxeter Bus Station for the Town Circular service. *(AP)*

E478 NSC, a Mercedes-Benz 811D with Alexander body fitted with 25 dual-purpose seats, was new in 1988, and acquired in April 1994 from Porter, Dummer, becoming no.241. The driver takes a break in the bus, having arrived from Burton via Tutbury, presumably on a Sunday. *(TM)*

Les Smith kindly drew the vehicle forward to assist the photographer and now prepares to leave Spath yard to take up a journey from Uttoxeter via Hanbury to Burton early one Saturday morning. G901 MNS, another Mercedes-Benz 811D, but this time with a Reeve-Burgess body seating 32, was new in 1989 and acquired from Whitelaw, Stonehouse, in September 1991. *(EW)*

Ancillary Vehicles and Engineering

PCW 945 was very nicely converted into a tree-lopper cum tow-bus, and it is seen being used in the latter capacity as it brings in failed DMS OJD 151R (28) to receive attention at Spath. (EW)

DRC 543J, an Alexander-bodied Daimler Fleetline, was new to Trent Motor Traction but passed to Ribble, from where it was acquired via Lister (dealer), Bolton for tree-lopping duties. By its side at Spath is OSG 998G, a Bedford KM, originally a refuse vehicle in Scotland, which was converted to become Spath depot's recovery vehicle. (EW)

Sealandair's recovery vehicle, Q172 GDH, was despatched to Macclesfield depot to recover Olympian 99, Q246 FVT, and the two vehicles are seen at Spath just before 99 completes its final journey. (EW)

For a while the recovery vehicle at Spath was VAN 524M, an ERF 'B' series, modified from an ex-London Fire Brigade fire tender. Collett's of West Bromwich converted it for use as a recovery vehicle, but Ray Worbey, who worked in the bodyshop at Spath, rebuilt it when it was acquired by Stevensons. I am told that although it had an automatic gearbox it performed well when required, albeit noisily due to its Perkins V6 engine. The real benefit was its turn of speed when travelling to a breakdown. *(EW)*

An early tree-lopper was ex-no.1 RWT 613, a Burlingham-bodied Guy Arab. The 'conversion' was minimal; a ladder was secured inside the saloon from the floor to the opening roof window, thereby allowing access to the roof, where the operative was able to work within a rectangular framework which had the look of something made from Meccano. Possibly Health and Safety would not be amused today! As it stands in Horninglow Road North on 17th August 1971, it can be seen that its alternative use was that of driver-training vehicle. *(TJ)*

Having worked for Stevensons for just over nine years, TTT 780 (3) was converted very neatly to a recovery tree-lopping vehicle, and was re-numbered 3A in December 1977, then 05 in February 1981. It always ran on trade plates 576 RF; in June 1982 it went to Bloor (dealer) Spath, and finally succumbed to the scrap-man's torch. *(EW)*

This Karrier Bantam short-wheelbase lorry was used at Spath for a while; it is seen there in July 1980. *(EW)*

Olympian 99 lived on to some degree after withdrawal, for its roof was used to replace that on decapitated EEH 904Y. On the top of 99 is Ray Buckley who masterminded the operation. *(EW)*

Mercedes-Benz F985 EDS received front-end accident damage, as seen in this view behind Spath Garage. A look at the destination blind may give you the opinion that the driver was attempting to apologise! The new body and paint shop is to the right, situated on the former railway land. *(EW)*

On a pit in the workshop at Willenhall depot, which opened in 1993, is Dennis Dart L305 NFA. *(EWC)*

More Personalities

Drivers Stefan Senkow and Keith Russell stand against a backdrop of ex-Leicester 82 HBC at Spath in late 1983. *(EW)*

On the same day driver Peter Birtles, to the right, watches on as (l to r) retired fitter George Smith, driver Harry Henchcliffe and conductor Tom Smith share a joke. Unfortunately, Tom passed away not long afterwards. *(EW)*

At Spath in July 1980, Tom Ginnis is standing beside his bus, MLK 457L. Tom was a most pleasant person and a good driver, and beside his driver's badge he wore one of the early chrome **SBS** uniform badges *(TJ)*

Driver Cyril Stretton of Spath depot is seen beside an ex-Portsmouth Atlantean at Wetmore Bus Park on 23rd September 1978, at the time of his retirement after 37 years service. *(TJ)*

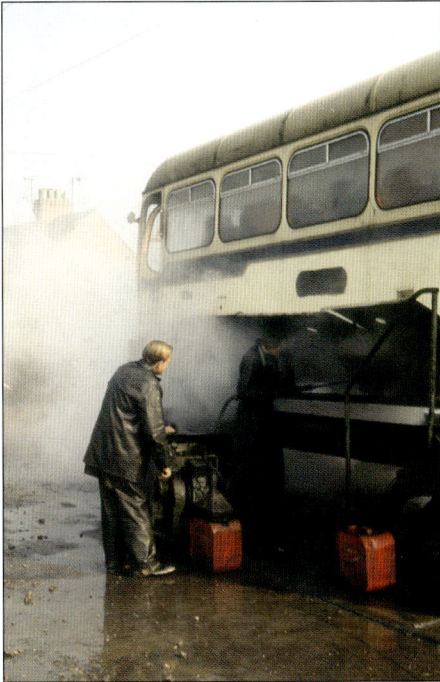

On 18th March 1972 conductor/cleaner Ken Charlesworth was assisting with steam cleaning of ex-Sheffield 5909 W before it went into the workshops for preparation. *(TJ)*

Dave Gaskin shelters beside the **AEC Swift, NJW 709E,** at Uttoxeter Bus Station on 7th August 1980, which seems to have been a rather inclement summer's day! Dave later became Traffic Office Supervisor at Wetmore Road depot. *(TJ)*

SPATH DEPOT GROUP PHOTOGRAPH

Left to right. Back row: Matthew Evans, Frank Kirkham, Alan Amison, Eric Wain, Konstantin Grynowski, Les Smith, Barry Hurst, Harry Hubble, Oliver Ball, Alan Peaty, Peter Wright, John Wheildon, Gerald Anthony, Richard Yoxall, Tim Stubbs, Adrian Johnson, Dave Pritchard.
2nd row: Doug Walker, Tim Jeffcoat, Philip Smith, Paul Rowley, Neil Blurton, George Bird, Bill Stanton, Bill Philips, Malcolm Woods, Gordon Cooke, Simon Hawksworth, Steve Lovatt, John Sharp, John Williams, Ray Worbey, Julian Peddle (Managing Director)

3rd row: Mark Bowd, Bill Davies, Les Cope, Russell Moore, Peter Birtles, Brian Kershaw, Chris Hawley, Lawrence Shuitor, Ken Penlington, David Penlington, Charlie Allen, Ray Buckley, George Stevenson, Andy Starbuck.
Front row: Linda Stanton, Mel Jones, Kathy Hackett, Hazel Barlow, Elsie Cork, Nan Smith, Shirley Cox, Jenny Ratcliffe, Sue Cotton, Yvonne Newey, Jane Bailey.
Stevensons of Uttoxeter Ltd 1989)

BURTON DEPOT GROUP PHOTOGRAPH

Left to right. Tim Starbuck, Paul Fletcher, Pete Robinson, Mike Whyman, Dave Morgan, Dave Elliot, Zoe Kidger, Brian Matthews, Andy Cooper, Dave Gaskin, Pete Collinge, John Hincks, John Orton, Richard Emery, Heather Dewey, Rob Lawrence, Phil Plant, Tony Price, Ray Elson, Will Evans, Tim Stubbs, Andy Starbuck, Andrew Coltman, Keith Myatt, Kevin Wagstaffe, Clive Whatling, Matt Evans.

Stevensons of Uttoxeter Ltd 1989)

SWADLINCOTE DEPOT GROUP PHOTOGRAPH

Left to right. Geoff Coltman, Phillip Ashmore, Andy Roberts, Steven Hunt, Andy Grief, Paul Foster, Paul Dyche, Ian Hough, Richard Tuck, Kevin Rutter, Ronald Redfern, Reginald Shorthouse, Roger Wood, Phillip Wileman, Jayne Eustace, Mick Maw, Gordon Tomlinson, Percy Laud, Barry Kennard, Brian Humphries, Steven Wright, Tony Hyde, Robert Buswell, Paul Oldham, Peter Sims.

(Stevensons of Uttoxeter Ltd 1989)

More views of depots

Stevensons' operations in Rugeley were originally run from the Burton and Uttoxeter garages but from 1983 vehicles were kept at Middleton's yard in Armitage Road, Rugeley, the only infrastructure there being a portacabin. This arrangement continued until the Spring of 1988, when this brand-new garage building and concreted parking area was opened in a cul-de-sac off Power Station Road. *(EW)*

This 1980s view of the premises at Spath shows, left to right, the section of the garage altered in 1946 to house double-deckers, the old offices, the car Mo bay (which had formerly been the 'long garage' where John Stevenson rebuilt the bodies of many single-deckers in the 1930s and 1940s), the toilet and mess room, and the Stevenson family house 'Brooklands', by now in use as offices. *(EW)*

This is a 1980 aerial view of Spath. In the foreground is 'Brooklands' with its gardens and orchard. The garage buildings standing behind have a nucleus dating from 1930 but have been partially rebuilt for double-deckers in 1946 then extended at the back in the 1970s. The course of the Uttoxeter to Ashbourne railway line on the right-hand side is betrayed by the long hedgerow, and this land has now been incorporated into the bus company's property. The double-decker nearest the camera stands where the new bodywork and paint shop was constructed a few years later. The main road to Ashbourne passes the garage and off to the right, but this was superseded by a new route off the picture in the 1980s. The road to Stramshall runs straight ahead. In the angle between the two roads is the site of Spath House. On the left is the bus and staff car parking area opened after the Second World War as the fleet outgrew the accommodation available for it. At the time of the photo, part of this land was still in use as vegetable gardens, though previously these had been much more extensive. *(TJC)*

Following the purchase of Crystal Coaches in 1984, their base at Hassell Street in Newcastle remained in use. These premises were however very cramped and inadequate. In 1989 the operation moved into a brand-new garage and yard four miles away at Hot Lane Industrial Estate at Burslem. This gave space for extra vehicles, enabling the company to bid for additional tendered bus service work in the area. *(EW)*

Stevensons Fleet List

Fleet No.	Reg. No.	Chassis	Body	Seating	New	Acq	With drawn	Notes
8/1926 to 1940. Note fleet numbers were first allocated at some time between 1938 and 1941								
	RF 2202	Reo Pullman	?	B26F	8/26	New	2/30	Lost in fire
	RA 1765	Reo	?	B20F	3/27	3/27	12/37	(a) Later B24F
	TO 4624	Reo Speed Wagon	?	B18F	3/27	8/27	Post 1934	Later B20F
(3)	TO 4626	Reo Speed Wagon	?	B18F	3/27	8/27	Post 1937?	Later B24F
	RF 1798	?	?	C??	4/26	1/28	?	Ex-Roberts, Newborough
1	RA 4996	Bristol B	Roe	B32F	2/28	2/28	12/52	(b)
	RF 5178	Guy CX 6-wheeler	Guy	B41F	11/28	New	2/30	B36F by 1930, lost in fire
3	RF 7091	Bristol B	Lawton	B32F	4/30	New	4/54	(c)
	VO 390	Minerva	?	B30F	2/29	4/30	?	(d)
	RF 7352	Sunbeam Pathan	Burlingham	C32D	6/30	New	2/41	Scrapped
4	RF 8719	Morris Dictator	Burlingham	C32R	7/31	New	12/52	(e)
	EH 9136	TSM B10A	Lawton	B32F	1/27	?/32	11/44?	(f)
10	CRF 349	Sunbeam Pathan	Burlingham	C32R	3/34	New	2/41	(g)
11	CRE 13	Maudslay SF40	Burlingham	DP40F	7/35	New	9/57	(h)
2	VT 1195	Bristol B	Lawton	B32F	4/28	5/35	By 10/46	(i)
8	TE 4414	Leyland PLC1	Strachan & Brown	B26F	9/28	?/36	11/44?	Ex-Burnley, Colne & Nelson JTC
14	VT 4482	TSM B10A2	?	B34F	3/34	?/36	6/50	(j)
12	EVT 422	Bedford WTB	Duple	C25F	6/37	New	3/60	
	VT 4202	Bristol B (Chassis only, from Milton Bus Co)			2/30	?/37	10/37	(n)
5	VT 6211	TSM B10A2	Lawton	B32F	4/31	?/38	7/44	(k)
6	VT 9766	TSM B39A7	Lawton	C32R	8/33	?/38	4/52	(l)
7	VT 7640	TSM B49A7	Beadle	B35F	3/32	?/38	(m)	Ex-Associated Bus Co, Hanley
9	VT 4759	Leyland LT7	Lawton	B34F	5/30	?/38	12/53	Ex-Tilstone, Tunstall. 32 seats by 3/48

Notes:
(a) Believed to have been ex-Williamson, Heanor (dealer) in 3/27.
(b) Believed to have been ex-Williamson, Heanor (dealer) early in 1928. The body is presumed to have been mounted on the (longer) chassis of ex-Milton Bus VT 4202, lengthened and rebuilt, at an unknown date probably in 1937/8.
(c) In 1951 rebuilt with Gardner 4LW engine, and a 1935 ECOC body ex-North Western RCC, DB 9416, becoming no.7.
(d) New to Bloomfield, Nottingham, acquired ex-Nottingham Corporation.
(e) Rebuilt B35F, re-numbered 21, and received a Leyland radiator in 1948.
(f) Ex-Tilstone, Tunstall (Lawton's first 'overtype' body); carried fleet no.4 in 1944.
(g) Leyland petrol engine fitted at an unknown date. Sold to Worthington Motor Tours, Stafford.
(h) To DP38F c 1946; withdrawn due to accident.
(i) Ex-Tilstone, Tunstall; with Homer (showman) by 4/54.
(j) New to Hawthorn, Stoke-on-Trent, acquired from PMT. Withdrawn, possibly in early 1940s, became a hen house. Rebuilt and fitted with 32 slatted seats in 1944; had a Leyland radiator by 1949.
(k) New to Allen, Sneyd Green, acquired from PMT. Later renumbered 21.
(l) New to Hawthorn, Stoke-on-Trent, acquired from PMT. Fitted with a Leyland radiator in 1945. Rebuilt (possibly B32R) and renumbered 2 in 1947.
(m) VT 7640 was withdrawn at some time between 15/1/50 and 3/7/50.)
(n) This chassis would appear to have been used in the rebuilding of RA 4996

Fleet No.	Reg. No.	Chassis	Body	Seating	New	Acq	With drawn	Notes
From 1941 (Formation of John Stevenson (Uttoxeter) Ltd) to 1950								
	TF 2973	Leyland LT2	Leyland	B32F	8/30	11/43	4/47	Ex-Burnley, Colne & Nelson JTC
15	GO 4307	Leyland LT2	?	B31F	4/31	by 3/44		(a)
16	RA 4517	Bristol B	Roe	B32F	12/27	by 3/44	6/51	(b)
5	RB 6093	Morris Dictator	Reeve & Kenning	DP32F	5/32	9/44	1/51	(c)
17	LRE 199	Guy Arab III 5LW	Park Royal	H30/26R	2/45	New	8/64	
10	WG 37	Leyland TS3	Cowieson	C26F	3/31	By 3/45	?/54	(d)
12A	VD 3432	Leyland LT5A	Leyland	B32R	?/34	9/45	9/56	(e)
6	WG 3256	Leyland LT5A	Alexander	B38F	3/35	By 3/46	9/6/60	(f)
18	MRE 391	Guy Arab III 5LW	Santus	C33F	10/46	New	10/65	Sun roof removed at some time
19	GE 7222	Leyland TD1	Croft	L27/24R	2/30	?/46	7/54	(g)
4	NRE 36	Leyland PD1	Burlingham	H30/26R	3/3/47	New	?/66	
8	PRE 607	Leyland PS 1/1	Barnard	C33F	19/6/48	New	12/69	(h)
20	PRE 608	Leyland PS 1/1	Barnard	C33F	19/6/48	New	6/65	
22	RRF 330	Guy Arab III 6DC	Burlingham	C33F	8/4/49	New	11/65	Gardner 5LW engine later
3	RRF 773	Guy Arab III 6DC	Massey	H30/26R	5/49	New	4/69	(i)
24	WJ 9970	Leyland LT5A	Cravens	C32F	6/34	?/49	5/56	(j)

Notes:

(a) New to Knight, London; later received a Cov-Rad radiator. It was withdrawn at some time between 9/50 and 1/51.

(b) New to Williamson, Heanor, to Midland General then to Lewis (dealer) 1937; possibly acquired before 1944.

(c) New to Truman, Shirebrook. Received a Leyland radiator by 1950.

(d) New to W Alexander & Sons Ltd Falkirk. To War Department use 8/40 to 6/43, passing to Millburn Motors, then to Stevenson 6/44. The body was repaired and modified by Lawton Coachbuilders to C30F, and it entered service by 3/45. Cov-Rad radiator fitted at unknown date.

(e) New to Central SMT, Motherwell. In 1949 received the Willowbrook DP39F body, of 1938, from ERB 92 of Tailby & George, Willington. Renumbered 23 in 1949.

(f) New to W Alexander & Sons Ltd, Falkirk. Received a Gardner 4LW engine in 1951, then a 5LW in 1/54. Renumbered 9 in 1951.

(g) New to Glasgow Corporation with Cowieson H27/24R body, to Young's, Paisley via dealer, re-bodied as noted c 1942, and to Stevensons. Later received a Leyland Retriever radiator, a fully-floating rear axle, and a Gardner 5LW engine.

(h) Received a new Burlingham FC35F body in 1953.

(i) Later fitted with a Gardner 5LW engine, and platform doors by 5/65.

(j) New to A Kitson, Sheffield, passing to Sheffield United Tours Ltd 2/35. Received a new Burlingham C33F body in 1950, and was fitted with a Cov-Rad radiator.

Fleet No.	Reg. No.	Chassis	Body	Seating	New	Acq	With drawn	Notes
			1950 to 1960					
14	AVW 453	Dennis Lancet I 5LW	ECOC	B35R	5/34	7/50	2/57	(a)
15	BOL 38	Daimler COG5	MCCW	B34F	3/36	1/51	21/58	Ex-Birmingham City Transport
5	AOP 59	Daimler COG5	MCCW	B34F	7/35	1/51	6/59	Ex-Birmingham City Transport
6	AOP 70	Daimler COG5	Strachans	B34F	10/35	1/51	3/60	Ex-Birmingham City Transport
16	VRF 139	Leyland PSU1/15	Burlingham	C39C	1/6/51	New	11/70	
2	BOL 32	Daimler COG5	MCCW	B34F	2/36	5/52	3/59	Ex-Birmingham City Transport
25	GVT 508	Leyland TS8	Willowbrook	C35F	2/39	5/52	11/57	(b)
1	EOG 237	Leyland TD6c	English Electric	H28/26R	2/39	12/52	1/64	(c)
26	YRF 871	Bedford SB	Plaxton	C37F	6/53	New	12/69	
21	FA 8532	Guy Arab III 5LW	Guy	B35R	3/47	2/54	6/63	Ex-Burton Corporation
27	FA 8419	Guy Arab III 5LW	Brush	B34F	11/46	2/54	12/64	Ex-Burton Corporation
7	FA 8424	Guy Arab III 5LW	Brush	B34F	11/46	2/54	3/65	Ex-Burton Corporation
28	FA 8420	Guy Arab III 5LW	Brush	B34F	11/46	2/54	6/63	Ex-Burton Corporation
19	FON 326	Leyland TD7	Leyland	H30/26R	5/42	7/54	6/64	Ex-Birmingham City Transport
10	FON 630	Leyland TD7	Leyland	H30/26R	7/42	10/54	2/65	Ex-Birmingham City Transport
24	599 LRE	Bedford SBG	Duple	C41F	5/56	New	9/72	
14	KGK 724	AEC Regent III	Cravens	H30/26R	7/49	4/57	2/72	(d)
23	KGK 725	AEC Regent III	Cravens	H30/26R	8/49	4/57	7/71	(d)
11	ERB 92	Daimler COG5/40	Willowbrook	DP35F	6/38	11/57	12/65	(e)
25	GUS 293	Daimler CVD6	Plaxton	C33F	7/49	6/58	7/66	(f)
15	EP 9503	Guy Arab III 5LW	Duple	C33F	?/47	11/58	2/62	(g)
2	CNU 872	Daimler COG5/40	Willowbrook	DP39F	3/36	2/59	5/64	(e)
5	BRB 645	Daimler COG5/40	Willowbrook	DP39F	12/35	6/59	1/62	(e)
29	KGU 216	Leyland 7RT	Park Royal	H30/26R	6/49	11/59	5/76	(d)
12	4799 RF	Ford 570E	Duple	C41F	6/60	New	4/75	

Notes:

(a) New to Eastern National OC as DP32R; 1940 to Ministry of Works and Buildings, to Wavell (Enterprise Bus Service) Newport, I-O-W, thence to Stevensons. In service by 1/7/50 at least (hires book).

(b) New to Davies, Stoke-on-Trent; had a diesel engine from new.

(c) New to Birmingham City Transport with MCCW body which was destroyed by enemy action. Replaced with this Manchester-style body in 1942.

(d) Ex-London Transport Executive (LTE), via Bird (dealer) in 1/57 (14, 23), or 10/59 (29). Fitted with platform doors in 10/65 (29), 1965 (23), or by 6/65 (14).

(e) New to Tailby and George, Willington. The body on 11, new in 1948, replaced the original Willowbrook DP39F body . Renumbered 23 in 1949.

(f) New to Northern Roadways, Glasgow, to Findlow, Biddulph, then Stevensons. Renumbered 9 in 1951.

(g) New to Mid Wales Motorways, Newtown; acquired via Yeates (dealer), entering service in 12/58.

Fleet No.	Reg. No.	Chassis	Body	Seating	New	Acq	With drawn	Notes
			1961 to 11/1971					
9	HTF 822	Leyland PD2/1	Leyland	H30/26R	11/47	1/61	7/70	(a)
6	KWB 86	AEC Regent III	NCB	H30/26R	11/47	3/61	12/65	New to Sheffield Corporation
30	KUE 950	AEC Regal IV	Burlingham	B44F	8/51	11/61	6/68	New to De Luxe Buses, Mancetter
5	UBA 554	AEC Reliance	Yeates	C41F	8/61	3/62	8/76	New to Hankinson, Salford
15	50 AMC	AEC Reliance	Park Royal	B44F	7/53	11/62	6/67	(b)
28	GAY 171	Leyland PS1/1	Willowbrook	DP35F	5/50	5/63	6/72	Ex-Allen, Mountsorrel
21	GAY 170	Leyland PS1/1	Willowbrook	DP35F	5/50	6/63	6/72	(c) Ex-Allen, Mountsorrel
1	RWT 613	Guy Arab UF	Burlingham	B44F	3/56	1/64	2/72	(d) Ex-Morgan (Blue Line), Armthorpe
2	DJP 841	Leyland PSUC1/2T	Plaxton	C41F	6/58	5/64	3/73	Ex-Florence Excursions, Morecambe
19	RVM 37	Daimler D650HS	Duple	C41C	6/55	7/64	7/69	Ex-Lock, Stonehouse
17	LYF 65	Leyland 7RT	Park Royal	H30/26R	2/51	10/64	6/75	(e)
10	HLW 203	AEC Regent III	Weymann	H30/26R	11/47	2/65	5/71	(e)
27	MXX 371	Guy Special	ECW	B26F	6/54	3/65	10/72	(e)
20	DHE 347	Leyland PSU1/9	Brush	B43F	5/51	6/65	8/72	(f)
7	DHE 352	Leyland PSU1/9	Brush	B43F	5/51	10/65	3/70	(f)
18	DHE 339	Leyland PSU1/9	Brush	B43F	5/51	11/65	5/72	(f)

Fleet No.	Reg. No.	Chassis	Body	Seating	New	Acq	With drawn	Notes
22	DHE 342	Leyland PSU1/9	Brush	B43F	5/51	11/65	5/71	(f)
11	KLB 908	Leyland 6RT	Leyland	H30/26R	12/49	1/66	10/77	(e)
25	HJU 546	Leyland PSU1/9	Leyland	B44F	5/52	4/66	11/73	(g)
6	VBF 118D	Ford R192	Duple	C45F	6/66	New	4/76	
30	EHE 160	Leyland PSU1/13	Roe	B43F	8/52	2/67	6/74	(h)
15	KGU 69	Leyland 7RT	MCCW	H30/26R	12/49	6/67	10/68	(i)
15	KXW 110	AEC Regent III	Weymann	H30/26R	1/50	3/68	6/71	(j)
4	CTT 423C	AEC Reliance	Duple Northern	C51F	3/65	6/68	7/80	Ex-Trathen, Yelverton
	ORE 576F	Ford Transit	Martin Walter	B12-	6/68	New	4/73	
3	TTT 780	AEC Regent V	MCCW	H33/26RD	7/56	9/68	10/77	(k)
	ROD 770	AEC Regent V	MCCW	H33/26R	1/56	12/68	?	Ex-Devon General, not operated
	URF 690G	BMC 250JU	BMC	B12-	5/69	New	4/73	
19	JEE 123	Leyland PSUC1/2	Duple	C41F	?/57	7/69	4/73	Ex-Stark, Tetney
8	966 CWL	AEC Regent V	Weymann	H37/28R	3/58	1/70	8/77	(l) Re-seated to 41/32 before 2/70
9	959 AJO	AEC Regent V	Park Royal	H33/28R	5/57	5/70	3/78	(l)
26	DHD 192	AEC Reliance	Park Royal	B43F	?/59	10/70	12/74	(m)
7	DHD 193	AEC Reliance	Park Royal	B43F	?/59	10/70	9/76	(m)
16	DEK 106	Leyland PD2/20	Massey	H32/26R	10/57	10/70	7/78	(n)
10	564 FTF	Leyland PD3/4	MCCW	H41/32R	9/58	3/71	10/78	(o)
15	1500 WJ	Leyland L1	Weymann	C41F	7/59	6/71	6/79	(p)
1	1501 WJ	Leyland L1	Weymann	C41F	8/59	6/71	4/78	(p)
22	CLT 95H	Ford R226	Plaxton	C53F	4/70	6/71	3/78	Ex-Thorpe, London
23	3908 WE	Leyland PD3/1	Roe	H41/32RD	6/59	7/71	12/79	Ex-Sheffield Corp, to service 10/71
17	3914 WE	Leyland PD3/1	Roe	H41/32RD	6/59	7/71	7/79	Ex-Sheffield Corp, to service 11/71

Notes:

(a) Ex-Accrington Corporation; platform doors fitted 3/64.

(b) New to ACV, Southall, as the original AEC Reliance demonstrator. The body was completed by Roe on Park Royal frames. Ex-Armstrong, Newcastle upon Tyne; fitted for one man operation.

(c) Towing vehicle by 2/73, also used as tree-lopper 6/73-1974; Preserved.

(d) Tree-lopper during 1972.

(e) Ex-London Transport, doors fitted 10/64 (17), 1965 (10), 1966 (11). 27 was fitted for one man operation. No.11 is preserved.

(f) Ex-Yorkshire Traction Co Ltd, Barnsley (20 via Hulley, Baslow – not operated by them); equipped for one man operation.

(g) New to Allen, Mountsorrel, acquired from BMMO.

(h) Ex-Yorkshire Traction Co Ltd, via Green Bus Co, Rugeley (not operated by them). Tree-cutting/towing vehicle from 10/74, scrapped 7/77.

(i) Ex-London Transport; badly damaged in accident, stripped for spares, and scrapped.

(j) New to London Transport; acquired from Gibson, Barlestone. Platform doors fitted 10/68 when it entered service.

(k) Ex-Devon General; became Tree-cutting/ towing vehicle 12/77 numbered 3A, later 05.

(l) Ex-City of Oxford Motor Services. Platform doors fitted as follows – no.8 before entering service in 2/70, no.9 8/70.

(m) New to Yorkshire Woollen; acquired from Smythe, London (7), Drewery, Woodford Bridge (26).

(n) New to Wigan Corporation. Platform doors fitted 10/68 when it entered service. Sold for preservation.

(o) Ex-Lancashire United Transport. Platform doors fitted in 1971, entered service in 5/71. Sold for preservation, but scrapped in April 2015.

(p) Ex-Sheffield Corporation, to service 8/71 (15), 9/71 (1).

Stevensons of Uttoxeter Limited 11/1971 to 12/1975

Fleet No.	Reg. No.	Chassis	Body	Seating	New	Acq	With drawn	Notes
	NPT 597D	Ford Transit	Stevensons	B12-	?/66	2/72	12/73	(a)
24	WCD 72	Leyland PD2/37	Weymann	H33/28R	3/59	3/72	7/79	(b) Re-numbered 24A, 6/79
18	5907 W	Leyland L1	Burlingham	DP41F	7/60	3/72	7/78	(c) Re-numbered 18A 3/78
20	5909 W	Leyland L1	Burlingham	DP41F	8/60	3/72	8/76	(c)
28	1914 WA	Leyland L1	Weymann	C41F	4/61	3/72	10/78	(c)
27	6349 WJ	AEC Regent V	Roe	H39/30RD	4/60	6/72	10/76	(c)
21	LRE 783K	Ford R192	Duple	C45F	7/72	New	12/82	Re-numbered 16, 1/81
31	6306 W	Leyland L1	Weymann	B44F	7/60	11/72	10/80	(c) Re-numbered 31A in 9/80
2	6307 W	Leyland L1	Weymann	B44F	7/60	11/72	2/80	(c) Re-numbered 2A in 2/80
	TRE 321L	Ford Transit	Deansgate	B12	4/73	New	4/76	
	VRF 260L	Ford Transit	Moseley	B12	5/73	New	10/76	
19	VRF 338L	Ford R1114	Plaxton	C49F	5/73	New	11/83	(d)
32	SFA 82	Daimler CCG5	Massey	H33/28R	3/63	8/73	3/77	Ex-Burton-upon-Trent Corporation
33	SFA 84	Daimler CCG5	Massey	H33/28R	3/63	8/73	3/77	Ex-Burton-upon-Trent Corporation
34	DFC 365D	AEC Renown	Park Royal	H38/27F	5/66	11/73	3/79	Ex-City of Oxford MS
25	WBF 842M	Seddon Pennine 6	Duple	C57F	3/74	New	4/77	
	DRE 569E	Bedford J1Z2H	Hawson	B12	?/67	6/74	5/77	
30	KRA 200D	Bedford SB5	Plaxton	C41F	3/66	6/74	5/79	Ex-Stubbs, Manchester
12	EMB 159K	Ford R226	Plaxton	C53F	4/72	10/74	8/80	(e) Ex-Shearing Group, Altrincham
35	EMB 162K	Ford R226	Plaxton	C53F	4/72	10/74	8/80	(f) Ex-Shearing Group, Altrincham
26	VHE 205	Leyland PD3A/1	NCME	H41/32F	6/61	11/74	1/81	Ex-Middleton, Rugeley

Fleet No.	Reg. No.	Chassis	Body	Seating	New	Acq	With drawn	Notes
36	JRF 785N	Bedford YRT	Duple	C53F	5/75	New	5/80	
	TVW 156E	Ford Transit	Ford	B12	?/67	7/75	12/75	(a)
	LUT 899F	Bedford J1Z2H	Hawson	B12	?/68	7/75	5/77	
14	204 BTP	Leyland PDR1/1 Mark II	MCCW	H43/33F	6/63	8/75	1/81	Ex-Portsmouth via East Staffs District Council
29	NJW 709E	AEC Swift	Strachans	B54D	6/67	12/75	2/81	(g)

Notes:
(a) Acquired as non-PSV and converted to PSV standards.
(b) Ex-Brighton Corporation, entering service 5/72.
(c) Ex-Sheffield Corporation, entering service 5/72 (18, 28), 8/72 (20), 11/72 (27), 3/73 (2), 4/73 (31).
(d) Re-numbered 11 in 4/80. Sold via Yeates (dealer) to unidentified operator, Famagusta, Cyprus.
(e) 4/80 re-numbered 12A.
(f) 5/80 re-numbered 35A.
(g) New to Wolverhampton Corporation, to West Midlands PTE, acquired from Sykes (dealer), Barnsley. Re-built to B58F prior to entry into service in 5/76; had new lower front panel c 1978.

				1976 – 1980				
5	NTU 178L	Ford R1114	Plaxton	C53F	5/73	1/76	7/84	(a) Ex-Jackson, Altrincham
7	217 BTP	Leyland PDR1/1 Mark II	MCCW	H43/33F	7/63	4/76	7/81	(b) Ex-City of Portsmouth
27	219 BTP	Leyland PDR1/1 Mark II	MCCW	H43/33F	7/63	4/76	12/82	(b) Ex-City of Portsmouth
6	OEH 512P	Ford R1014	Duple	C45F	5/76	New	2/84	No.15, from 1/81, later 18, 18A
--	OFA 325P	Ford Transit	Tricentrol	B12	c6/76	New	7/77	Was non-PSV with Stevensons
39	OEA 519P	Ford Transit	Tricentrol	B12	8/76	New	7/83	No.26 from 9/81, later 55
20	CHG 551C	Leyland PD2A/27	East Lancs	H37/27F	9/65	9/76	7/83	(c) To service 8/76; later 31, 51
3	PCW 942	Leyland PD2A/27	NCME	H37/27F	1/64	10/76	1/82	(c) To service 10/76; later 32, 32A
--	PCW 943	Leyland PD2A/27	NCME	H37/27F	1/64	9/76	?	(c) Not operated
32	PCW 944	Leyland PD2A/27	NCME	H37/27F	1/64	10/76	3/80	(c) To service 6/77. 9/81 to 32A
8	PCW 945	Leyland PD2A/27	NCME	H37/27F	1/64	10/76	10/81	(c) To service 10/76. 1/81 to 28
33	CHG 548C	Leyland PD2A/27	East Lancs	H37/27F	9/65	10/76	5/82	(c) To service 10/76. Later 33A, 53
9	PCW 946	Leyland PD2A/27	NCME	H37/27F	1/64	11/76	9/90	(c) To service 10/76. 1/81 to 29
37	XMA 210M	Ford R1114	Plaxton	C53F	6/74	12/76	11/83	(d) To service 4/77. 1/81 to no.10
25	TEH 761R	Ford R1114	Plaxton	C53F	4/77	New	12/83	No.8 from 1/81
40	TRF 411R	Ford Transit	Dormobile	B16	5/77	New	9/80	
38	JCB 234	Bedford VAS5	Plaxton	C29F	7/73	7/77	4/81	(e) Ex-JC Bamford, Rocester
11	DGE 339C	Leyland PDR1/1	Alexander	H44/34F	12/65	9/77	9/79	(f) Ex-Greater Glasgow PTE
16	XRE 305S	Leyland PSU3E/4R	Plaxton	C53F	10/77	New	BB	(h) (BB = passed to British Bus in June 1994)
18	6 MPT	Leyland PSU3/3R	Plaxton	B55F	3/64	12/77	10/82	(g) To service 2/78
22	JLG 559L	Ford R1114	Plaxton	C53F	3/75	2/78	2/85	(d) 1/81 became no.9
1	PUP 123P	Bedford SB5	Duple	C41F	2/76	3/78	3/80	Ex-Hunt, Sunderland
24	FHG 158E	Leyland PD2A/27	East Lancs	H37/27F	1/67	5/78	4/83	(c) To service 9/78 1/81 to no.30
10	FVO 428D	Leyland PSU3E/3RT	Weymann	DP53F	5/66	8/78	11/80	(i) To service 12/78
28	FVO 434D	Leyland PSU3E/3RT	Weymann	DP53F	4/66	8/78	8/81	(i) To service 11/78
--	207 BTP	Leyland PDR1/1 Mark II	MCCW	H43/33F	6/63	2/79	--	(j) Not operated
--	208 BTP	Leyland PDR1/1 Mark II	MCCW	H43/33F	6/63	2/79	--	(j) Not operated
34	OKM 145G	Leyland PDR1/1 Mark II	Massey	H43/31F	7/68	3/79	7/81	(k) To service 3/79
30	OKM 146G	Leyland PDR1/1 Mark II	Massey	H43/31F	9/68	3/79	7/82	(k) To service 3/79. Later 37, 37A
23	JKE 335E	Leyland PDR1/1 Mark II	Massey	H43/31F	3/67	4/79	12/82	(k) To service 4/79. Later 38, 53
15	JKE 339E	Leyland PDR1/1 Mark II	Massey	H43/31F	2/67	4/79	4/82	(k) To service 6/79. Later 35, 35A
11	NKK 243F	Leyland PDR1/1 Mark II	Massey	H43/31F	3/68	4/79	7/82	(k) To service 5/79. Later 36, 36A
45	JGF 196K	Daimler CRG6LXB	Park Royal	H44/24D	11/71	7/79	6/90	(l) (m)
47	JGF 241K	Daimler CRG6LXB	Park Royal	H44/24D	1/72	7/79	12/89	(l) (m). Later 37
48	JGF 298K	Daimler CRG6LXB	Park Royal	H44/24D	1/72	7/79	1/91	(l) (m). Later 38
42	JGF 314K	Daimler CRG6LXB	Park Royal	H44/24D	2/72	7/79	7/88	(l) (m)
17	JGU 284K	Daimler CRG6LXB	MCW	H44/24D	8/72	7/79	2/90	(l) (n). Later 41
46	MLH 303L	Daimler CRG6LXB	MCW	H44/24D	10/72	7/79	7/90	(l) (m)
44	MLH 315L	Daimler CRG6LXB	MCW	H44/24D	10/72	7/79	11/89	(l) (m)
--	JGF 362K	Daimler CRG6LXB	Park Royal	H44/24D	6/72	9/79	-	(l) Not operated
43	MLK 457L	Daimler CRG6LXB	Park Royal	H44/24D	10/72	10/79	10/90	(l) (m)
17	NGD 971P	Ford R1014	Plaxton	C45F	2/76	11/79	10/83	(o)
2	LBF 454V	Ford R1114	Plaxton	C53F	2/80	New	5/82	(p)
1	LFA 872V	Leyland PSU3E/4R	Duple	C53F	2/80	New	11/88	2/86 to no.102, 1/87 to AEH 607A
3	MRE 530V	Ford R1114	Plaxton	C53F	3/80	New	6/83	To service 5/80; burnt out 6/83
19	HHA 163L	Ford R192	Plaxton	B45F	12/72	7/80	11/83	Ex-Midland Red

174

Fleet No.	Reg. No.	Chassis	Body	Seating	New	Acq	With drawn	Notes
20	HHA 173L	Ford R192	Plaxton	B45F	12/72	7/80	11/83	Ex-Midland Red
4	NVT 451W	Ford R1114	Plaxton	C53F	8/80	New	8/85	
5	NVT 452W	Ford R1114	Plaxton	C53F	8/80	New	5/85	
--	8859 VR	AEC Regent V	Neepsend	H41/32R	1/64	9/80	11/80	(q)
60	8860 VR	AEC Regent V	Neepsend	H41/32R	1/64	9/80	12/80	(q)
21	MUS 103P	Leyland PSU3C/4R	Duple	B53F	12/75	11/80	4/92	(r)
22	TGD 218R	Leyland PSU3C/4R	Duple	B53F	12/76	11/80	3/91	(r)
23	GUS 368N	Ford R1014	Duple	B46F	11/74	11/80	9/84	(s)
50	PFA 50W	Bristol VRTSL3/6LXB	ECW	CH41/29F	11/80	New	9/88	13ft 8ins high

Notes:
(a) Later no.12.
(b) To service 6/76 (7), 9/76 (27).
(c) Ex-Burnley & Pendle JTC. In 7/81 PCW 945 converted to tree-lopper/recovery vehicle becoming 028.
(d) Ex-Shearings Holidays, Altrincham; 22 received the Trent Valley livery for a while.
(e) 6/80 re-registered YVT 937M, later re-numbered 23.
(f) Entered service in 10/77.
(g) New to Stanhope Motor Services, Stanhope, acquired from The Eden Bus Services, West Auckland; entered service in 2/78. Currently preserved.
(h) Delivered 10/77 and stored, entered service 3/78. 1/81 became no.7; 4/86 fitted for one-man-operation, re-registered 422 AKN, later VOV 926S.
(i) New to East Midland Motor Services, Chesterfield.
(j) Ex-City of Portsmouth.
(k) Ex-Maidstone Borough Council via TPE (dealer) Macclesfield. Purchased 1/79 but arrived at Stevensons ready painted on the dates shown in the fleetlist. To service 3/79 (30/4), 4/79 (23), 5/79 (11), 6/79 (15).
(l) Ex-London Transport Executive (LTE); 17, 44 and 46 direct from LTE, the remainder via Wombwell Diesels (dealer).
(m) Rebuilt to H44/29F and to service 9/79 (42), 1/80 (44), 2/80 (43), 8/80 (45), 10/80 (46). 11/80 (47), 1/81 (48).
(n) Ex-LTE; entered service 9/79 as H44/24D, re-seated to 44/28 in 1/80, and re-built to H44/29F in 5/82.
(o) New to Northern Roadways, Glasgow; bought from Salopia, Whitchurch.
(p) Sometimes operated as an 'executive' with tables.
(q) On loan from Maynes, Manchester, 8860 VR was purchased becoming no.60.
(r) Ex-Garelochhead Coach Services, Garelochhead, entering service in 12/80 (21), 9/81 (22). 21 was withdrawn in 10/83, converted to Leyland PSU3E/4R standard, and received a new Plaxton C46FT body in 1984, returning to service in 8/84 as no.12. 11/84 re-registered TFA 13. To C53F 12/86. 22 was withdrawn in 8/84, converted as no. 21, and received a new Plaxton C53F body in 1984, returning to service in 3/85 as no.9. Re-registered 961 PEH in 6/85.
(s) Ex-Garelochhead Motor Services, Garelochhead, entering service 8/81.

1981-1982

Fleet No.	Reg. No.	Chassis	Body	Seating	New	Acq	With drawn	Notes
--	YYS 254H	Leyland PSU3/3R	Plaxton	C51F	7/70	1/81	-	Not operated (Ex-Garelochhead)
--	PTW 168K	Ford R192	Plaxton	B44F	1/72	1/81	-	Not operated (Ex-Garelochhead)
28	RCN 699	AEC Routemaster	Park Royal	H41/31F	4/64	1/81	5/86	(a)
--	JRV 504F	AEC Reliance	Plaxton	C51F	6/68	1/81	-	Ex-Middleton, Rugeley, not operated
6	PFA 6W	Leyland PSU3E/4R	Plaxton	C53F	2/81	New	8/94	(b)
31	THM 708M	Daimler CRL6/30	MCW	H44/27D	9/74	3/81	9/82	(c) Withdrawn 9/82, accident damage
49	THM 711M	Daimler CRL6/30	MCW	H44/27D	10/74	3/81	8/90	(c) Later 39.
40	THM 716M	Daimler CRL6/30	MCW	H44/27D	10/74	4/81	12/89	(c)
32	GUM 704N	Daimler CRL6	MCW	H44/27D	1/75	4/81	7/90	(c)
33	KUC 973P	Leyland FE30ALR	MCW	H44/24D	5/76	9/81	7/90	(c)
34	KUC 974P	Leyland FE30ALR	MCW	H44/24D	5/76	9/81	3/91	(c)
24	OJD 89R	Bristol LH6L	ECW	B45F	4/77	10/81	2/84	(e)
49	UVT 49X	Bristol VRTSL3/6LXB	ECW	CH41/29F	10/81	New	9/88	13ft 8ins high
--	TGX 754M	Daimler CRL6/30	Park Royal	H44/24D	12/73	11/81	-	(c) Not operated
38	THM 689M	Daimler CRL6/30	MCW	H44/24D	10/74	11/81	3/91	(c) (d) Later 31, CBF 31Y.
35	JGU 251K	Daimler CRG6LXB	MCW	H44/27F	8/72	2/82	3/90	(f)
36	MLK 445L	Daimler CRG6LXB	Park Royal	H44/27F	9/72	2/82	8/88	(f)
37	MLK 449L	Daimler CRG6LXB	Park Royal	H44/27F	10/72	2/82	2/90	(f) Later 62, 55.
13	UVT 13X	Leyland TRCTL11/2R	Plaxton	C53F	3/82	New	2/90	
14	UVT 14X	Leyland TRCTL11/2R	Plaxton	C53F	3/82	New	2/89	
16	MFR 41P	Leyland PSU4C/2R	Alexander AY	B45F	2/76	4/82	BB	(g) (BB= passed to British Bus in July 1994)
--	THM 540M	Daimler CRL6/30	MCW	H44/24D	11/73	5/82	-	(c) Not operated
--	THM 552M	Daimler CRL6/30	MCW	H44/24D	12/73	5/82	7/82	(c) Operated for a short while
52	THM 586M	Daimler CRL6/30	MCW	H44/24D	1/74	5/82	10/82	(c)
--	BNC 879B	Leyland PD3A/2	Massey	H41/29F	1/62	7/82	-	(h) Not operated
--	OJD 163R	Leyland FE30AGR	Park Royal	H44/24D	12/76	7/82	-	(c) Not operated
26	OJD 133R	Leyland FE30AGR	Park Royal	H44/24D	10/76	8/82	3/91	(c)
27	OJD 136R	Leyland FE30AGR	Park Royal	H44/24D	10/76	8/82	8/90	(c)
28	OJD 151R	Leyland FE30AGR	Park Royal	H44/24D	2/77	8/82	8/92	(c)
52	OUC 42R	Leyland FE30AGR	MCW	H44/24D	11/76	9/82	12/89	(i) 10/85 re-numbered 82
--	OUC 51R	Leyland FE30AGR	MCW	H44/24D	11/76	9/82	-	(c) Not operated
18	WTE 351T	Leyland PSU3E/4R	Plaxton	C53F	5/79	10/82	11/88	(j)

Fleet No.	Reg. No.	Chassis	Body	Seating	New	Acq	With drawn	Notes
--	EGP 81J	Daimler CRG6LXB	Park Royal	H44/24D	3/71	11/82	-	(c) Not operated
30	PAX 466F	Leyland PD3/4	Massey	L35/33RD	6/68	11/82	8/94	(k)
16	LAB 101T	Leyland PSU5C/4R	Plaxton	C32FT	3/79	12/82	8/89	(l) 11/86 re-registered AEH 560A
48	BTX 540J	Bristol VRTSL6G	NCME	H44/33F	4/71	12/82	6/84	(m)
--	HRE 683K	Seddon Pennine 6	Plaxton	C55F	3/72	12/82	-	(n) Not operated

Notes:

(a) Ex-Northern General, to service 7/81; 2/83 re-numbered 52. Now preserved.

(b) The chassis was intended to have a horse box body fitted for J Mowlem & Company, Brentford, but was acquired from them as a chassis. To Viking livery 2/88.

(c) Ex-London Transport Executive via Ensign (dealer). Many re-built to H44/29F as follows: 11/81 (33), 4/82 (34), 10/82 (27), ?/82 (OJD 163R), 1/83 (26/8), 12/84 (52), 5/81 (31), 8/81 (32), 9/81 (49), 5/86 (40). To service in 5/81 (31, 49), 6/81 (40), 9/81 (34), 10/81 (32), 2/82 (33), 11/82 (52-THM 586M), 12/82 (27), 4/83 (28), 1/83 (38), 5/83 (26). Gardner 6LXB engines fitted in 8/82 (33), 11/82 (40), 12/82 (49), 2/83 (32), c7/84 (34), 9/84 (38).

(d) 38 (THM 689M) had its chassis re-built using parts from other similar vehicles, the new chassis number being SBS/FEL/001. In 10/82 the body was re-built to H44/29F, and the vehicle entered service in 2/83 as CBF 31Y, with fleet number 31.

(e) Ex-London Transport Executive (LTE).

(f) New to LTE, re-built by Ensign to H44/27F for OK Motor Services, Bishop Auckland, from where they were purchased.

(g) Ex-Lancaster City Council. To service 8/82, and received the coach seats from VYS 254H in 8/82 becoming DP45F. Renumbered 25 (1/83), 65 (4/85).

(h) New to Wigan Corporation, acquired from Greater Manchester PTE.

(i) New to LTE, operated by CK Coaches, Cardiff; to PR Whaddon, Caerphilly, and re-built to H44/29F before sale to Stevensons.

(j) New to Monks, Leigh. 1/83 became no.15, re-registered 82 HBC in 2/85.

(k) New to Bedwas and Machen UDC, passing to Rhymney Valley DC in 4/74. Although in the Stevensons' fleet, it was owned by Julian Peddle personally. 3/86 Leyland 0.680 engine fitted from KUC 933P; no.30 is now preserved.

(l) Ex-Everton Coaches, Droitwich; re-seated to C55F in 6/83.

(m) New to Gelligaer UDC, passing to Rhymney Valley DC in 4/74. To service with Stevensons in 1/83.

(n) New to Green Bus Company, Rugeley, passing via various operators to Stevensons.

1983

Fleet No.	Reg. No.	Chassis	Body	Seating	New	Acq	With drawn	Notes
83	OUC 44R	Leyland FE30AGR	MCW	H44/24D	11/76	1/83	5/89	(a) Numbered 83 in 10/85
53	OUC 53R	Leyland FE30AGR	MCW	H44/24D	12/76	1/83	4/91	(a)
--	EGP 107J	Daimler CRG6LXB	Park Royal	H44/24D	4/71	1/83	-	(a) Not operated
--	MLH 454L	Daimler CRG6LXB	Park Royal	H44/24D	6/73	3/83	-	(a) Not operated
--	OJD 131R	Leyland FE30AGR	Park Royal	H44/24D	10/76	3/83	-	(a) Not operated
--	OJD 162R	Leyland FE30AGR	Park Royal	H44/24D	3/77	3/83	-	(a) Not operated
47	OUC 47R	Leyland FE30AGR	MCW	H44/24D	11/76	3/83	8/88	(a) Numbered 47 in 4/84
2	CBF 2Y	Leyland TRCTL11/2R	Plaxton	C53F	3/83	New	8/89	
--	EGP 18J	Daimler CRG6LXB	Park Royal	H44/24D	1/71	5/83	-	(a) Not operated
--	EGP 120J	Daimler CRG6LXB	Park Royal	H44/24D	7/71	5/83	-	(a) Not operated
21	LPT 902P	Leyland PSU3C/4R	Willowbrook	B55F	8/75	5/03	3/88	(b) Re-numbered 61 in 4/85
54	82 HBC	Leyland PD3A/1	East Lancs	H41/33RD	3/64	6/83	5/87	(c) Re-numbered 54A in 5/87
99	Q246 FVT	Leyland ONLXB/1R	ECW	H43/30F	?/79	6/83	BB	(d)
56	CNB 854T	Ford Transit	Deansgate	B12	?/79	6/83	9/84	(e)
--	XRD 23K	Bristol VRTLL6G	NCME	H47/30D	9/71	7/83	9/83	(f)
20	HUP 132N	Leyland PSU3B/4R	Willowbrook	B55F	3/75	8/83	6/87	(g) Re-numbered 60 in 4/85
55	JRC 168V	Ford Transit	Ford	C8R	?/80	9/83	8/85	(h)
3	WYX 320G	Leyland PSU3A/4R	Plaxton	C51F	2/69	10/83	12/83	(i)
17	XNE 886L	Leyland PSU3B/4R	Plaxton	C53F	7/73	10/83	11/92	(j) Re-numbered 23 in 5/85
8	OTD 828R	Leyland PSU3D/4R	Plaxton	C51F	7/77	10/83	BB	(k)
10	LMA 60P	Leyland PSU3C/4R	Plaxton	C51F	7/75	12/83	BB	(l)
11	LMA 61P	Leyland PSU3C/4R	Plaxton	C51F	7/75	12/83	BB	(l)

Notes:

(a) Ex-LTE via Ensign (dealer); the following were re-built to H44/29F in 6/83 (53), 12/83 (OJD 131R, 47), 12/84 (83). The following entered service in 6/83 (53), 4/84 (47), 10/85 (83). 53 was loaned to Pegg, Rotherham at various dates between 6/89 and 8/89.

(b) Was new to Trimdon Motor Services, Trimdon Grange, acquired from Everton, Droitwich.

(c) New to Leicester Corporation, acquired from Astill & Jordan, Ratby, where it was fitted with platform doors in 11/79. In 2/85 was re-registered RRF 109B.

(d) Stevensons acquired this un-registered prototype Olympian test bed in an un-finished state, fitted panelling, seats, and completed the electrics. The vehicle was classified as a 'Morgan' when registered and entered service in 1/85.

(e) Ex-Main Street Carpets, Newhall; operated as a non-PSV by Stevensons.

(f) Ex-Reading Corporation; loaned to Berresford's Cheddleton in 7/83 before sale.

(g) Ex-Trimdon Motor Services, Trimdon Grange.

(h) Ex-Betamax Construction, Derby; operated as a non-PSV by Stevensons.

(i) Ex-Lacey, East Ham, London; was used to test the possible fitment of a Gardner engine in a Leyland Leopard chassis.

(j) Ex-Greater Manchester PTE, entered service in 12/83, temporarily numbered 11.

(k) Ex-Greater Manchester PTE; entered service in 12/83, re-seated to 53 in 12/84. Post-1992, re-registered AAX 562A.

(l) Ex-Selwyn, Runcorn. Later re-registered 488 BDN (10), YSG 339 (11).

1984

Fleet No.	Reg. No.	Chassis	Body	Seating	New	Acq	With drawn	Notes
--	RYA 700L	Bristol VRTSL6G	ECW	H44/31F	6/73	1/84	-	(a) Not operated
48	AJA 418L	Bristol VRTSL6G	ECW	H43/32F	?/73	2/84	7/87	(b)
51	AJA 421L	Bristol VRTSL6G	ECW	H43/32F	?/73	2/84	8/87	(b)
3	A53 HRE	Leyland TRCTL11/2R	Plaxton	C53F	3/84	New	7/88	
--	EGP 40J	Daimler CRG6LXB	Park Royal	H44/24D	1/71	3/84	-	(c) Not operated
--	JGF 307K	Daimler CRG6LXB	Park Royal	H44/24D	2/72	3/84	-	(c) Not operated

Fleet No.	Reg. No.	Chassis	Body	Seating	New	Acq	With drawn	Notes
24	MFR 125P	Leyland PSU4C/2R	Alexander AYS	B45F	2/76	3/84	BB	(d) Re-numbered 64, 4/85
18	MFR 18P	Leyland PSU3C/2R	Alexander AY	C49F	2/76	4/84	BB	(d) Re-numbered 68, 2/87
61	HWU 61N	Leyland PSU5A/4R	Plaxton	C57F	6/75	4/84	5/92	(e)
--	SHG 128K	Seddon RU 6HLX	Pennine	DP42F	6/72	5/84	-	(f) Not operated
--	MLH 460L	Daimler CRG6LXB	MCW	H44/27F	6/73	5/84	-	(g) Not operated
91	MLH 584L	Daimler CRL6/30	Park Royal	H44/27F	4/73	5/84	7/88-	(g) Numbered 91, 11/85
19	MWJ 469P	Leyland PSU3C/4R	Duple	C53F	5/76	7/84	3/85	(f)
--	MGA 747E	Leyland PSU3/3RT	Plaxton	C47F	5/67	8/84	-	(h) Not operated
74	GJU 853V	Ford Transit	Moseley	B12F	1/80	8/84	4/87	(i) Re-numbered 174, 3/87
55	HNK 145G	Leyland PSU3A/4R	Plaxton	C51F	5/69	9/84	8/86	(j) (k)
71	VRF 660S	Ford Transit	Deansgate	C12F	10/77	9/84	12/89	(j) (l) Re-numbered 171, 3/87
72	XRE 10S	Ford Transit	Deansgate	B12F	3/78	9/84	by ?/90	(j) Re-numbered 172, 3/87
76	SDK 96S	Ford A0609	Dormobile	C25F	?/78	9/84	1/88	(j) (m) Re-numbered 176, 2/87
70	SVT 783R	Ford Transit	Deansgate	C12F	2/80	9/84	12/89	(j) (n) Re-numbered 170, 3/87
73	ORE 830W	Ford Transit	Crystal	B12F	9/80	9/84	7/88	(j) (o) Re-numbered 173. 3/87
--	ONF 893H	Daimler CRG6LXB	MCW	H47/29D	?/70	9/84	1/85	(p)
--	TGX 710M	Daimler CRL6/30	Park Royal	H44/27F	9/73	9/84	-	(g) Not operated
17	TWH 687T	Leyland PSU3E/4R	Plaxton	C51F	10/78	9/84	BB	(q) Later re-registered WYR 562
19	YBN 629V	Leyland PSU3E/4R	Plaxton	C51F	8/79	9/84	6/87	(q)
20	YBN 630V	Leyland PSU3E/4R	Plaxton	C51F	8/79	9/84	7/88	(q)
22	XNE 882L	Leyland PSU3B/4R	Plaxton	C45F	?/73	10/84	7/92	(r) Re-numbered 62, 2/86
23	MFR 126P	Leyland PSU4C/2R	Alexander AYS	B45F	2/76	10/84	BB	(d) Re-numbered 63, 4/85
90	MLK 635L	Daimler CRL6/30	Park Royal	H44/27F	5/73	10/84	3/90	(g) Numbered 90, 11/85; 90A, 10/89
1	APP 264K	Leyland PSU3B/4R	Plaxton	C49F	8/71	11/84	10/89	(s) Numbered 1 in 5/86.

Notes:

(a) New to Hutchings and Cornelius, South Petherton as H39/31F; to West Wales Motors, Tycroes where it was altered to 44/31.

(b) Ex-Greater Manchester PTE. 48 was fitted with power steering by Alder Valley Engineering in 12/84.

(c) Ex-LTE via Ensign (dealer).

(d) Ex-Lancaster City Council. 18 was re-seated to DP49F in 1/87, then DP45F in 11/87, and to B53F in 1988.

(e) Ex-Berline Coaches, Gloucester, entering service in 5/84. Re-numbered 21 in 4/85, re-registered 488 BDN in 6/85, and in 1986 was fitted for one-man-operation. Re-numbered 119 in 12/87.

(f) New to Burnley, Colne & Nelson JOC; acquired from Errington (dealer), Evington.

(g) Now to LTE, passing to Lancashire United Transport, then Greater Manchester PTE; all were re-built to H44/27F by Ensign.

(h) Ex-Webber, Blisland.

(i) Ex-Jalna Coaches, Church Gresley.

(j) Ex-Crystal Coaches, Newcastle-under-Lyme.

(k) Re-numbered 24 in 4/85, then 105 in 10/85.

(l) The body was completely re-built by Stevensons, using the original running units, becoming Stevensons C12F.

(m) New to Les Bywater, Rochdale, then to Roy Lewis Taxis (Coventry) and Yeates (dealer).

(n) New in 5/77 to Lunt, May Bank, to Crystal in 9/80. It was completely re-built by Stevensons using a new Ford body shell, and the original running units. Re-registered Q248 FVT in 4/85.

(o) New to Durber, Newcastle-under-Lyme as ERE 858N with Deansgate B12F body. It passed to Crystal in 9/80 where it was fitted with a new Crystal 12-seat body using the original running parts, and was re-registered ORE 830W at that time.

(p) New to South East Lancashire and North East Cheshire Passenger Transport Executive (SELNEC), it passed to various owners before purchase from Crompton, Chorley. It operated a few school contracts, then went on loan to Astill & Jordan, Ratby from 11/84 to 22/12/84.

(q) Ex-Greater Manchester PTE, re-seated to 53 in 12/84, and 17 received Viking livery in 1/89.

(r) Ex-Greater Manchester PTE, and re-seated to 53 in 12/84.

(s) New to Red Rover Omnibus, Aylesbury, via various operators (latterly Eagle Travel, Heath Hayes). It received a new Plaxton C53F body in 11/85, and entered service with Stevensons in 5/86 as o.1. Re-registered AEH 227A in 9/86.

1985

Fleet No.	Reg. No.	Chassis	Body	Seating	New	Acq	With drawn	Notes
25	LUA 255V	Volvo B58-56	Plaxton	C53F	3/80	2/85	10/94	(a)
4	LOT 777R	Volvo B58-61	Duple	C57F	8/76	4/85	BB	(b)
--	HTW 197H	Leyland PSU3A/4R	Plaxton	C49F	6/70	4/85	-	(c) Not operated
5	MNT 596W	Volvo B58-56	Plaxton	C49F	3/81	5/85	8/94	(d) Re-registered AEH 607A in 8/89
--	MLH 311-2L	Daimler CRG6LXB	MCW	H44/27F	10/72	5/85	-	(e) Not operated
--	MLH 346L	Daimler CRG6LXB	MCW	H44/27F	12/72	5/85	-	(e) Not operated
93	JGU 259K	Daimler CRG6LXB	MCW	H44/27F	8/72	5/85	11/88	(e) Numbered 93 in 5/86, 93A in 10/88
--	MLK 437L	Daimler CRG6LXB	Park Royal	H44/24D	9/72	5/85	-	(f) Not operated
52	MLH 360L	Daimler CRG6LXB	MCW	H44/27F	1/73	6/85	10/89	(e) Numbered 52 in 11/86
--	VBW 821L	Leyland PSU3B/4R	Duple	C53F	7/73	7/85	-	(g) Not operated
4	TSJ 678S	Leyland PSU3B/4R	Plaxton	C53F	12/77	7/85	8/94	(h) Numbered 4 in 5/86, 104 in 1/87
75	BNE 589Y	Mercedes-Benz L508D	Whittaker	C19F	9/82	7/85	3/90	(i) Re-numbered 175 in 3/87
104	MFA 704G	Daimler SRG6LW	Willowbrook	B44F	3/69	10/85	11/85	(j)
105A	MFA 805G	Daimler SRG6LW	Willowbrook	B44F	4/69	10/85	11/85	(j)
109	RFA 406J	Daimler CRG6LX	NCME	H42/33F	11/70	10/85	7/86	(j)

Fleet No.	Reg. No.	Chassis	Body	Seating	New	Acq	With drawn	Notes
107	RFA 407J	Daimler CRG6LX	NCME	H42/33F	11/70	10/85	12/85	(j)
108	RFA 408J	Daimler CRG6LX	NCME	H42/33F	11/70	10/85	12/85	(j)
67	HTD 324K	Bristol RESL6L	East Lancs	B47F	12/71	10/85	9/88	(j) Re-numbered 109 in 5/87
66	YED 274K	Bristol RESL6L	East Lancs	DP40F	1/72	10/85	11/88	(j) Re-numbered 108 in 2/87
68	STC 890L	Bristol RESL6L	East Lancs	B47F	10/72	10/85	4/86	(j)
110	GFA 10L	Daimler CRG6LX	Willowbrook	H44/33F	7/73	10/85	2/87	(j)
111	GFA 11L	Daimler CRG6LX	Willowbrook	H44/33F	7/73	10/85	10/86	(j)
112	NFA 12M	Daimler CRG6LX	Willowbrook	H44/33F	8/73	10/85	2/86	(j)
113	NFA 13M	Daimler CRG6LX	Willowbrook	H44/33F	8/73	10/85	3/86	(j)
114	NFA 14M	Daimler CRG6LX	Willowbrook	H44/33F	8/73	10/85	3/86	(j)
115	NFA 15M	Daimler CRG6LX	Willowbrook	H44/33F	8/73	10/85	1/86	(j)
116	NFA 16M	Daimler CRG6LX	Willowbrook	H44/33F	8/73	10/85	4/86	(j)
117	NFA 17M	Daimler CRG6LX	Willowbrook	H44/33F	8/73	10/85	4/86	(j)
118	NFA 18M	Daimler CRG6LX	Willowbrook	H44/33F	8/73	10/85	2/86	(j)
119	NFA 19M	Daimler CRG6LX	Willowbrook	H44/33F	8/73	10/85	4/86	(j)
120	NFA 20M	Daimler CRG6LX	Willowbrook	H44/33F	9/73	10/85	2/87	(j)
121	NFA 21M	Daimler CRG6LX	Willowbrook	H44/33F	9/73	10/85	4/86	(j)
22	XRF 22S	Dennis Dominator DD101A/109	East Lancs	H43/32F	6/78	10/85	10/85	(j)
23	XRF 23S	Dennis Dominator DD101A/109	East Lancs	H43/32F	5/78	10/85	10/85	(j)
94	XRF 24S	Leyland AN68A/1R	East Lancs	H43/32F	5/78	10/85	8/90	(j) Re-numbered 57 in 9/88
95	XRF 25S	Leyland AN68A/1R	East Lancs	H43/32F	5/78	10/85	8/90	(j) Re-numbered 58 in 9/88
96	XRF 26S	Leyland AN68A/1R	East Lancs	H43/32F	5/78	10/85	8/90	(j) Re-numbered 59 in 9/88
27	FBF 127T	Dennis Dominator DD110A	East Lancs	H43/32F	5/79	10/85	10/85	(j)
28	FBF 128T	Dennis Dominator DD110A	East Lancs	H43/32F	5/79	10/85	10/85	(j)
29	FBF 129T	Dennis Dominator DD110A	East Lancs	H43/32F	5/79	10/85	10/85	(j)
30	LBF 230V	Dennis Dominator DD120A	East Lancs	H43/32F	4/80	10/85	10/85	(j)
31	LBF 231V	Dennis Dominator DD120A	East Lancs	H43/32F	4/80	10/85	10/85	(j)
32	LBF 232V	Dennis Dominator DD120A	East Lancs	H43/32F	4/80	10/85	10/85	(j)
33	LBF 233V	Dennis Dominator DD120A	East Lancs	H43/32F	4/80	10/85	10/85	(j)
34	LBF 234V	Dennis Dominator DD120A	East Lancs	H43/32F	4/80	10/85	10/85	(j)
37	PRE 37W	Dennis Dominator DD120A	East Lancs	H43/32F	1/81	10/85	12/85	(j)
100	PDD 110M	Leyland PSU3B/4R	Duple	C53F	3/74	10/85	1/90	(k) Re-numbered 100A in 6/89
--	TUP 161M	Bedford YRT	Plaxton	C53F	7/74	10/85	-	(k) Not operated
--	HPB 672N	Bedford YRT	Plaxton	C53F	2/75	10/85	-	(k) Not operated
103	HWU 73N	Leyland PSU3C/4R	Duple	C53F	?/75	10/85	10/89	(k) Re-numbered 103A in 6/89
106	LWW 6P	Leyland PSU3C/4R	Duple	C53F	11/75	10/85	11/88	(k)
--	LUX 517P	Bedford YLQ	Duple	C45F	4/76	10/85	-	(k) Not operated
--	LYU 545P	Bedford YMT	Willowbrook	C51F	5/76	10/85	-	(k) Not operated
57	EWS 819D	Leyland PDR1/1	Alexander	H43/31F	10/66	10/85	11/85	(l)
--	PSC 323G	Leyland PDR1A/1	Alexander	H45/30D	9/69	10/85	-	(l) Not operated
56	AJA 360L	Leyland PSU3B/4R	ECW	C47F	?/73	10/85	BB	(l)
--	AJA 402L	Bristol VRTSL6G	ECW	H43/32F	?/73	10/85	-	(l) Not operated
80	KUC 933P	Daimler CRL6	MCW	H44/24D	11/75	10/85	1/91	(m)
77	CSC 818W	Mercedes-Benz L508D	Reeve Burgess	C21F	3/81	11/85	10/93	(n) Re-numbered 177 in 3/87, 180 in 4/89
22	DEN 245W	Volvo B58-61	Plaxton	C55F	8/80	11/85	1/93	(o)
23	DEN 246W	Volvo B58-61	Plaxton	C55F	8/80	11/85	9/94	(o)
24	DEN 247W	Volvo B58-61	Plaxton	C55F	8/80	11/85	BB	(o)
81	OUC 34R	Leyland FE30ALR	MCW	H44/24D	11/76	11/85	9/91	(p) Re-numbered 36 in 5/89
85	OJD 204R	Leyland FE30ALR	MCW	H44/24D	3/77	11/85	12/87	(p)
86	OJD 208R	Leyland FE30ALR	MCW	H44/24D	4/77	11/85	5/88	(p)
87	OJD 223R	Leyland FE30ALR	MCW	H44/24D	5/77	11/85	5/88	(p)
84	OJD 187R	Leyland FE30ALR	MCW	H44/24D	1/77	12/85	5/88	(p) Re-numbered 84A in 4/88
88	OJD 229R	Leyland FE30ALR	MCW	H44/24D	6/77	12/85	5/88	(p)
89	OJD 241R	Leyland FE30ALR	MCW	H44/24D	7/77	12/85	5/89	(p) Re-numbered 89A in 5/88, then 48 in 9/88

Fleet No.	Reg. No.	Chassis	Body	Seating	New	Acq	With drawn	Notes

Notes:

(a) Ex-Wallace Arnold Tours; Leeds, re-registered AJF 405A in 4/85, fitted for one man operation by 1986, and received Viking livery in 11/88. Re-numbered 101 in 12/87, it became no.3 in 6/89.

(b) Ex-Coliseum Coaches, Southampton after accident damage; the body was removed, the chassis refurbished to B10M standard, and then it received a new Plaxton C53F body, entering service in 2/87 as no.4, re-registered 614 WEH.

(c) Ex-Blue Bus Services, Rugeley via Lister (dealer), Bolton.

(d) Ex-Mayer, Freckleton, entering service in 6/85; re-painted in Viking livery in 12/88.

(e) New to LTE, re-built to H44/27F by Ensign (dealer), then to West Midlands PTE; acquired from Lister (dealer), Bolton, entering service in 5/86 (93), 11/86 (52).

(f) New to LTE, acquired from Red Rover, Aylesbury.

(g) New to Holder, Charlton-on-Otmoor, acquired from Lister (dealer), Bolton.

(h) New to Clyde Coast Services, Ardrossan, acquired from Thomas Tours, Stockport, entering service in 5/86 as no.4. Later re-registered PCW 946, and re-numbered 104.

(i) Ex-Butterworth, Freckleton, entering service in 8/85.

(j) Ex-East Staffordshire District Council, Burton-upon-Trent. 32 had been on loan from ESDC from 19/8/85 to 23/8/85. XRF 25S (95, later 58) re-seated to CH43/27F. MFA 805G was numbered 105 by Stevensons; however, ex-Crystal Coaches HNK 145G had been numbered 105, so MFA 105G was regarded as 105A but the suffix was not carried.

(k) Ex-Erewash Travel Services, Ilkeston, entering service in 10/85 (100, 103), 11/85 (106). 103 was re-seated DP53F in 1/87.

(l) Ex-Blue Bus Services, Rugeley. 56 was new to South East Lancashire and North East Cheshire (SELNEC). The ECW body was removed, the chassis up-graded to Tiger standard, including the fitting of a TL11 engine, and it received a Duple 320 C53F body. It entered service in 5/87 as no.18, and was re-registered 479 BOC. 57 was new to Edinburgh Corporation Transport.

(m) Ex-LTE and ran in London Transport commemorative livery until 7/87. It received a Gardner 6LXB engine in 3/86.

(n) Ex-Nelson, Bellshill, it was fitted with folding doors by PMT Engineering and re-seated to C19 in 4/87, then to DP21 by 10/88.

(o) Ex-Greater Manchester PTE. 22 was re-seated to C46FT (executive) in 2/87, and was re-registered 784 RBF in 3/87. 23 received Viking livery in 2/88, was re-seated and fitted with side lift equipment in 11/88, becoming C49FL. Later re-registered 852 YYC. 24 received Viking fleetnames (but not the livery) in 2/89. Later re-registered 124 YTW.

(p) Ex-LTE, entering service in 12/85 (86/7), 1/86 (81), 3/86 (85/8), 4/86 (84/9). 81 received a Gardner 6LXB engine in 12/85. Re-built to H44/29F in 1/86 (81) and 3/86 (89).

1986

Fleet No.	Reg. No.	Chassis	Body	Seating	New	Acq	With drawn	Notes
101	NRF 454W	Ford Transit	Ford	B8	?/81	2/86	1/87	(a)
78	C78 WRE	Mercedes-Benz L608D	PMT	C19F	2/86	New	by 11/94	Re-numbered 178 in 3/87
92	TGX 710M	Daimler CRL6-30	Park Royal	H44/27F	9/73	4/86	3/89	(b) Re-numbered 92A in 3/89
56	TGX 742M	Daimler CRL6-30	Park Royal	H44/29F	1/74	6/86	3/89	(b)
107	XNE 887L	Leyland PSU3B/4R	Plaxton	C49F	6/73	7/86	2/90	(c)
25A	HSD 710N	Volvo B58-61	Alexander	C53F	?/75	7/86	BB	(d)
--	AWH 62L	Leyland PSU3B/4R	ECW	C47F	?/73	8/86	-	(c) Not operated
--	MLH 321L	Daimler CRG6LXB	MCW	H44/27F	10/72	9/86	-	(e) Not operated
--	MLH 324L	Daimler CRG6LXB	MCW	H44/27F	10/72	9/86	-	(e) Not operated
--	JGU 294K	Daimler CRG6LXB	MCW	H44/27F	8/72	10/86	-	(e) Not operated
59	MLH 460L	Daimler CRG6LXB	MCW	H44/27F	6/73	10/86	3/89	(e) Re-numbered 59A in 9/88
57	WWH 40L	Daimler CRG6LXB	Park Royal	H43/32F	?/73	10/86	9/87	(c)
58	XJA 551L	Daimler CRG6LXB	Park Royal	H43/32F	?/73	10/86	7/87	(c)
179	D179 CRE	Freight Rover 300	PMT	B20F	10/86	New	10/87	
--	MLH 336L	Daimler CRG6LXB	MCW	H44/27F	11/72	11/86	-	(e) Not operated
--	BYX 104V	MCW DR101/9			10/79	11/86	-	(f)
77	GBU 3V	MCW DR101/6	MCW	H43/30F	10/79	12/86	4/94	(g)
78	GBU 7V	MCW DR101/6	MCW	H43/30F	10/79	12/86	BB	(g)
79	GBU 10V	MCW DR101/6	MCW	H43/30F	10/79	12/86	12/93	(g)
--	PKG 600M	Bristol VRTSL6G	ECW	H43/31F	?/74	12/86	-	(h)

Notes:

(a) Ex-National Coal Board, non-PSV with Stevensons.

(b) New to LTE, acquired from Astill & Jordan, Ratby, and had been sold to them previously by Stevensons. 59 entered service in Astill & Jordan livery and returned on loan to that company in 12/86 for a few weeks. 92 entered service in 5/86 and received a Gardner 6LXB engine in 9/87.

(c) Ex-Greater Manchester PTE. In 10/86 57/8 entered service and 107 was re-seated to DP53F, then entered service in 11/86.

(d) New to Western SMT, Kilmarnock as C42FT, it was acquired from RAF Cosford without seats, being fitted as shown before entry into service in 5/87. It always had the 'A' suffix in the fleet number since the numbers reserved for coaches had all been allocated.

(e) New to LTE, re-built to H 44/27F by Ensign (dealer) for West Midlands PTE. Acquired from PVS (dealer), Carlton.

(f) New to London Buses, the chassis was acquired for spares, the body having been burned out.

(g) Ex-Greater Manchester Buses, they entered service in 2/87 (78), 3/87 (77/9).

(h) New to Cardiff Corporation, acquired via Lister (dealer) Bolton for spares.

1987

Fleet No.	Reg. No.	Chassis	Body	Seating	New	Acq	With drawn	Notes
180	D180 DRE	Freight Rover 300	PMT	C20F	1/87	New	10/87	
181	D181DRE	Freight Rover 300	PMT	B20F	2/87	New	12/87	
--	JWU 251N	Leyland PSU4C/4R	Plaxton	B43F	7/75	2/87	-	(a) Not operated
105	JWU 253N	Leyland PSU4C/4R	Plaxton	B43F	7/75	2/87	2/92	(a)
73	UWW 512X	MCW DR101/15	Alexander RH	H43/32F	3/82	2/87	BB	(a)
76	UWW 517X	MCW DR101/15	Alexander RH	H43/32F	3/82	2/87	BB	(a)
182	D906 MVU	Mercedes-Benz L609D	Made to Measure	C27F	2/87	New	9/94	
66	JWU 247N	Leyland PSU4C/4R	Plaxton	DP43F	6/75	3/87	11/88	(a)
--	WYG 256S	Leyland AN68A/1R	Roe	H43/33F	10/77	3/87	-	(b) Not operated
74	UWW 513X	MCW DR101/15	Alexander RH	H43/32F	3/82	3/87	BB	(a)
75	UWW 515X	MCW DR101/15	Alexander RH	H43/32F	3/82	3/87	BB	(a)
--	D573 LSJ	Leyland LX112TL11/ZR1	Leyland	B51F	10/86	3/87	3/87	(c)
54	THM 584M	Daimler CRL6-30	MCW	H44/31F	1/74	4/87	10/90	(d)

Fleet No.	Reg. No.	Chassis	Body	Seating	New	Acq	With drawn	Notes
--	SHA 873G	Daimler CRG6LXB	Alexander	H45/30D	7/69	5/87	-	(e) Not operated
--	UHA 192H	Daimler CRG6LXB	Alexander	H45/30D	9/69	5/87	-	(e) Not operated
--	DRC 543J	Daimler CRG6LXB	Alexander	H44/33F	3/71	5/87	-	(f) Re-built as tree-lopper
67	XTF 807L	Leyland PSU3B/4R	Duple	C49F	7/73	5/87	9/87	(g)
60	XTF 827L	Leyland PSU3B/4R	Duple	C49F	?/73	5/87	7/90	(g)
--	VAV 255X	Leyland TRCTL11/3R	-	-	3/82	5/87	-	(h)
98	UWW 6X	Leyland ONLXB/1R	Roe	H47/29F	3/82	5/87	2/91	(a)
70	C103 UHO	Leyland National 2	NL116HLXCT/1R	B52F	8/85	5/87	10/89	(i)
71	C104 UHO	Leyland National 2	NL116HLXCT/1R	B52F	8/85	5/87	10/89	(i)
--	THM 636M	Daimler CRL6/30	MCW	H44/29F	4/74	7/87	-	(j) Not operated
130	NOE 565R	Leyland National	11351A/1R	B49F	11/76	7/87	12/87	(k)
127	GGE 157T	Leyland National	10351A/1R	B41F	3/79	7/87	7/88	(l)
126	GGE 136T	Leyland National	10351A/1R	B41F	3/79	7/87	7/88	(l)
48	THM 653M	Daimler CRL6/30	MCW	H44/29F	5/74	8/87	7/88	(k)
120	HWY 718N	Leyland PSU3B/4R	Alexander AY	C49F	3/75	8/87	6/88	(k)
121	HWY 719N	Leyland PSU3B/4R	Alexander AY	C49F	3/75	8/87	6/88	(k)
122	HWY 720N	Leyland PSU3B/4R	Alexander AY	C49F	3/75	8/87	7/88	(k)
123	HWY 722N	Leyland PSU3B/4R	Alexander AY	C49F	3/75	8/87	12/87	(k)
126	GOL 416N	Leyland National	11351/1R	B49F	5/75	8/87	10/87	(k)
127	JOX 494P	Leyland National	11351/1R	B49F	5/76	8/87	10/87	(k)
67	PHH 613R	Leyland PSU3D/4RT	Duple	C49F	3/77	8/87	1/89	(k)
124	XCW 154R	Leyland PSU3E/4R	Willowbrook	C47F	5/77	8/87	3/88	(k)
125	XCW 156R	Leyland PSU3E/4R	Willowbrook	C47F	11/77	8/87	3/88	(k)
128	EON 827V	Leyland National 2	NL116L11/1R	B49F	5/80	8/87	6/89	(k)
129	EON 830V	Leyland National 2	NL116L11/1R	DP39FL	6/80	8/87	4/92	(k)
136	C536 TJF	Ford Transit	Rootes	B16F	3/86	8/87	12/87	(k)
137	C537 TJF	Ford Transit	Rootes	B16F	3/86	8/87	12/87	(k)
138	C538 TJF	Ford Transit	Rootes	B16F	3/86	8/87	11/88	(k)
139	C539 TJF	Ford Transit	Rootes	B16F	3/86	8/87	9/92	(k)
140	C540 TJF	Ford Transit	Rootes	B16F	3/86	8/87	3/92	(k)
141	C541 TJF	Ford Transit	Rootes	B16F	3/86	8/87	11/88	(k)
142	C542 TJF	Ford Transit	Rootes	B16F	3/86	8/87	8/91	(k)
143	C543 TJF	Ford Transit	Rootes	B16F	3/86	8/87	11/88	(k)
144	C544 TJF	Ford Transit	Rootes	B16F	3/86	8/87	9/87	(k)
145	C545 TJF	Ford Transit	Rootes	B16F	3/86	8/87	9/91	(k)
146	C546 TJF	Ford Transit	Rootes	B16F	3/86	8/87	9/91	(k)
147	C547 TJF	Ford Transit	Rootes	B16F	3/86	8/87	2/92	(k)
148	C548 TJF	Ford Transit	Rootes	B16F	3/86	8/87	11/88	(k)
149	C549 TJF	Ford Transit	Rootes	B16F	3/86	8/87	11/89	(k)
150	C550 TJF	Ford Transit	Rootes	B16F	3/86	8/87	4/90	(k)
151	C551 TJF	Ford Transit	Rootes	B16F	3/86	8/87	3/92	(k)
152	C552 TJF	Ford Transit	Rootes	B16F	3/86	8/87	5/90	(k)
153	C553 TJF	Ford Transit	Rootes	B16F	3/86	8/87	6/91	(k)
154	C554 TUT	Ford Transit	Rootes	B16F	3/86	8/87	8/92	(k)
155	C555 TUT	Ford Transit	Rootes	B16F	3/86	8/87	11/92	(k)
156	C556 TUT	Ford Transit	Rootes	B16F	3/86	8/87	9/91	(k)
157	C557 TUT	Ford Transit	Rootes	B16F	3/86	8/87	3/93	(k)
158	C558 TUT	Ford Transit	Rootes	B16F	3/86	8/87	by 6/93	(k)
159	C559 TUT	Ford Transit	Rooted	B16F	3/86	8/87	4/90?	(k)
160	C560 TUT	Ford Transit	Rootes	B16F	3/86	8/87	by 1/91	(k)
173	C573 TUT	Ford Transit	Dormobile	B16F	3/86	8/87	11/92	(k)
174	C574 TUT	Ford Transit	Dormobile	B16F	3/86	8/87	11/92	(k)
175	C575 TUT	Ford Transit	Dormobile	B16F	3/86	8/87	4/91	(k)
176	C576 TUT	Ford Transit	Dormobile	B16F	3/86	8/87	4/91	(k)
177	C577 TUT	Ford Transit	Dormobile	B16F	3/86	8/87	-/91	(k)
417	KCG 625L	Leyland National	1151/1R/0402	B49F	6/73	10/87	10/87	(l)
515	JOX 515P	Leyland National	11351A/1R	B49F	7/76	10/87	11/87	(m)
556	NOE 556R	Leyland National	11351A/1R	B49F	11/76	10/87	11/87	(m)
131	LUA 311V	Leyland National2	NL106L11/1R	B41F	4/80	10/87	11/91	(n)

Fleet No.	Reg. No.	Chassis	Body	Seating	New	Acq	With drawn	Notes
132	LUA 324V	Leyland National 2	NL106L11/1R	B41F	3/80	10/87	1/92	(n)
133	LUA 325V	Leyland National 2	NL106L11/1R	B41F	3/80	10/87	by 9/93	(n)
134	LUA 326V	Leyland National 2	NL106L11/1R	B41F	3/80	10/87	10/91	(n)
135	LUA 328V	Leyland National 2	NL106L11/1R	B41F	3/80	10/87	by 4/92	(n)
--	NMS 563M	Leyland PSU3/3R	Alexander AYS	B53F	8/73	11/87	-	(o) Not operated
--	NMS 574M	Leyland PSU3/3R	Alexander AYS	B53F	9/73	11/87	-	(o) Not operated
--	SCS 332M	Leyland PSU3/3R	Alexander AYS	B53F	6/74	11/87	-	(o) Not operated
481	JOX 481P	Leyland National	11351/1R	B49F	11/75	11/87	1/88	(m)
563	NOE 563R	Leyland National	11351/1R	B49F	11/76	11/87	12/87	(m)
57	BHL 621K	Daimler CRG6LX	NCME	H43/33F	3/72	11/87	7/88	(p)
58	BHL 625K	Daimler CRG6LX	NCME	H43/33F	3/72	11/87	10/88	(p) Re-numbered 58A in 9/88
190	TFP 25R	Ford R1014	Plaxton	C45F	7/77	11/87	3/88	(p)
191	TRY 3S	Ford R1114	Plaxton	C53F	8/77	11/87	3/88	(p)
192	EBC 280T	Ford R1114	Plaxton	C53F	6/79	11/87	3/88	(p)
197	EBC 672T	Ford R1114	Plaxton	C53F	6/79	11/87	3/88	(p)
--	GJF 400V	Ford R1114	Plaxton	C53F	10/79	11/87	11/87	(p)
--	OFA 10	Ford R1114	Plaxton	C53F	7/80	11/87	12/87	(p)
--	LJF 742V	Ford R1114	Plaxton	C53F	7/80	11/87	12/87	(p)
--	RJU 383W	Ford R1114	Plaxton	C51F	?/81	11/87	12/87	(p)
136	DDM 33X	Leyland PSU3F/4R	Willowbrook	C47F	3/82	11/87	3/92	(p)
137	LOA 834X	Leyland PSU3F/4R	Willowbrook	C49F	6/82	11/87	3/92	(p)
21	LFO 800Y	Leyland TRCTL11/2R	Duple	C53F	5/83	11/87	7/88	(p)
25	JGL 53	DAF MB200DKFL600	Plaxton	C53F	6/83	11/87	BB	(p)
19	A834 PPP	Leyland TRCTL11/3R	Plaxton	C41F	3/84	11/87	4/91	(p)
183	E183 BNN	Fiat 49.10	Robin Hood	B25F	11/87	New	2/90	
184	E184 BNN	Fiat 49.10	Robin Hood	B25F	11/87	New	2/90	
1703	A703 HVT	Leyland TRCTL11/2R	Duple	B51F	2/84	12/87	2/88	(m)
1709	A709 HVT	Leyland TRCTL11/2R	Duple	B51F	3/84	12/87	12/87	(m)

Notes:

(a) Ex-West Yorkshire PTE, entering service in 3/87 (66, 73), 4/87 (105), 5/87 (76), 7/87 (74/5, 98).

(b) Ex-Lister (dealer).

(c) Owned by AA Motor Services, Ayr, it was on loan from Leyland Buses Ltd for one day only (12/3/87).

(d) New to LTE; acquired from Cottrell, Mitcheldean, entering service in 5/87, still in Cottrell's livery. It received a Gardner 6LXB engine in 1/88.

(e) New to BMMO (Midland Red), they were acquired from Lister (dealer), Bolton.

(f) New to Trent Motor Traction, was acquired from Lister (dealer), Bolton. Converted to tree-lopper.

(g) 60 was new to North Western, and 67 was new to Ribble Motor Services; both were acquired from Lister (dealer), Bolton, entering service in 5/87 (67), 6/87 (60).

(h) New to Premier Travel, Cambridge; was destroyed by fire and acquired from Ripley (dealer), Carlton as chassis only, but was found unsuitable for repair.

(i) Ex-Provincial Bus Company, Fareham, entering service in 5/87 (70, in Provincial livery before receiving an all-over advert livery), and 6/87 (71).

(j) New to LTE; converted to H44/29F by Ensign (dealer), to Western National, then Midland Fox, (as a training vehicle).

(k) Ex-Midland Fox. They were new to the following: Cumberland Motor Services, Whitehaven (67), West Riding, Wakefield (120-3), National Travel (West), Manchester (124/5), Midland Red, Birmingham (126-130); 129 was new as B49F, becoming DP39FL in 5/85, as a 'Mobility Coach'. It received Viking livery in 11/87. 130 entered service with Stevensons in 7/87. 136/7, 144, 150/9/60 never carried their Stevensons fleet numbers.

(l) On loan from Trent Motor Traction, Derby in 10/87.

(m) On loan from Midland Red (North) as follows: 515 (28/10/87-11/11/87), 556 (28/10/87-16/11/87), 481 (11/11/87-11/1/88), 563 (16/11/87-4/12/87), 1709 (14/12/87-24/12/87), 1703 (24/12/87-9/2/88).

(n) Ex-Yorkshire Rider, Leeds, entering service in 3/88 (131/3), 5/88 (132/4/5).

(o) Ex-Strathtay Scottish Omnibuses, Kilmarnock.

(p) Ex-Viking Motors, Woodville. 19 was new to Armchair Passenger Transport, Brentford; it was re-seated to 53 by Stevensons. 21 was new to Morris, Bromyard. 25 (JGL 53) re-registered DFP 707Y in 10/88, then to 82 HBC in 8/89. 57/8 were new to West Riding, Wakefield. 136 (DDM 33X), 137 (LOA 834X), 190/1, were ex-Victoria Motorways, Woodville. 136 was new to Crosville Motor Services, Chester. It received Stevensons' livery in 12/88. 137 was new to Midland Red (Express) Ltd, Birmingham; it received Stevensons' livery in 1/89.

1988

Fleet No.	Reg. No.	Chassis	Body	Seating	New	Acq	With drawn	Notes
72	E72 KBF	Leyland LX112CL10/FR1	Leyland	B51F	2/88	New	BB	
--	MSF 751P	Seddon Pennine 7	Alexander	C42FT	6/76	2/88	-	(a) Not operated
115	BSD 847T	Seddon Pennine 7	Alexander AY	B53F	5/79	2/88	?/92	(b)
118	BSD 850T	Seddon Pennine 7	Alexander AY	B53F	5/79	2/88	2/92	(b)
111	ASD 838T	Seddon Pennine 7	Alexander AY	B53F	3/79	3/88	1/94	(b)
112	ASD 839T	Seddon Pennine 7	Alexander AY	B53F	3/79	3/88	4/93	(b)
113	ASD 841T	Seddon Pennine 7	Alexander AY	B53F	3/79	3/88	12/91	(b)
114	BSD 846T	Seddon Pennine 7	Alexander AY	B53F	5/79	3/88	8/94	(b)
116	BSD 848T	Seddon Pennine 7	Alexander AY	B53F	5/79	3/88	12/91	(b)
117	BSD 849T	Seddon Pennine 7	Alexander AY	B53F	5/79	3/88	7/91	(b)
123	CCY 817V	Leyland National 2	NL116L11/1R	DP48F	12/79	3/88	12/89	(c)
124	CCY 818V	Leyland National 2	NL116L11/1R	DP48F	12/79	3/88	12/89	(c)
125	CCY 819V	Leyland National 2	NL116L11/1R	DP48F	12/79	3/88	3/90	(c)
130	CCY 820V	Leyland National 2	NL116L11/1R	DP48F	12/79	3/88	6/89	(c)

Fleet No.	Reg. No.	Chassis	Body	Seating	New	Acq	With drawn	Notes
84	EWF 469V	MCW DR102/13	MCW	H46/27D	2/80	3/88	c9/93	(d)
85	EWF 473V	MCW DR102/13	MCW	H46/27D	2/80	3/88	11/92	(d)
86	JWF 490V	MCW DR102/13	MCW	H46/27D	8/80	3/88	BB	(d)
87	JWF 493V	MCW DR102/13	MCW	H46/27D	8/80	3/88	8/94	(d)
88	JWF 494V	MCW DR102/13	MCW	H46/27D	8/80	3/88	8/94	(d)
--	KUC 220P	Daimler CRL6	MCW	CO45/32F	2/76	4/88	-	(e) Not operated
89	BSN 878V	MCW DR102/5	MCW	H45/28D	9/79	4/88	BB	(f)
--	THM 636M	Daimler CRL6/30	MCW	H44/29F	4/74	7/88	-	(g) Not operated
20	124 YTW	Bova FLD12-250	Bova	C53F	6/84	7/88	?/90	(h)
21	125 EJU	Bova FLD12-250	Bova	C53F	6/84	7/88	7/89	(h)
181	D176 LNA	Mercedes-Benz 609D	Made to Measure	DP27F	10/86	8/88	9/94	(i)
186	F186 PRE	Mercedes-Benz 709D	Reeve Burgess	B25F	8/88	New	BB	
187	F187 REH	Mercedes-Benz 609D	Whittaker	B20F	8/88	New	BB	
188	F188 REH	Mercedes-Benz 609D	PMT	B20F	8/88	New	BB	
185	F185 PRE	Mercedes-Benz 709D	Robin Hood	B29F	9/88	New	BB	
93	TTT 172X	Leyland ONLXB/1R	East Lancs	H43/31F	3/82	9/88	2/91	(j)
94	TTT 173X	Leyland ONLXB/1R	East Lancs	H43/31F	3/82	9/88	2/91	(j)
95	TTT 174X	Leyland ONLXB/1R	East Lancs	H43/31F	3/82	9/88	2/91	(j)
--	JRB 744N	Leyland PSU3C/4R	Duple	DP53F	7/75	9/88	9/88	(k)
--	LAL 747P	Leyland PSU3C/4R	Duple	DP53F	8/75	9/88	9/88	(k)
--	LAL 750P	Leyland PSU3C/4R	Duple	DP53F	8/75	9/88	9/88	(k)
179	A343 ASF	Mercedes-Benz L608D	Stevensons	B25F	11/83	10/88	8/94	(l)
189	F189 RRF	Mercedes-Benz 709D	Robin Hood	B29F	10/88	New	BB	
190	F190 RRF	Mercedes-Benz 709D	Robin Hood	B29F	11/88	New	BB	
--	D420 FEH	Freight Rover	PMT	B20F	7/87	11/88	11/88	(m)
--	E26 ECH	Scania K92	Alexander PS	B51F	6/88	11/88	11/88	(n)
96	F96 PRE	Leyland ONCL10/1RZ	Alexander RL	H47/32F	12/88	New	BB	
97	F97 PRE	Leyland ONCL10/1RZ	Alexander RL	H47/32F	12/88	New	BB	

Notes:
(a) Ex-Eastern Scottish, Edinburgh, acquired for spares.
(b) New to Western SMT, and acquired from Clydeside Scottish Omnibuses, entering service in 3/88 (116/8), 4/88 (113/4), 6/88 (111/5), 7/88 (112/7).
(c) Ex-South Wales Transport, Swansea, entering service in 4/88.
(d) Ex-South Yorkshire Transport Ltd, Sheffield, entering service in 3/88 (84), 4/88 (85), 5/88 (86/8), 6/88 (87).
(e) New to LT as H44/27D; converted to convertible open-top by Ensign (dealer), then to South Wales Transport from where it was acquired.
(f) New to Tayside Regional Council, Dundee. It was acquired from Enterprise and Silver Dawn and saw service in their livery for a while.
(g) Ex-Cound (dealer), Cheltenham to where it had been sold previously by Stevensons.
(h) New to Shamrock and Rambler Coaches, Bournemouth; acquired via Kirkby (dealer), South Anston, entering service in 7/88. 21 received Viking fleetnames, but not livery, in 12/88.
(i) Ex-Marriott, Clayworth, entering service in 8/88.
(j) Ex-Plymouth Citybus Ltd.
(k) On loan from City of Nottingham Transport Ltd during 9/88.
(l) New to Scottish Council for Spastics, Edinburgh as an ambulance. Stevensons fitted a service bus door and 25 bus seats, and it entered service in 4/89.
(m) On loan from PMT (dealer) from 11/11/88 to 25/11/88.
(n) On loan from Scania (GB) Ltd (dealer) for one day only (8/11/88); it was not used in service.

1989

Fleet No.	Reg. No.	Chassis	Body	Seating	New	Acq	With drawn	Notes
91	B101 PHC	Leyland ONLXCT/2RSp	East Lancs	CH47/23F	4/85	1/89	7/93	(a) Converted to DPH47/23F
92	B102 PHC	Leyland ONLXCT/2RSp	East Lancs	CH47/23F	5/85	1/89	7/93	(a) Converted to DPH47/23F
110	F110 SRF	Scania K93 CRB	Alexander PS	B51F	2/89	New	BB	
61	F61 PRE	Leyland LX 112L10ZR1R	Leyland	B51F	3/89	New	BB	
120	DSR 132V	Daimler SRG 6LX	Marshall	B51F	3/70	3/89	12/89	(b)
--	DSR 133V	Daimler SRG 6LX	Marshall	B51F	3/70	3/89	12/89?	(b)
--	B400 WTC	Ford Transit	Robin Hood	B16F	3/85	3/89	4/89	(c)
30	C30 EUH	Leyland ONTL11/1R	East Lancs	CH47/31F	9/85	3/89	4/89	(d)
194	B882 HSX	Mercedes-Benz L608D	?	?	12/84	3/89	BB	(e)
81	F181 YDA	MCW Metrobus II DF104/64	MCW	H43/30F	8/88	3/89	BB	Ex-MCW demonstrator
191	F191 SRF	Mercedes-Benz 709D	Robin Hood	B29F	4/89	New	9/94	
192	F192 VFA	Mercedes-Benz 709D	Robin Hood	B29F	5/89	New	9/94	
100	DDW 65V	Leyland PSU4E/2R	East Lancs	B47F	10/79	5/89	7/93	(f)
101	DUH 76V	Leyland PSU3E/2R	East Lancs	DP47F	3/80	5/89	5/93	(f)
102	DUH 77V	Leyland PSU3E/2R	East Lancs	DP47F	3/80	5/89	11/93	(f)
103	DUH 78V	Leyland PSU3E/2R	East Lancs	DP47F	3/80	5/89	11/93	(f)
80	TOJ 592S	MCW DR101/2	MCW	H43/28D	11/77	6/89	BB	(g)
193	F326 PPO	Mercedes-Benz 709D	Phoenix	B29F	?/89	7/89	9/94	(h)
109	G109 YRE	Scania K93	Alexander PS	B51F	8/89	New	BB	

Fleet No.	Reg. No.	Chassis	Body	Seating	New	Acq	With drawn	Notes
21	G21 YVT	Volvo B10M-60	Van Hool	C51FT	8/89	New	BB	(i)
25	G25 YVT	Volvo B10M-60	Plaxton	C53F	8/89	New	BB	(i)
--	LSC 934T	Seddon Pennine 7	Alexander AY	B53F	6/79	10/89	?	(j)
--	LSC 935T	Seddon Pennine 7	Alexander AY	B53F	6/79	10/89	?	(j)
121	SSX 598V	Seddon Pennine 7	Alexander AYS	B53F	2/80	10/89	2/92	(j)
122	SSX 599V	Seddon Pennine 7	Alexander AYS	B53F	2/80	10/89	2/92	(j)
123	SSX 600V	Seddon Pennine 7	Alexander AYS	B53F	2/80	10/89	-/92	(j)
124	SSX 601V	Seddon Pennine 7	Alexander AYS	B53F	2/80	10/89	2/90	(j)
125	YSG 651W	Seddon Pennine 7	Alexander AYS	B53F	12/80	10/89	7/93	(j)
126	YSG 652W	Seddon Pennine 7	Alexander AYS	B53F	12/80	10/89	8/94	(j)
127	YSG 653W	Seddon Pennine 7	Alexander AYS	B53F	12/80	10/89	4/92	(j)
128	JFS 977X	Seddon Pennine 7	Alexander AYS	B53F	3/82	10/89	8/92	(j)
129	JFS 978X	Seddon Pennine 7	Alexander AYS	B53F	3/82	10/89	4/92	(j)
90	B45 NDX	Leyland ON6LXB	East Lancs	CH40/33F	8/85	10/89	7/93	(k)
160-3	G160-3 YRE	Mercedes-Benz 709D	LHE	B29F	11/89	New	BB	
25B	RSE 875N	Bedford YRT	Duple	C53F	1975	12/89	4/90	(l)
25C	WYR 562	Volvo B58	Plaxton	C53F	1973	12/89	4/90	(l)
13A	XOI 2907	Volvo B58	Plaxton	C53F	1980	12/89	8/90	(l)
14	POI 9786	Volvo B58	Duple	C51F	1981	12/89	4/90	(l)
16	2488 KB	Volvo B58	Plaxton	C48FT	1981	12/89	11/93	(l)
15	VOI 6874	Volvo B10M	Plaxton	C53F	1983	12/89	BB	(l)
1	HIJ 3652	Volvo B10M	Plaxton	C51F	1984	12/89	BB	(l)
82	BOK 72V	MCW DR 102/12	MCW	H43/30F	1980	12/89	BB	(m)
83	BOK 75V	MCW DR 102/12	MCW	H43/30F	1980	12/89	BB	(m)
195	F272 OPX	Mercedes-Benz 811D	LHE	C29F	1989	12/89	8/94	Ex-LHE demonstrator

Notes:
(a) Ex-Eastbourne Borough Transport. On both vehicles, windows were inserted in the former luggage compartment area, and ex-DMS bus seats were fitted throughout the lower saloon, coach seating being retained in the upper saloon, becoming DPH47/35F. They were completed in 3/89 (91), 5/89 (92), entering service in 9/89.
(b) New to Dundee Corporation with Alexander B46D bodies, registered KTS 216/24H; re-bodied and re-registered as shown in 4/80, then to AA Motor Services, Ayr, (Dodds, Troon), from where purchased, 120 entering service in 3/89.
(c) On loan from Midland Fox, Leicester.
(d) New to Rhymney Valley District Council, passing to Inter Valley Link, Caerphilly, via G&G (dealer), Leamington to Stevensons. Sold to Midland Fox, Leicester 4/89.
(e) New to Scottish Council for Spastics, Edinburgh, as B16FL, although it was acquired without seats. Fitted out at Spath becoming 'Stevensons' B21F.
(f) New to Rhymney Valley DC, passing to Inter Valley Link, Caerphilly, from where they were acquired.
(g) Formerly a demonstrator with MCW, Birmingham, it was acquired in poor condition, virtually without seats, and fitted with a Gardner five-cylinder engine, which belonged to Gardner and was removed. A small bustle was added at the rear so as to accommodate a Gardner six-cylinder engine, and the completed vehicle entered service in 1991.
(h) Formerly a demonstrator with Phoenix, Southampton.
(i) 21 had a demountable toilet arrangement, to enable C51FT and C55F configurations. Both 21 and 25 were delivered in Viking livery.
(j) Ex-Kelvin Central Buses Ltd.
(k) New to Ipswich Borough Transport, it was acquired from Eastbourne Borough Transport Ltd. Bus seats were fitted in due course.
(l) Ex-Bagnall, Woodville.
(m) Ex-West Midlands Travel via dealer.

1990

Fleet No.	Reg. No.	Chassis	Body	Seating	New	Acq	With drawn	Notes
164/5	G164/5 YRE	Mercedes-Benz 709D	LHE	B29F	1/90	New	BB	
108	G108 CEH	Scania N113	Alexander PS	B51F	2/90	New	5/93	
14	A655 EMY	Leyland Royal Tiger	Roe	C49F	1994	2/90	BB	(a)
166-73	G166-73 YRE	Mercedes-Benz 709D	LHE	B29F	3/90	New	BB	
174	G174 YRE	Mercedes-Benz 811D	Carlyle	B33F	3/90	New	BB	
70/1	KJW 318/20W	MCW DR 102/22	MCW	H43/30F	1981	4/90	BB	(b)
119	VSX 762R	Seddon Pennine 7	Alexander AY	B53F	1978	4/90	-/94	(c)
183/4	G183/4 DRF	Mercedes-Benz 709D	LHE	B29F	6/90	New	BB	
22	G122 DRF	Volvo B10M	Van Hool	C53F	6/90	New	BB	
175	G175 DRF	Mercedes-Benz 811D	LHE	B33F	7/90	New	BB	
48	BOK 68V	MCW DR 102/12	MCW	H43/30F	1980	7/90	BB	(b)
49/50	GOG 223/72W	MCW DR 102/18	MCW	H43/30F	1981	7/90	BB	(b)
51	KJW 296W	MCW DR 102/22	MCW	H43/30F	1981	7/90	BB	(b)
52	KJW 301W	MCW DR 102/22	MCW	H43/30F	1981	7/90	BB	(b)
53/4	KJW 305/6W	MCW DR 102/22	MCW	H43/30F	1981	7/90	BB	(b)
55	KJW 310W	MCW DR 102/22	MCW	H43/30F	1981	7/90	BB	(b)
56	KJW 322W	MCW DR 102/22	MCW	H43/30F	1981	7/90	BB	(b)
44-47	JHE 189-92W	MCW DR 104/6	MCW	H46/31F	1981	10/90	BB	(d)
57	JHE 193W	MCW DR 104/6	MCW	H46/31F	1981	10/90	BB	(d)
58/9	JHE 137-8W	MCW DR 104/6	MCW	H46/31F	1981	10/90	BB	(d)
43	JHE 144W	MCW DR 104/6	MCW	H46/31F	1981	10/90	12/93	(d)

Fleet No.	Reg. No.	Chassis	Body	Seating	New	Acq	With drawn	Notes
176/7	H176/7 JVT	Mercedes-Benz 814D	Wright	B29F	10/90	New	BB	
196-8	H196-8 JVT	Mercedes-Benz 814D	Wright	B33F	10/90	New	BB	(except 196 which was withdrawn 8/94)
199	H199 KEH	Mercedes-Benz 814D	Phoenix	DP31F	10/90	New	BB	
159	E564 YBU	Mercedes-Benz 709D	Reeve Burgess	B25F	1988	12/90	BB	(e)

Notes:
(a) Ex-Midland Fox.
(b) Ex-West Midlands Travel via dealer.
(c) Ex-Midland Scottish.
(d) Ex-South Yorkshire Transport. 44 (JHE 189W) was not operated, being dismantled at Burton. JHE 191W took fleet number 44 and a vehicle bought as stock (JHE 145W) eventually took fleet number 46.
(e) Ex-Starline, Knutsford.

1991

Fleet No.	Reg. No.	Chassis	Body	Seating	New	Acq	With drawn	Notes
210-4	B730-4 YUD	Ford Transit	Carlyle	B20F	1984	1/91		(a)
215	B875 EOM	Ford Transit	Carlyle	B20F	1984	1/91		(a)
216-8	B736-8 YUD	Ford Transit	Carlyle	B20F	1984	1/91		(a)
219-21	C725-7 JJO	Ford Transit	Carlyle	B20F	1986	2/91		(a)
66	H166 MFA	Leyland Swift ST2R44C97A4	Wadham Stringer	B39F	3/91	New	BB	
9	G417 WFP	Bova FHD12.290	Bova Futura	C30FT	1990	3/91	BB	(b)
200	F114 UEH	MCW Metrorider	MCW	C29F	1988	4/91	8/94	(c)
222-7	C41-4/51/4 HDT	Dennis Domino	Optare	B33F	1985	4/91		(d)
67	GMS 295S	Leyland PSU3E/4R	Alexander AYS	B53F	1978	4/91	BB	(e)
12	D205 SGB	Volvo B10M	Plaxton	C53F	1987	5/91	8/91	(f) Later LUY 742
14	E562 UHS	Volvo B10M	Plaxton	C49FT	1987	5/91	BB	(f) Later LUY 742 (after 8.91)
26	XOR 841	Volvo B10M	Van Hool	C53FT	1983	5/91	BB	(f)
27	TOU 962	Volvo B10M	Van Hool	C53FT	1983	5/91	BB	(f)
150	FFD 57Y	Dodge S56	Reeve Burgess	C25F	1981	5/91	2/92	(f)
231	LDH 940P	Ford R1114	Plaxton	C53F	1975	5/91	2/93	(f)
232	VFD 806S	Ford R1114	Plaxton	C53F	1977	5/91	2/93	(f)
233	VNX 229S	Ford R1114	Plaxton	C53F	1977	5/91	11/92	(f)
234	GDH 908T	Ford R1114	Plaxton	C53F	1979	5/91	4/92	(f)
235	JDH 882T	Ford R1114	Plaxton	C53F	1979	5/91	9/93	(f)
236	PFK 174W	Ford R1114	Plaxton	C53F	1980	5/91	6/94	(f)
237	VFX 660X	Ford R1114	Plaxton	C53F	1981	5/91	6/94	(f)
238	VFX 661X	Ford R1114	Plaxton	C53F	1981	5/91	7/94	(f)
239	468 KPX	AEC Reliance	Plaxton	C57F	1973	5/91	7/93	(g) Later FEA 55L
240	803 HOM	AEC Reliance	Duple	C53F	1976	5/91	3/92	(g)
241	YPL 71T	AEC Reliance	Duple	C49F	1979	5/91	7/91	(g) May not have been operated
242	7970 RU	AEC Reliance	Van Hool	C53F	1980	5/91	8/91	(g)
243	SWW 143R	Leyland PSU3	Duple	C53F	1977	5/91	7/91	(g)
244	OLJ 194W	Leyland PSU5	Duple	C57F	1980	5/91	4/92	(g)
245	SDR 444T	Volvo B58-61	Duple	C57F	1979	5/91	9/93	(g)
246	MDS 231V	Volvo B58-61	Plaxton	C57F	1981	5/91	9/93	(g) 803 HOM post-3/92
152	LUY 742	Mercedes-Benz L609D	Coachcraft	C24F	1988	5/91	9/93?	(h) To E926 LNR, Viking livery
247	PSV 323	Volvo B58-61	Plaxton	C57F	1981	5/91	8/94	(h)
67	F956 XCK	Leyland Swift LBM6N/2RAO	Wadham Stringer	B39F	1988	5/91	BB	Ex-Stones, Glazebury
68	G98 VMM	Leyland Swift LBM6T/2RA	Wadham Stringer	B39F	1989	5/91	BB	Ex-Green, Kirkintilloch
00	ECT 912	Bedford OB	Duple	C29F	1950	5/91	7/92	(i)
60	D401 MHS	Leyland LX5636LXCTFR1	Leyland	B51F	1986	6/91	BB	Ex-Kelvin Central
156	F77 ERJ	Mercedes-Benz L609D	Reeve Burgess	C29F	1988	7/91	BB	Ex-Starline, Congleton
228/9	C46/7 HDT	Dennis Domino	Optare	B33F	1985	7/91	10/93	(d)
201/2	H201/2 LRF	Mercedes-Benz 814D	Wright	B33F	5/91	New	BB	
203-7	J203-7 REH	Mercedes-Benz 814D	Wright	B31F	8/91	New	BB	
149	G901 MNS	Mercedes-Benz 811D	Reeve Burgess	B32F	1989	9/91	BB	Ex-Whitelaw, Stonehaven
118	GNL 841N	Leyland PSU3C/4R	Alexander AY	B62F	1975	9/91	2/95	(j)
146	E219 SOL	MCW Metrorider	MCW	C25F	1987	9/91	9/94	Ex-Buchanan, Stoke-on-Trent
145/53	G897/6 TGG	Mercedes-Benz 814D	Reeve Burgess	B33F	1989	10/91	BB	Ex-Whitelaw, Stonehaven
117	RSR 844H	Leyland PSU4	Plaxton	C40F	1970	11/91	11/92	Ex-Stagecoach, Perth
141	D126 OWG	Dodge S56	Reeve Burgess	B25F	1987	11/91	1/93	Ex-South Yorkshire Transport
31/2	J31/2 SFA	Leyland Swift ST2R44C97A4	Wright	B39F	12/91	New	BB	
143	J143 SRF	Mercedes-Benz 709D	Wright	B29F	12/91	New	BB	

Fleet No.	Reg. No.	Chassis	Body	Seating	New	Acq	With drawn	Notes

Notes:
(a) Ex-City of Oxford MS. Withdrawn by Stevensons in 8/94 (210/1/3-5/7/8), 4/91 (216), 2/95 (212).
(b) Ex-Boyden, Castle Donington.
(c) Ex-PMT. Later re-registered 565 LON
(d) Ex-South Yorkshire Transport; withdrawn by Stevensons in 10/92 (224), 10/93 (228-9), 11/92 (remainder).
(e) Ex-Henley, Abertillery, re-numbered 120 later.
(f) Ex-Sealandair, West Bromwich.
(g) Ex-Collett, West Bromwich.
(h) Ex-Classic Coaches, Wombourne.
(i) Ex-Kime, Folkingham, bought for specialised private hire and nostalgia tours. Sold for preservation.
(j) Ex-Globe, Barnsley (had 3x2 seating).

Fleet No.	Reg. No.	Chassis	Body	Seating	New	Acq	With drawn	Notes
			1992					
260/1	HXI 3010/1	Leyland Lynx LX563TL11FR	Alexander N (Belfast)	B53F	1986	1/92	BB	(a)
144	IDZ 8561	Mercedes-Benz 811D	Wright	B26F	1990	1/92	BB	Ex-Crown, Cramlington
150	D111 OWG	Dodge S56	Reeve Burgess	B25F	1987	1/92	8/93	Ex-South Yorkshire Transport
147/40	D117/22 OWG	Dodge S56	Reeve Burgess	B25F	1987	1/92	1/93	Ex-South Yorkshire Transport
19	VRR 447	Volvo B10M	Van Hool	C48F	1982	1/92	BB	(b)
256	HXI 3006	Leyland Lynx LX5636LXCTFR	Alexander N (Belfast)	B53F	1986	2/92	BB	(a)
257-9	HXI 3007-9	Leyland Lynx LX5636LXBFR	Alexander N (Belfast)	B53F	1986	2/92	BB	(a)
262	HXI 3012	Leyland Lynx LX563TL11FR	Alexander N (Belfast)	B53F	1986	2/92	BB	(a)
33/5	H313/4 WUA	Leyland Swift ST2R44C97A4	Reeve Burgess	DP39F	1991	2/92	BB	(c)
41	G141 GOL	Dennis Dart 9SDL3002	Duple	B39F	1990	2/92	BB	Ex-Starline, Congleton
34/6	J34/6 SRF	Leyland Swift ST2R44C97A4	Wright	B39F	2/92	New	BB	
12	AAX 562A	DAF	Plaxton	C51FT	1986	2/92	?	Ex-Telling-Golden Miller
240/2	AAL 303/404A	Leyland PSU5D/4R	Plaxton	C53F	1980	3/92	BB	(d) Previously BUH 226/222V
208/9	J208/9 SRF	Mercedes-Benz 709D	Wright	B27F	4/92	New	BB	
115/6	YSF 86/93S	Leyland PSU3E/4R	Alexander AYS	B53F	1978	4/92	BB	Ex-Fife Scottish
151	J151 WEH	Mercedes-Benz 709D	Dormobile	B29F	4/92	New	9/94	
134	D38 NDW	Dodge S56	East Lancs	DP24F	1987	4/92	5/93	Ex-National Welsh
135	D39 NDW	Dodge S56	East Lancs	B25F	1987	4/92	3/93	Ex-National Welsh
113	YSF 85S	Leyland PSU3E/4R	Alexander AYS	B53F	1978	5/92	BB	Ex-Fife Scottish
131/2	E647/642 DCK	Dodge S56	Dormobile	B25F	1987	7/92	8/94	Ex-Fife Scottish
216	C112 HKG	Ford Transit	Robin Hood	B16F	1986	7/92	8/92	Ex-National Welsh
270-5	C83/5/9/91/2/4 AUB	Ford Transit	Carlyle	B20F	1985	8/92	8/94	Ex-Yorkshire Rider
276/7	C97/100 AUB	Ford Transit	Carlyle	B20F	1985	8/92	8/94	Ex-Yorkshire Rider
278/9	D521/6 HNW	Ford Transit	Carlyle	B20F	1985	8/92	8/94	Ex-Yorkshire Rider
280/2/3	E223/22/20 PWY	MCW Metrorider	MCW	C23F	1987	8/92	5/94	Ex-Yorkshire Rider
281/4	E232/224 PWY	MCW Metrorider	MCW	C23F	1987	8/92	8/94	Ex-Yorkshire Rider
42	H851 NOC	Dennis Dart 9.8SDL3004	Carlyle	B43F	1991	8/92	BB	Ex-Chisolm, Reigate
128-30	D133/5/41 NUS	Mercedes-Benz L608D	Alexander	B21F	1986	8/92	BB	Ex-Kelvin Central
38	F907 PFH	Leyland Swift LBM6T/2RA	GC Smith	B32FL	1989	8/92	BB	Ex-Gloucester County Council
136/7	K136/7 ARE	Mercedes-Benz 709D	Wright	B29F	9/92	New	BB	
131/2	K131/2 XRE	Mercedes-Benz 709D	Dormobile	B29F	10/92	New	9/94	
40	J556 GTP	Dennis Dart 9SDL3002	Wadham Stringer	B35F	1991	11/92	BB	Ex-Irwell Valley
37	G616 WGS	Leyland Swift LBM6T/2RA	Reeve Burgess	B35F	1989	12/92	BB	Ex-Chambers, Stevenage
150	K150 BRF	Mercedes-Benz 709D	Wright	B29F	12/92	New	BB	
147	K947 BRE	Mercedes-Benz 709D	Dormobile	B29F	12/92	New	BB	
148	K148 BRF	Mercedes-Benz 709D	Dormobile	B29F	12/92	New	BB	
267/9	D527/522 HNW	Ford Transit	Carlyle	B20F	1987	12/92	3/93	Ex-Yorkshire Rider
268	D528 HNW	Ford Transit	Carlyle	B20F	1987	12/92	4/93	Ex-Yorkshire Rider

Notes:
(a) Ex-Belfast Citybus; 256 was a Leyland Lynx prototype. These were the only Leyland Lynxes to operate in the UK mainland with other than Leyland bodywork.
(b) Ex-Cumberland MS, originally UHH 575X. Acquired after accident damage which was repaired by Stevensons. Re-registered 468 KPX.
(c) Ex-Pennine, Gargrave; operated in Pennine livery for a while.
(d) Ex-Rhondda Buses (later nos.12, 13).

Fleet No.	Reg. No.	Chassis	Body	Seating	New	Acq	With drawn	Notes
			1993					
134	F822 GDT	Mercedes-Benz 811D	Reeve Burgess	C25F	1989	2/93	BB	Ex-Gordon, Rotherham
135	G807 FJX	Mercedes-Benz 811D	PMT	C33F	1990	2/93	BB	Ex-Traject, Halifax
223-5	C802/23/22 SDY	Mercedes-Benz L608D	Alexander	B20F	1985	2/93	BB	Ex-East Midland
107	F170 DET	Scania K93 CRB	Plaxton	B57F	1989	3/93	BB	Ex-Frontrunner, Dagenham
133	J480 XHL	Mercedes-Benz 709D	Alexander AM	B25F	1991	3/93	8/94	(a)
29	LFR 532F	Leyland PD3/11	MCCW	H41/30R	1967	4/93	7/94	Ex-Eastbourne Buses
138/9	K138/9 BRF	Mercedes-Benz 811D	Dormobile	B31F	4/93	New	BB	

Fleet No.	Reg. No.	Chassis	Body	Seating	New	Acq	With drawn	Notes
105	E829 AWA	Leyland TRCTL11/2RP	Plaxton	B54F	1987	5/93	BB	Ex-Liverline, Liverpool
140-2	K140-2 BFA	Mercedes-Benz 811D	Dormobile	B31F	5/93	New	BB	
154	K154 BRF	Mercedes-Benz 811D	Dormobile	B27F	5/93	New	BB	
106	SOA 676S	Leyland PSU3E/4R	Plaxton	C49F	1978	6/93	BB	(b)
155	K155 CRE	Mercedes-Benz 709D	Dormobile	B27F	6/93	New	8/94	
156-8	K156-8 BRF	Mercedes-Benz 709D	Dormobile	B27F	6/93	New	8/94	
152	G702 NGR	Mercedes-Benz 709D	Scott	C25F	1990	7/93	8/94	Ex-Rush, Newcastle-on-Tyne
226	F226 FEH	Mercedes-Benz 709D	Dormobile	B29F	7/93	New	BB	
227/8	L227/8 HRF	Mercedes-Benz 709D	Dormobile	B29F	7/93	New	8/94	
45	H192 JNF	Dennis Dart 9SDL3002	Wadham Stringer	B35F	1990	7/93	BB	Ex-Stones, Glazebury
100	L100 SBS	Mercedes-Benz 0405	Wright	B51F	8/93	New	BB	
39	G727 RGA	Leyland Swift LBM6T/2RA	Reeve Burgess	B39F	1990	8/93	BB	Ex-Kelvin Central
112	GNL 838N	Leyland PSU3B/4R	Alexander AY	DP49F	1975	8/93	BB	Ex-Chase, Chasetown
264-7	E802-5 UDT	MCW Metrorider	MCW	B25F	1987	8/93	8/94	Ex-East Midland
285/7	E808/10 UDT	MCW Metrorider	MCW	B25F	1987	8/93	8/94	Ex-East Midland
286	E809 UDT	MCW Metrorider	MCW	B25F	1987	9/93	8/94	Ex-East Midland
288/9	E811/2 UDT	MCW Metrorider	MCW	B25F	1987	9/93	8/94	Ex-East Midland
263/8	E801/6 UDT	MCW Metrorider	MCW	B25F	1987	9/93	8/94	Ex-East Midland
251/2	D71/2 WTO	MCW Metrorider	MCW	B25F	1986	9/93	8/94	Ex-East Midland
290	E604 VKC	MCW Metrorider	MCW	B23F	1987	9/93	8/94	Ex-East Midland
121-3	E990/2/3 NMK	Leyland Swift LBM6T/2RS	Wadham Stringer	B37F	1987	9/93	BB	Ex-Armchair, Brentford
229-33	L229-33 HRF	Mercedes-Benz 709D	Dormobile	B27F	9/93	New	BB	(except 231/33 withdrawn 9/94)
180	G301 RJA	Mercedes-Benz 709D	Reeve Burgess	B25F	1989	9/93	BB	Ex-Starline, Congleton
94/5	L94/5 HRF	DAF DB250RS200505	Optare Spectra	H48/29F	10/93	New	BB	
20	D319 VVV	Volvo B10M	Jonckheere P50	C51F	1986	11/93	BB	(c)
108	F258 GWJ	Leyland Lynx LX112L10ZR1R	Leyland	B51F	1989	11/93	BB	Ex-Wright, Penycae
117	F155 DKU	Leyland Swift LBM6T/2RA	Reeve Burgess	B39F	1989	11/93	BB	Ex-K Line, Kirkburton
222	H880 NFS	Mercedes-Benz 709D	PMT	B29F	1991	12/93	BB	Ex-Chapman, Airdrie
234/5	G142/3 GOL	Mercedes-Benz 709D	Carlyle	B29F	1990	12/93	9/94	Ex-Kentish Bus

Notes:
(a) Ex-Mercedes-Benz, Barnsley (ex-demonstrator).
(b) Ex-Rhondda Buses. The body was re-built and re-seated to C53F.
(c) Ex-Telling-Golden Miller, Cardiff. Re-seated to C53F and re-registered 784 RBF.

1994

Fleet No.	Reg. No.	Chassis	Body	Seating	New	Acq	With drawn	Notes
250	F835 BCW	Mercedes-Benz 811D	Reeve Burgess	B33F	1989	1/94	BB	Ex-Knighton, Blackburn
350	TPD 178M	Leyland National 1051/1R0402	Leyland	B41F	1973	1/94	BB	Ex-Dearsley, Barking
351	MEX 772P	Leyland National 11351A/1R	Leyland	B52F	1976	1/94	BB	Ex-Holt Drive, Bolton
352	KOM 797P	Leyland National 11351A/2R	Leyland	B37F	1976	1/94	BB	Ex-Evag Cannon, Bolton
353	THX 126S	Leyland National 11351A/2R	Leyland	B34F	1978	1/94	BB	Ex-Evag Cannon, Bolton
111	VAJ 785S	Leyland PSU3E/4R	Willowbrook	B48F	1977	1/94	BB	(a)
248	G65 SNN	Mercedes-Benz 709D	Carlyle	DP29F	1990	2/94	BB	Ex-Skill, Nottingham
106	H408 YMA	Leyland Lynx LX2R11C15Z4R	Leyland	B51F	1990	2/94	BB	Ex-Wright, Penycae
249	F836 BCW	Mercedes-Benz 811D	Reeve Burgess	B33F	1989	2/94	BB	Ex-Knighton, Blackburn
89-93	D676/8/80/2/3 MHS	MCW Metrobus DR102/52	Alexander RL	DPH78F	1986	3/94	BB	Ex-Kelvin Central
102	L102 MEH	Volvo B6	Plaxton Pointer	B42F	3/94	New	BB	
244	G399 FSF	Mercedes-Benz 811D	PMT	B33F	1990	3/94	BB	Ex-Henderson, Hamilton
245	F985 EDS	Mercedes-Benz 811D	Alexander	DP33F	1988	3/94	BB	Ex-Rhondda Buses
242/3	H801/3 SKY	Mercedes-Benz 709D	Reeve Burgess	B25F	1990	4/94	BB	Ex-Kinch, Mountsorrel
241	E478 NSC	Mercedes-Benz 709D	Alexander	DP25F	1988	4/94	BB	Ex-Porter, Dummer
43	L43 MEH	MAN 11.190	Optare Vecta	B41F	5/94	New	BB	
300	L300 SBS	Dennis Dart	Plaxton Pointer	B40F	6/94	New	BB	
301	L301 NFA	Dennis Dart	Plaxton Pointer	B40F	6/94	New	BB	
253-5	L253-5 NFA	Mercedes-Benz 709D	Wadham Stringer	B29F	6/94	New	BB	
240	H802 SKY	Mercedes-Benz 709D	Reeve Burgess	B25F	1990	6/94	BB	Ex-Kinch, Mountsorrel
302-5	L302-5 NFA	Dennis Dart	Plaxton Pointer	B40F	7/94	New	BB	
221	G900 TJA	Mercedes-Benz 811D	Mellor	B32F	1989	7/94	8/94	Ex-Sampwell, Woburn

Notes:
(a) Ex-South Lancs Transport, St Helens.
Subsequent vehicles were purchased in British Bus ownership.

E. A. Wain, January 2016 ©
With acknowledgement to David Stanier for his assistance with the compilation of this fleet list

Appendix 1

Garages And Outstations To June 1994

Location	From	To	Notes
Uttoxeter			
The Garage, Spath	September 1926	June 1994	Passed with sale of Stevensons to British Bus
Burton-up on-Trent			
Adjacent to Drill Hall, Horninglow Street	September 1938	September 1939	Commandeered by military at outbreak of war
Unknown location	September 1939	June 1940	
Canal Wharf, Horninglow Road North	June 1940	End of 1964	Compulsorily purchased for new route of A38
Rolleston Road, Horninglow	End of 1964	May 1981	
Wetmore Road	May 1981	October 1985	1985-1988, not an operational depot, used for storage etc
ESDC Depot, Derby Street	October 1985	October 1988	Three-year lease following amalgamation with ESDC Transport Dept
Wetmore Road	October 1988	June 1994	Passed with sale of Stevensons to British Bus
Donisthorpe Outstation			
Cosy Coaches Garage, Hill Street	Early 1980s		Two school contract buses outstationed
Rugeley			
Middleton's Yard, Armitage Road	September 1983	March 1988	
Power Station Road	March 1988	June 1994	Passed with sale of Stevensons to British Bus
Potteries			
Hassell Street, Newcastle under Lyme	September 1984	May 1989	Obtained with Crystal Coaches business
Nevada Close, Hot Lane Ind Est, Burslem	May 1989	June 1994	Passed with sale of Stevensons to British Bus
Ilkeston			
Hallam Fields Road	October 1985	November 1988	Obtained with Erewash Travel business - operation passed to Nottingham City Transport
Swadlincote (buses)			
Midland Road, Swadlincote	August 1987	June 1994	Former Midland Fox garage - passed with sale of Stevensons to British Bus
Lichfield & Brownhills Outstations			
London Road, Lichfield	August 1987	December 1988	Former Midland Fox outstation - subsequently relocated to Brownhills
Lichfield Road, Brownhills	December 1988	May 1989	Allocation transferred to Rugeley
Swadlincote (coaches)			
Ashby Road, Woodville	November 1987	May 1990	Obtained with Viking Coaches business
Ryder Close, Cadley Hill	May 1990	June 1994	Obtained with Bagnall's Coaches business - passed with sale of Stevensons to British Bus
Cheddleton Outstation			
Berresford's Garage, Cheadle Road	1988	1989	Two school contract buses outstationed
West Midlands			
Darlaston, Heath Road Ind. Estate	October 1989	February 1993	Allocation transferred to Willenhall
Tunnel Road, Hill Top, West Bromwich	May 1991	September 1991	Obtained with Collett's Tours business, used briefly then prepared for use as bus garage
Tunnel Road, Hill Top, West Bromwich	September 1991	late 1992	Used as bus garage, then allocation transferred to Oak Road.
Tunnel Road, Hill Top, West Bromwich	late 1992	June 1994	Used as coach garage - passed with sale of Stevensons to British Bus
Oak Road, West Bromwich	May 1991	late 1992	Obtained with Sealandair business, used as coach garage, then allocation transferred to Hill Top
Oak Road, West Bromwich	late 1992	June 1994	Used as bus garage - passed with sale of Stevensons to British Bus
Costin's Haulage, Morgan Cl, Willenhall	September 1992	October 1992	Former PMT Red Rider garage - only used briefly then allocation transferred to Oak Road
Morgan Close, Willenhall	February 1993	June 1994	Passed with sale of Stevensons to British Bus
London Street, Smethwick	April 1994	May 1994	Allocation transferred to Oak Road and Willenhall
Stockport			
Ashton Road, Bredbury	March 1991	1991	'Pacer' subsidiary - temporary base
Rooth Street, Stockport	1991	September 1992	Business passed to PMT
Involvement in other operations			
Rotherham and District	December 1989	December 1990	50% share in business
Edinburgh Transport	1992	1994	75% share in business
Rhondda Buses	January 1992	June 1994	10% share in business

Appendix 2

Stage Carriage Services
Commenced Between 1926 and 1979

Uttoxeter-Tutbury-Burton. (Originally New Street, then Horninglow St, later Wetmore Road Motor Park)

11th September 1926, daily service, originally six return journeys each day, soon doubled. (Please refer to page 6 and 7 for route originally licensed and subsequent variation). 10/26 the route was formalised to run via Tutbury, thence via Horninglow Road to terminate in Horninglow Street, Burton (Wetmore Road Motor Park from 1st October 1927). 17th June 1931, first road service licence granted 'for continuation of service already operating'. **About 1939 became service 1**. 1939, war emergency timetable. 1945, basically the pre-war timetable with 15 round trips. 28/11/60, service altered to serve Holts Lane and Park Lane in Tutbury. 17th February 1979, route altered to serve Burton town centre, service renumbered **401**. 31st May 1980, certain journeys diverted via Doveridge Village, others were added progressively. 26th October 1986, certain journeys were lost on tender to other operators for various durations. 1st March 1987, Sunday service re-routed via Rolleston. 27th February 1989, most journeys diverted to serve Doveridge Village, Sunday journeys extended across Uttoxeter on Town Circular route.

Uttoxeter-Sudbury-Draycott-in-the-Clay-Hanbury-The Acorn Inn-Henhurst Hill-Burton (New Street Motor Park)

Roberts, Newborough, had operated a Thursday service between Hanbury and Burton (New Street Motor Park) which ran via Henhurst Hill and Shobnall Road. This service ceased to operate from 14th January 1928, and on 19th January John Stevenson started this service between Uttoxeter and Burton via Sudbury and Draycott to Hanbury, thence on the route followed by Roberts. 17th June 1931, first road service licence granted 'for continuation of service already operating'. 1933, Mon/Thu/Sat operation, one bus. At some time, connections introduced at Sudbury to/from Uttoxeter on some journeys. 1935, Sunday operation added and timetable changes. **About 1939 became service 2**. 1939, war emergency – Thu/Sat only. January 1945, Sunday service reinstated. 19th October 1946, licence cancelled, journeys modified to run via Anslow and Beam Hill. (See new service 2 below)

Sudbury (Portaway Head)-Cubley-Darley Moor-Ashbourne

19th September 1928, reported in Burton County Borough Minutes that a Sudbury-Ashbourne service was being considered. Started as a daily operation. 4th May 1931, first road service licence granted 'to continue the service of stage carriages operated by him between Sudbury and Ashbourne'. Full route started 8th August 1933 Uttoxeter to Ashbourne via Sudbury, reduced to Tue/Thu/Sat/Sun, connections at Sudbury for Uttoxeter or Burton on many journeys. 1938, Tuesday service withdrawn. **About 1939 became service 3**. 1939, war emergency timetable, Saturdays only operation. 1948, daily service again, but Sunday service only operated April – September. 1st February 1950, almost all journeys withdrawn consequent upon introduction of new service 5 Burton-Ashbourne. 1962, remaining Uttoxeter-Ashbourne trips withdrawn.

Uttoxeter-Doveridge-Somersal Herbert

Wednesday only service, commenced at some time between July 1929 and May 1931. 17th June 1931, first road service licence granted 'for continuation of service already operating'. 24th April 1933, extended to Cubley Village and Darley Moor (Norbury Lane End). **About 1939 became service 4**. 1951, timetable reduced. 6th November 1963, service withdrawn.

Burton Wetmore Bus Park-Tutbury-Scropton

Saturday evening operation, granted 16th June 1934. **About 1939 became service 5**. 1939, war emergency timetable. Early 1948, diversion round Park Lane, Tutbury, and service massively expanded to run daily. 1st February 1950, absorbed into new Burton-Tutbury-Ashbourne service, retaining service no.5 (see below).

Burton Wetmore Bus Park-Beam Hill-Anslow Bell Inn

From 14th November 1936, Thu/Sat/Sun, three round trips each day of operation. **About 1939 became service 6**. 1939, war emergency timetable. 19/th October 1946, licence cancelled, journeys transferred to Uttoxeter-Hanbury-Burton service 2– see below.

Bramshall-Holly Road-Uttoxeter, Service 6.

From 5th October 1946, daily service. June 1948, extended to Doveridge Village. Late 1956, Mon-Fri evening and Sunday services suspended for Suez Crisis but not reinstated. December 1959, modified to run via Byrds Lane between Bramshall and Holly Road. 17th February 1979, service renumbered **406**. 28th june 1980, service withdrawn, Bramshall served by new service 404, and remaining Doveridge journeys transferred to 401 timetable.

Uttoxeter-Doveridge-Sudbury-Draycott-Hanbury-Anslow-Beam Hill-Burton Wetmore Bus Park, Service 2

19th October 1946, daily service, incorporating journeys from original service 2 Uttoxeter-Hanbury-Burton and 6 Burton-Anslow, with many connections to/from Uttoxeter at Sudbury. 1st February 1947, revised timetable, which had fewer connections at Sudbury. 1965, Sunday service confined to Burton-Anslow section. 26th October 1970, Sunday service withdrawn altogether. 21st April 1975, service re-routed via Marchington between Uttoxeter and Draycott. 17th February 1979, further changes, including alteration of route to serve Newborough and Burton town centre; service renumbered **402**.

Church Broughton-Hatton-Scropton-Uttoxeter

Wednesday only, one return journey from December 1949. September 1950, service ceased due to lack of patronage.

Burton Wetmore Bus Park-Tutbury (Green Lane-Park Lane-High St)-Scropton-Cubley-Darley Moor-Ashbourne, Service 5

1st February 1950, new service combining most of Uttoxeter-Sudbury-Ashbourne service 3 and all journeys from Burton-Scropton service 5. 1951 and 1952, timetables cut back considerably. October 1956, service re-routed into new Ashbourne Bus Station. Decemv56, fuel rationing due to Suez crisis, service reductions, including loss of Sunday service, which was not reinstated. 10th December 1962, route varied in Tutbury. At least by 17th February 1979, the service was Thursday and Saturday only. 17th February 1979, route altered to serve Burton town centre, service renumbered **405**. 21st June 1980, route altered to serve Church Broughton and Boylestone instead of Sudbury. 25th October 1986, cut back to operate between Tutbury and Ashbourne only, Saturday service withdrawn.

Abbots Bromley-Marchington-Draycott-Hanbury-Burton Wetmore Bus Park, Service 3

Thursdays only, from 15th December 1977. From 17th February 1979, Saturday service added, service renumbered **403**.

Uttoxeter-Abbots Bromley-Lichfield-Minworth-Birmingham (Carrs Lane), Service X48

Tuesdays only from 20th February 1979. From 5th April 1980, Saturday service added, first Saturday in the month, on a variation of the route from Uttoxeter, but this was discontinued after 14th March 1981.

Kings Bromley-Yoxall-Burton, Service 407

Thursdays only from 22nd February 1979. From 3rd April 1980, Thursdays round trip Kings Bromley-Rugeley added. 5th April 19/80, Saturday service added, last ran 24th May 1980.

Appendix 3
Final Operations

The Transport Act of March 1980 saw new legislation introduced, at which point the ability to introduce new bus services and make changes to them was transformed, and changes occurred much more frequently. Examples of these new services for each operating area have been given in the text, together with an indication of the extent of those operations. Following the implementation of the 1985 Transport Act, from October 1986 the company successfully tendered for many services, some of which were for full routes, others being for certain journeys on routes otherwise operated commercially by other companies. Many tendered services had quite limited durations. The following gives an overview of the operation by area at the time of the sale of the company in June 1994.

Spath	
18/19 Creswell – Cheadle – Ashbourne	234/5 Uttoxeter – Alton – Cheadle – Leek
239 Uttoxeter – Alton	248/411 Uttoxeter – Leigh area – Hanley
401 Uttoxeter – Tutbury – Burton	402 Uttoxeter – Hanbury – Burton
403 Abbots Bromley – Burton	404 Uttoxeter – Stafford
408 Uttoxeter – Abbots Bromley – Rugeley	409 Uttoxeter – Ashbourne – Belper
406 Uttoxeter Town Circular, Outer Circle, Park Avenue, Westlands Road	X48 Uttoxeter – Abbots Bromley – Lichfield – Birmingham

Burton (many linked as cross-town services)	
1 Burton – Horninglow	2 Burton – Horninglow
3 Burton – Winshill	5 Burton – Beans Covert
6 Burton – Eton Rd Estate	7 Burton – Old Wetmore
10 Burton – Acorn Inn	12 Burton – Barton
13 Burton – District hospital	14 Burton – Beam Hill – Stretton
15 Burton – Rolleston	16 Burton – Eton Road Estate – Stretton
17 Brizlincote – Burton – Clay Mills	18 Swadlincote – Burton – Stretton – Derby
405 Hatton – Scropton – Ashbourne	410 Burton – Bretby
417 (Derbs. CC) Etwall – Ashbourne	412 Stretton – Burton – Nottingham
112 Burton – Lichfield – Birmingham	
Some services were interworked between Burton and Spath depots, and to a greater extent, between Burton and Swadlincote depots.	

Swadlincote	
4/4B/4D Burton – Newhall – Swadlincote	6/9 Loughborough Town Services
8 Swadlincote – Linton – Ashby	9 Burton – Woodville – Ashby
177 Swadlincote – Osgathorpe – Loughborough	20/26 Burton – Stapenhill – Swadlincote
21A Burton – Coton Park – Swadlincote	24 Burton – Coton in the Elms – Swadlincote
27 Burton – Measham – Ashby	29 Hatton – Etwall – Swadlincote
97 Tamworth – Ashby – Coalville	118 Swadlincote – Leicester
163 Moira – Ibstock – Leicester	172 Ashby – Coalville – Derby
173 Coalville – Ashby – Derby	177 Loughborough – Worthington – Coalville
179 Hinckey – Ibstock – Coalville	

Rugeley (including Lichfield and Sutton Coldfield areas)	
53 Lichfield – Oakenfield Circular	54 Lichfield – Meadowbrook Road Circular
25 Erdington – Shard End – Chelmsley Wood	68 Sutton Coldfield – Castle Vale – Erdington
105 Roughley – Mere Green – Sutton Coldfield	109 Erdington – Old Oscott – Kingstanding
117 Erdington – Walmley – Sutton Coldfield	165 Erdington – Falcon Lodge – Sutton Coldfield
377 New Oscott – Walsall	382 Lichfield – Shenstone – Brownhlls/Aldridge
404 Hixon – Rugeley	407 Rugeley – Yoxall – Burton
421 Rugeley – Springfields Estate	422/ 445 Abbots Bromley – Rugeley – Walsall
423 Rugeley – Pear Tree Estate	424 Rugeley – Upper Brereton
429 Abbots Bromley – Yoxall – Lichfield	447 Springfields Estate – Fradley
601 Erdington – Bromford Bridge – Shard End	663 East Birmingham Hospital – Erdington
655 Aldridge – Great Barr	823 Rugeley – Stafford
840 Rugeley – Slitting Mill	901 Lichfield – Castle Vale – Birmingham
905/912 Lichfield – Sutton Coldfield – Birmingham	

Crystal Coaches	
7 Tunstall – Whitehill	12 Tunstall – Smallthorne – Norton
39 Hanley – Birches Head – Burslem – Middleport	70 Boothen – Stoke – Bentilee
75/77 Newcastle – Knutton – Wilmot Drive	86/7/8 Mow Cop – Biddulph – Congleton
94 Newcastle – Burslem – Chell Heath	106 Longton – Leek – Westwood (Sats)
177 Kidsgrove – Biddulph	313 Newcastle – Alsager – Sandbach (Th)
321/2/4 Hanley – Newcastle – Alsager – Hanley	350 Eccleshall – Newcastle – Hanley
15 Macclesfield – Tytherington Circular	19 Macclesfield – Prestbury
287 Macclesfield – Mottram – Wilmslow (Sat)	K52/3 Sandbach Town Circular (Th)

In addition, a number of tendered journeys were operated on otherwise commercially-operated services in the Potteries and, to a much lesser extent, in Cheshire. These comprised a mixture of early morning, peak, off-peak, school journeys, and evening timings.

West Midlands area, operated from Willenhall, Hill Top and West Bromwich	
2A/D Kidderminster – Hales Park	46A Birmingham – Pheasey
74 Dudley – West Bromwich	77 Wolverhampton – Rocket Pool
81 Birmingham – West Bromwich	88 Langley Green – Birmingham
127 Birmingham – Merry Hill	140 Dudley – Bearwood
158 Birmingham – Bloxwich	202/3/4 Bromsgrove – Halesowen
207 Dudley – Wrens Nest	212 Cradley Heath – Halesowen
223 Willenhall – Gornal Wood	224 Willenhall – Dudley
227 Bilston – Dudley	232 Halesowen – Stourbridge
248 Stourbridge – Dudley	255 Bobbington – Dudley
261 Wall Heath – Dudley	262 Bilston – Dudley
292 Kidderminster – Birmingham	303 County Bridge – Bilston
303/4 Kidderminster – Worcester	325 Bloxwich – Wednesbury
377 Walsall – Sutton Coldfield	379 Walsall – Streetley
411 West Bromwich – Wednesbury	441 West Bromwich – Halesowen
444 Londonderry – Bearwood	450 West Bromwich – Bearwood
459 West Bromwich – Birmingham	511 Wolverhampton – Underhill
522 Wolverhampton – Princes End	526 Wolverhampton – Stowlawn
529 Wolverhampton – Willenhall	530 Wolverhampton – Rocket Pool
536 Wolverhampton – Pattingham / Lower Penn	546 Wolverhampton – Bilston
571 Wolverhampton – Coppice Farm	572/3/4 Wolverhampton – Willenhall
582 Wolverhampton – Kinver	613 Wolverhampton – Northwood Park
631 West Bromwich – Greets Green	636 Walsall – Delves Road
637 Walsall – Hough Road	639 Walsall – West Bromwich
642 Dudley – Uplands Estate	644 Tipton – West Bromwich
640/650 Birmingham – Kings Heath	651 Handsworth Wood – Great Barr
663 Heartlands Hospital – Erdington	686/7 Dudley – Wednesbury
688 Dudley – West Bromwich	815 Birmingham Airport – B/ham Business Pk

All the above routes were transferred to West Midlands Travel with the sale of the West Midlands service bus depots on 14th August 1994. Also transferred was service 445 Smethwick – Brandhall (due to start on 21st August)

Bibliography

Stevensons of Uttoxeter, A W Peto/D J Stanier/D Penlington, ISBN 0-907864-11-2

Stevensons in the Eighties, David J Stanier, ISBN 0-948131-26-8

Fleet History of Stevensons of Uttoxeter, PD17, published by the PSV Circle, 1990

The Independent Stage Carriage Operators of Staffordshire, Fleet history 2PD7, published by The PSV Circle, November 1973

Additional information from various articles published in Bus Fayre, Buses, Buses Extra, Bus and Coach, Coaching Journal, from archives of the company and the Omnibus Society archive.

For Information

A good selection of Tim Jeffcoat's period colour photos, covering vehicles of Stevensons and other local operators, is available from Colour Classics. www.colourclassics.co.uk

The Magic Attic, Swadlincote provides a research facility for old local area newspapers. www.magicatticarch@googlemail.com

The Model Bus Federation caters for all those interested in model buses. www.model-bus-federation.org.uk
www.facebook.com/groups/209120979272898/

The Omnibus Society. www.omnibus-society.org

The PSV Circle. psvcircle.org.uk/

The Potteries Omnibus Preservation Society (POPS) caters for those interested in bus and coach operators (past and present) in the North Staffordshire area, and actively preserves a number of rare and interesting vehicles.
https://potteriesomnibus.wordpress.com/

Key to Photographers (where known)

AC	Alan Cross	HP	H Peers	RHC	Robin Hannay Collection
AJ	Andrew Jarosz	JB	James Boddice	RM	Roger Monk
AP	Adrian Pearson	JC/OS	John Clarke/Omnibus	RJ	Robin Jeffcoat
B&C	Bus & Coach Magazine		Society	RM/OS	Roy Marshall/Omnibus
CW	Colin White	LRC	Leon Richardson		Society
DH	Daniel Hill Photography		Collection	STEV	Stevensons' archive
DPC	David Penlington	MAC	The Magic Attic	TBG	The Bus Gallery
	Collection		Collection	TG	T Greaves
DS	David Stanier	OS	Omnibus Society	TJ	Tim Jeffcoat
EW	Author	PB	Photobus	TJC	Tim Jeffcoat Collection
EWC	Author's Collection	PS	Phillip Stephenson	TM	Tim Machin
GHB/RM	George Bullock/courtesy	PY/OS	Peter Yeomans/Omnibus	TS	Tony Smith
	Roger Monk		Society	UA	Uttoxeter Advertiser
GM	Geoffrey Morant	RDC	Ruth Day Collection		
GSC	George Stevenson	RFM	RF Mack		
	Collection	RH	Robin Hannay		

A new depot opened at Willenhall in February 1993 which was fitted out with pits to become the engineering centre for the West Midlands area; this allowed for the closure of Darlaston depot, the vehicles and forty drivers transferring to the new depot on 20th February. The last new vehicles purchased by Stevensons, in June 1994, prior to the sale to British Bus, were six Plaxton Pointer-bodied Dennis Darts. One of the batch, L302 NFA, sits outside Willenhall depot beside Wright-bodied Mercedes-Benz 814D H196 JVT of 1990. (EW)